Militants and Citizens

*The Politics of Participatory Democracy
in Porto Alegre*

Militants and Citizens

The Politics of Participatory Democracy

in Porto Alegre

Gianpaolo Baiocchi

STANFORD UNIVERSITY PRESS

Stanford, California   2005

Stanford University Press
Stanford, California
© 2005 by the Board of Trustees of the
Leland Stanford Junior University

Library of Congress Cataloging-in-Publication Data

Baiocchi , Gianpaolo.
    Militants and citizens : The politics of participatory
democracy in Porto Alegre / Gianpaolo Baiocchi.
        p. cm.
    Includes bibliographical references (p.   ) and index.
    ISBN 0-8047-5122-6 (cloth : alk. paper) —
    ISBN 0-8047-5123-4 (pbk. : alk. paper)
    1. Porto Alegre (Brazil)—Politics and government—
Citizen participation. 2. Political participation—Brazil—
Porto Alegre—History. 3. Political culture—Brazil—Porto
Alegre—History. 4. Civil society—Brazil—Porto Alegre—
History. I. Title.
JS2425.P67B34   2005
323'.042'098165—dc22

                                                    2004026598

Printed in the United States of America
Original Printing 2005
Last figure below indicates year of this printing:
14   13   12   11   10   09   08   07   06   05

Typeset at Stanford University Press in 10/13 Palatino

Contents

Tables

Figures

Preface

On the evening of January 24, 2003, the leader of Brazil's Partido dos Trabalhadores (PT), or Workers' Party, the former metalworker Luis Ignácio da Silva, known as Lula, walked onstage at the World Social Forum's single largest event as the country's newly elected president. Like its first two incarnations, the Third World Social Forum (WSF), a world-wide gathering of social justice activists, was held in Porto Alegre, having grown to an event of over 100,000 participants from more than 150 countries. When Lula came onstage, Porto Alegre's citizens mingled with *piqueteros* from Argentina, queer activists from India, living-wage activists from the United States, trade unionists from South Africa, and activists from literally thousands of different social movements. The electrified audience, already in a festive spirit, was mesmerized by his speech, which lent the event a sense of world-historical significance.

Flanked by well-known PT leaders like Benedita da Silva (the ex-governor of Rio de Janeiro) and Tarso Genro (Porto Alegre's ex-mayor), Lula called for international solidarity in support of his mandate in the face of the tough times ahead it would no doubt face.[1] Lula then publicly defended his decision to attend the World Economic Forum in Davos as one of a series of pragmatic decisions that would foster dialogue to solve common problems. He likened his term as president to the role of a soccer coach at a match; although there would no doubt be difficulties, his record ought to be examined at the end of the term rather than at its start. He closed by promising he would not deviate "one comma" from his socialist ideals. The crowd went wild and started to chant holding up two hands to signify the number eight, already calling for his reelection barely three weeks into his term.

The World Social Forum has catapulted Porto Alegre and its style of governance onto the world stage. Activists and scholars alike have recognized the WSF as a completely novel "movement of movements" that transcends traditional narratives of social movements:[2] it is a North-South transnational gathering without a hierarchy, unified ideology, or leadership that contains elements of previous nationally based movements without being easily definable as any of them.[3] The organizing committee chose Porto Alegre partially because of practical concerns; it had, after all, a sympathetic municipal government with the capacity to host such an event and the experience to carry it off, given its years of successful participatory meetings. But the choice was also symbolic on the part of organizers; the city's style of participatory democracy stood in for the alternatives that global social justice activists sought to craft. In Porto Alegre, progressive administrators based their decisions on real participatory input from the city's least privileged, and radical democracy and discussion from below had guided and transformed the Left's redistributive mission.

But Lula's victory in October 2002 also represents something quite novel as well. The story of the Workers' Party, a party of political outsiders, which barely made an impact in elections in the early 1980s, is one of a rupture with traditional Brazilian electoral politics and the traditional narratives of left-wing political parties. It is difficult to capture in terms of the distinctions between "social democratic and socialist" (or "reformist and revolutionary") usually used to describe leftist projects. In a sense, Lula and the PT officials who shared the podium with him faced their social movement mirror image in the multitude of global justice activists who stood before them. Lula had in the past been "one of them"; he was a social movement activist become president.

The history of the PT in the 1980s and 1990s is one of evolution of a vision and practice centered around citizenship, participatory democracy, and good governance. The party's spectacular electoral growth was marked by neither clientelist mobilization of the masses nor traditional cadre organizing, but by translating civil society's innovations and forging alliances with its various sectors through institutions of participatory democracy such as its participatory budget. The growing importance of the strategy of promoting citizenship through participatory institutions is apparent in documents from the PT's subsequent national congresses and resolutions.

At the center of the story of the PT's evolution is Porto Alegre's experiment in participatory democracy, which has been emulated in many places throughout the world. A large body of literature describes that experiment, but this book takes a different approach from many other accounts of it. The story I tell here is neither directly about the PT nor about governance itself, but rather about civic life and civic practices in a city where participatory democracy has become a way of life. What is the quality of democracy in participatory meetings? What sort of political culture has evolved in civil society in Porto Alegre?

Properly answered, these questions tell us something about the PT, I think, and shed some light both on Lula and his government and on the evolution of the Latin American left more broadly. For many, the fact that the national PT appears for the moment to have abandoned a redistributive platform has been a disappointing turn of events, but this has at least something to do with its strategies. In contrast to the Porto Alegre administration, the national government has not yet opened significantly empowered participatory avenues for popular decision making. Rather, it has sought parliamentary legitimacy in ever-broader coalitions and more conservative economic policies. It has had difficulty with organized sectors of society, some of which have played a limited consultative role in the new government. Prominent Porto Alegrenses in the administration have proposed broad participatory reforms in the manner of the city's Participatory Budget, or Orçamento Participativo, but to little avail.

But the book was written in the belief that there is something else to be learned far beyond Brazil from the story of Porto Alegre's neighborhood associations and movements. Taking this case seriously forces us to pay attention to facets of civic life and citizenship that are often obscured from view, exposing their "artifactuality."[4] It also suggests that trying to understand the ways in which social movements' claims and counterclaims can force the state into democratic innovations that in some cases shape the polity itself, in ways that blur distinctions between movement and state, may be more useful than the image of social movements as contenders "rattling at the gates of the state."[5] Movements, we are reminded, may change, but do not necessarily come to an end, when they engage the state. The implicit definition that often drives social movement studies, that movements are equal to protest activity, finds a limit case here—movements have declined protest activity, but have not demobilized; quite the contrary. But perhaps the most important innovation has to do with the explicit connection of civic participation to redistribution and to social justice, which calls for a kind of democratic theory that does not seek to "bracket" the effects of power at the door of the deliberative meeting; rather, it sees power, conflict, and, ultimately, the political as constitutive of the public sphere itself. This book is an attempt to add to that theory in light of the significant renewal that this experience represents.

This book was also written in the belief that the best testament to the experience of Porto Alegrenses is neither to romanticize them nor exaggerate their accomplishments, but to be fair, as well as true to my own interpretation. This was not easy, especially as I have, in some instances, come to disagree with people I really came to like and respect. Their insights nonetheless came to be important. I have, for instance, highlighted the civic consequences of participatory budgeting rather than its "good governance" or human development outcomes or its instrumental role in PT electoral successes. It is my belief that while these other aspects are important, the OP's significance lies with its contribution to the quality of democracy in a way that is more immediately visible than its impact on development indicators and that will probably outlast the PT in power. This book was also written on the assumption that its audience would not be made up only of Brazilianists or Porto Alegre experts, and I have therefore tried to avoid drowning readers in the alphabet soup of municipal agencies, the Brazilian tax structure, or Brazilian political parties. I have also attempted to resist the temptation of writing a "Porto Alegre compendium" and have spared readers some of the fine-grained institutional and historical detail that comes from seven years of research. As much as possible, I have relegated that to the endnotes, pointing readers to other sources, including the many policy reports and works that extensively document various features of participatory budgeting. The companion website to this book, www.participatorybudgeting.org, contains links to those reports, as well as to updated information on Porto Alegre.

In retrospect, authoring a book may be the best example of individual appropriation of collective production. This particular one would not have been possible without a number of people and organizations. The list is too long to give in full, but it includes scholars, friends, and co-survivors at the University of Wisconsin, as well as my family on both the Baiocchi and Chakravartty sides. Sociological co-conspirators Eduardo Bonilla-Silva, Amanda Lewis, Tyrone Forman, Black Hawk Hancock, and Brian Finch have helped me navigate the professional transitions since the Ph.D. I received funding from the U.S. National Science Foundation and the Inter-American Foundation at dissertation time; funding from the Latin American Studies and Global Studies Centers at the University of Pittsburgh allowed me to carry out follow-up research, while giving me teaching leave. I had a number of reliable and capable research assistants along the way, and I would like to single out the exceptional work of Alexandre Medeiros, Taeko Hiroi, Ashley Currier, Courtney Brown, and Catherine Wilson. The people of Porto Alegre who welcomed me and who appear in the book only under pseudonyms made this research possible, as did good friends at CIDADE, especially Regina Pozzobon, Sérgio Baierle, and Vera Amaro. My *gaúcho* family offered support and inspiration, and I am sorry that Laurinda did not get to see this book completed. My good friends Jane Pillar and Jorge Maciel were always generous and patient, and my fellow "gringo" researcher Ben Goldfrank was constant company in Porto Alegre; our daily research and ideas sessions propelled the research forward. At the *prefeitura*, I'll be forever indebted to Marlene Steffan, Assis Brasil, Antônio Girard, Carlos Schwank, Itamar Espanhol, and, most of all, Helena Monumat and Luciano Brunnet, whose *gentileza* and insight continue to inspire me and other researchers. A special mention goes to my fellow *orçamentólogo* Marcelo Silva, whose friendship and mentoring in all things to do with civil society made this book possible in more ways than one.

I've been also fortunate to have had a number of patient interlocutors: at Wisconsin, Paul Lichterman, Gay Seidman, Francisco Scarano, Ann Orloff, Nina Eliasoph, Mitch Duneier, and Mustafa Emirbaiyer offered helpful and kind commentary along the way. I am especially indebted to my dissertation co-chair Jane Collins for keeping me in graduate school, making sure this dissertation happened, and serving as a role model for a scholar-teacher, while offering research advice. Erik Wright, my other co-chair, is someone to whom I owe an immense intellectual and professional debt, and whose boundless enthusiasm for real utopias and clarity (especially the former) continues to be an influence. I've also learned a lot from a number of others with whom I've had the opportunity to exchange ideas, in particular, Leonardo Avritzer, Judith Tendler, Jane Mansbridge, Archon Fung, Marcus Melo, Zander Navarro, Evelina Dagnino, Patrick Heller, Shubham Chauduri, Jeff Alexander, Christopher Chase-Dunn, Kathy Blee, Barry Ames, Millie Thayer, and Joya Misra. I've had the benefit too of generously close commentary on the whole manuscript by John D. French, Peter Evans, Rich Wood, and Kate Wahl at Stanford University Press. My friends and colleagues John Markoff, Dan Clawson, Robert Zussman, Neil Gross, Mark Brenner, Annette Hunt, and Josh Whitford offered key comments on the text at various stages as well.

Anyone who knows the exigencies of two academic careers understands that at times the logic of exchange and the metaphors of reciprocity break down and movement forward is only possible with great acts of generosity and selflessness by one of the parties. I've been fortunate to have a *companheira* who has lovingly endured more talk of participatory governance than anyone ought to have to, while taking time from her own work to help me find coherence among jumbled thoughts and odd sentences. Paula more than anyone else made sure this book happened. To our delight, one of our daughter Aisha's first long words was "politics." She reminds us every day why we have to believe that a better world must be possible, and we hope her upbringing does not turn her away from politics.

Acronyms and Abbreviations

CIDADE	Centro de Assessoria e Estudos Urbanos (Center for Consultancy and Urban Studies)
CMDCA	Conselho Municipal dos Direitos da Criança e do Adolescente (Municipal Council on the Rights of Children and Adolescents)
COMATHAB	Conselho Municipal de Acesso à Terra e Habitação (Municipal Council of Access to Land and Housing)
COMPROMEL	Commissão Pró-Melhoria da Grande Santa Rosa (Committee for Improvements in the Greater Santa Rosa Neighborhood)
COP	Conselho do Orçamento Participativo (Participatory Budget Council)
CPP	Conselho Popular do Partenon (Popular Council of Partenon)
CPZN	Conselho Popular da Zona Norte (Popular Council of the Norte District)
CRC	Coordenação de Relações com a Comunidade (Office of Community Relations)
CROP(s)	*coordenador regional do Orçamento Participativo* (district facilitator of the participatory budget)
DEMHAB	Departmento Municipal de Habitação (Municipal Housing Department)
EPG	Empowered Participatory Governance

FASE   Fundação de Assistência Social Educativa (Foundation for Social and Educational Services)

FESC   Fundação de Educação Social e Comunitária (Social and Community Education Foundation)

FPB   Frente Brasil Popular (Brazilian Popular Front)

FRACAB   Federação Rio-Grandense das Associações Comunitárias e de Bairros (Federation of Community and Neighborhood Associations of Rio Grande do Sul)

FROP   Fórum Regional de Delegados do Orçamento Participativo (District Forum of Delegates of the Participatory Budget)

GAPLAN   Gabinete de Planejamento (planning department)

IBASE   Instituto Brasileiro de Análises Sociais e Econômicas

IBGE   Instituto Brasileiro de Geografia e Estatística (Brazilian Institute of Geography and Statistics)

ICMS   *imposto sobre circulação de mercadorias e serviços* (tax on the circulation of merchandise and services)

IPEA   Instituto de Pesquisa Econômica Aplicada

IPTU   *imposto predial e territorial urbano* (tax on buildings and urban lands)

ISSQN   *imposto sobre serviços de qualquer natureza* (services tax)

MCG   Movimento Comunitário Gaúcho (Community Movement of Rio Grande do Sul)

MDB   Movimento Democrático Brasileiro (Brazilian Democratic Movement)

OP   Orçamento Participativo (participatory budget)

PC do B   Partido Comunista do Brasil (Communist Party of Brazil)

PCB   Partido Comunista Brasileiro (Brazilian Communist Party)

PDS   Partido Democrático Social (Democratic Social Party); became the PPR, Partido Progressista Reformador (Reformist Progressive Party), in 1993

PDT   Partido Democrático Trabalhista (Democratic Labor Party; formerly the PTB)

PFL   Partido da Frente Liberal (Liberal Front Party)

PI	*plano de investimento* (yearly investment plan)
PMDB	Partido do Movimento Democrático Brasileiro (Brazilian Democratic Movement Party)
PMPA	Prefeitura Municipal de Porto Alegre (Municipal Prefecture of Porto Alegre)
PROCEMPA	Companhia de Processamento de Dados do Município de Porto Alegre
PSB	Partido Socialista Brasileiro (Brazilian Socialist Party)
PT	Partido dos Trabalhadores (Workers' Party)
PTB	Partido Trabalhista Brasileiro (Brazilian Labor Party; subsequently the PDT)
SIMPA	Sindicato dos Municipários de Porto Alegre (Union of Municipal Employees of Porto Alegre)
UAMPA	União das Associações de Moradores de Porto Alegre (Union of Neighborhood Associations of Porto Alegre)
UNDP	United Nations Development Programme
WSF	World Social Forum

Militants and Citizens

The Politics of Participatory Democracy
in Porto Alegre

At the citywide **Budget Council, councilors** chosen from among **delegates** make final decisions on the budget. At the municipal level, **UAMPA** is an independent organization that represents the interests of neighborhood associations.

In the districts, at weekly meetings of the **Budget Forum** of the Orçamento Participativo, **delegates** from the neighborhoods decide on local projects and priorities. **Institutional councils** with delegates from neighborhoods advise the municipality on service provision in areas such as health. **Popular councils** are independent organizations that represent neighborhood associations and local movements.

In many of the city's working-class and poor neighborhoods there are **neighborhood associations** and **cooperatives.** These are independent and voluntary entities, and most participate in the **Budget Forum.**

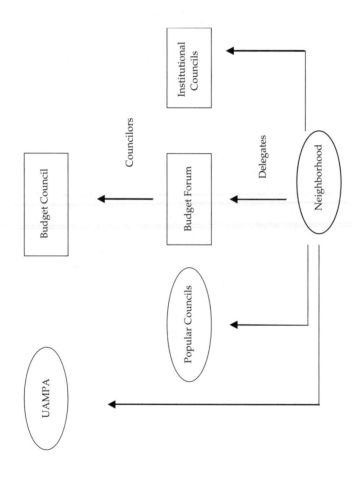

Legend:

○ Independent organization

▢ State-sponsored setting

FIG. 1. Civil society organizations and participatory settings in Porto Alegre

CHAPTER ONE

"Attention, Companheiros!"

Every Monday night, at eight o'clock, in the back room of the São Judas Tadeu Church, across busy Ipanema road and in sight of the city's Catholic University, where students are just arriving for night courses around this time, a ritual takes place in the Partenon district of Porto Alegre.[1] A dozen or so older community activists, mostly retired men and women, convene at the front of the borrowed classroom to call to order a meeting of the Conselho Popular do Partenon (CPP), or Popular Council of Partenon. The principal activists, who include a retired policeman, a hotel manager, and a mechanic, speak in hushed tones for a few minutes, lining up the remaining items on the agenda. One of them writes the agenda on the blackboard, another goes to fetch people who are smoking a last cigarette outside. Someone else eyes the clock. A volunteer is found to take the minutes. The atmosphere is relaxed. This is clearly also a place to meet for friends who may not see one another during the week. They sit close together on school chairs, joking back and forth until the meeting starts, with someone at the front calling it to order with a loud "Attention, *Companheiros!*"

The meeting then proceeds with its series of small rituals, with *companheiros* calling on one another as they go through the weekly announcements, the meeting's agenda, and the decision-making process, until the firm deadline of ten o'clock, when the meeting disbands and people meander home. Although the participants call each other *companheiro* ("fellow [citizen]" or "brother" would be the best translation), and the CPP's bylaws list it as an "embryo of popular power," much of the conversation at the meeting would be indistinguishable from that heard at a PTA meeting in the United States, if not at one of the celebrated New England town meetings. The CPP's meetings are dedicated to a broad discussion of community affairs, and much of the agenda is usually filled with discussion of mundane items such as broken pipes, rude bus drivers, and problems at the public health clinic. Some of the agenda items are grander; once every few weeks, there is an invited guest, such as a professor from a local university speaking on Brazilian politics or the world economy.

Often, agenda items from the municipal system of participatory governance filter down to the CPP's agenda. This municipal participatory program, the Orçamento Participativo (OP), or Participatory Budget, revolves around decision making on municipal budget items. On the successive Wednesdays of most weeks in the Partenon district, some fifty residents from various parts of the district meet to discuss the relative merits of investment priorities for their district in semi-structured meetings facilitated by a representative of City Hall. In the OP, citizens at the local level, like those of Partenon, decide on needed projects for their area and prioritize them, based on their financial and technical feasibility. A budget council made up of representatives chosen from the city's districts makes final, binding decisions about the destination of municipal funds.

The OP has attracted a lot of international attention in recent years. The image of poor slum residents participating week in and week out to actually decide on urban improvements contrasts starkly with the dystopian images of an urban Brazil characterized by increasing violence, urban blight, and social segregation in the past few decades. Media images sensationalize the extent of the problems, but Brazil's big cities are today among the most violent, unequal, and problem-ridden in the world. They are home to both the country's richest and poorest people. While roughly one-fourth of urban residents live in makeshift slum housing, often without access to any urban services, Brazl's elite lives in closed high-security buildings, working and socializing in equally private environments. Against this backdrop, and at a time when scholars and activists throughout the world decry the state of representative democracy, the OP stands out as a system that has not only provided services and improvements for the urban poor but involved large numbers of them in active civic life.

Established by Porto Alegre's Partido dos Trabalhadores (PT) municipal administration in the early 1990s, the OP has drawn tens of thousands of participants each year to its meetings around the city to deliberate and decide on a variety of municipal matters. The majority of the participants have been from among Porto Alegre's poorer citizens who live in its working-class neighborhoods and poor slum areas. Many, having originally come to the OP to discuss a specific problem, have stayed on to take part in organizations like the CPP, if not in local neighborhood associations, which have come to thrive. In fact, the OP has become a central feature of community life in the city's sixteen districts, and many voluntary organizations like the CPP receive a powerful impetus from it.

The activities of CPP community activists and participants in the OP challenge a number of powerful assumptions about civic engagement in the academic literature. First, and most obviously, they challenge the assumption, on the part of social capital scholars and public sphere enthusiasts, that civic engagement takes place *fully outside* of the state realm, in an autonomous "lifeworld." While CPP meetings are voluntary and autonomous, they receive a powerful impetus from government sponsorship, and their activities are closely integrated with the city administration. The recent history of the CPP, and of the rest of civil society in Porto Alegre, reflects the impact of the establishment of municipal participatory programs. At a time when scholars are pointing to a crisis of the welfare state as a threat to industrial democracies, here we see an instance of an innovation by municipal government that has empowered local citizenry, fostered new activism in civil society, and created a novel form of coordination across the state-civil society divide.[2]

Second, the CPP's day-to-day practice offers a subtle commentary on the assumptions about the proper prerequisites to democracy, at a time when very many indicators of Brazilian democracy have pointed to stagnant, or declining, civic engagement after the country's transition from authoritarian rule to democracy (1984–88).[3] Increasing distrust of and declining support for democracy have been noted.[4] Brazil's democracy has often been described as fragile and unconsolidated. But Porto Alegre's civil society presents a different image. Not only are there active civic organizations of various kinds throughout the city, but many of the participants in these organizations are poor, not formally educated, and have lived through two decades of authoritarian rule, making them incomparably different from the participants of the salons and other settings of the bourgeois public sphere, not to mention at odds with time-hallowed models of civic engagement that point to the importance of education and income in predicting civic participation.[5] While the imagery of the "marginal urban poor" no longer holds sway, as it once did, the portrayal of the Latin American urban poor as entangled in social pathology and clientelism, and as unlikely candidates for democratic orientation, still has some influence.[6]

More subtly, the activities of the CPP call into question the often-unstated analytic separation between social movement activity and civic engagement, which Archon Fung has called the "mischievous" and "cooperative" faces of civil society.[7] Social movements are disruptive, rowdy, and contestatory; civic engagement is virtuous, civil, and cooperative. CPP activists, many of whom participated in the prodemocracy movement, and most of whom would consider themselves "militants" on behalf of their communities, often describe their activities as part of "the movement" struggling for social justice in Brazil. But much of what they do also clearly falls under the rubric of civic engagement and virtue; they express concern about broad problems of the community and the city, encourage fellow residents to get involved in the activities of the OP, and invoke the importance of "average citizen" involvement in their community and local government. They use the language of citizenship to describe rights and responsibilities, and they describe themselves as citizens.

Community activists in Porto Alegre, such as those in the CPP, are both militants and citizens. They consider themselves part of a broad movement for social justice, engaged in what they believe is a process of social transformation. However, in order to achieve substantive change, they act in civic and cooperative ways. They are engaged in their communities and believe they must both monitor local government and bring more citizens to participate. While assuming both identities is not without contradictions, and there are settings where assuming one or the other role is considered more proper, practices within organizations like the CPP highlight the fact that the analytic distinction is artificial and born of an academic vision that evokes romantic images of virtuous citizens engaged in selfless discussion, which may not reflect the conflict inherent in such situations.[8]

Understanding these three puzzles about civic engagement in Porto Alegre—how and why municipal programs have fostered civic engagement, how it has been particularly successful at empowering the city's poorest participants, and how this has evolved into a political culture that straddles notions of citizenship and militancy—requires un-

FIG. 2. A meeting of the Conselho Popular do Partenon (CPP), 1999

derstanding the content of these civic practices in their "proper relational context," that is, exposing the web of enabling and constraining
relationships that bear on civic life.[9] Resolving these three puzzles con-
stitutes the central theoretical question of this book: What is the impact
of participatory governance on civic life?

The question is relevant not only to Porto Alegre or Brazil but also to
debates about social movements, democratic theory, and public policy
at large, not to mention to activists and reformers in other countries. In
terms of social movements, it helps explain what happens when social
movements' innovative practices are extended to broader publics.
Much as social movements are contexts in which activists engage in the
practices and relationships they would like to see extended to society at
large, "prefiguring" them, in the democratic world such movements
rarely extend beyond a small fraction of a population.[10] In Brazil, reinventing and reclaiming "citizenship" was a dominant theme in social
movements in the 1980s and 1990s.[11] In Porto Alegre, a prefigurative social movement innovation—norms of claims making and collective access to the public good—became institutionalized and extended to a
whole city. Understanding the travails of such an innovation and its im-

pact on civic practices is an important issue for new and old democracies alike, addressing the neglected issue of coordination across "voluntary and empowered publics."[12] As local-level participatory reforms become more common throughout the developing world as a result of the decentralization of national states, this question assumes significant practical importance as well. Many scholars have discussed the benefits of participatory reforms, but fewer have addressed the impact of such reforms on civic life.[13]

The City of Porto Alegre

The city of Porto Alegre, today with a population of 1.314 million, lies at the center of a metropolitan area of almost three million.[14] As the major industrial and financial center of Rio Grande do Sul, it is relatively well served by municipal services, and with high social indicators by Brazilian standards.[15] Its current literacy rate of 96.5 percent is among the highest in the country for a large city, as are the average life expectancy (71.5 years) and gross primary school enrollment (92.2 percent) rates. In 2000, Porto Alegre ranked eleventh in human development indicators among Brazilian municipalities overall and second among state capitals.[16]

Since the 1950s, Brazil has rapidly urbanized; today, roughly 80 percent of Brazilians live in cities, whereas fifty years ago, less than a third of the population did. In most urban centers, the quality of life deteriorated steadily in the 1980s. With continued investment in large-scale agriculture, the rate of rural out-migration was much higher than could be absorbed by the urban labor market.[17] Social problems in peripheral urban areas were also exacerbated because of rapid deindustrialization and the "informalization" of many jobs. Porto Alegre lost 30 percent of

TABLE 1

Irregular Settlements in Porto Alegre, 1965–1995

	1965	1975	1981	1987	1995	2000
Number of settlements	56	124	145	183	215	
Population	65,595	105,833	171,419	326,608	196,007	290,394
Percentage of city's population	8.1	9.5	15.2	24.7	15.5	22.1

SOURCE: Pozzobon 1998: 9; PMPA/SMP 1998; Marquetti 2001.

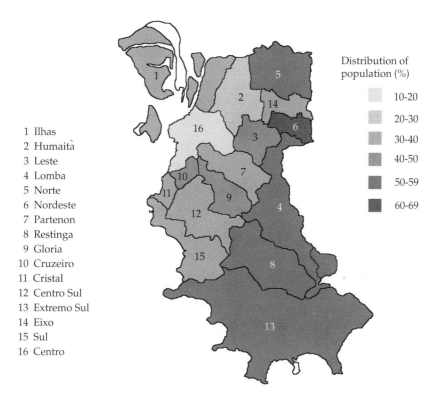

1 Ilhas
2 Humaità
3 Leste
4 Lomba
5 Norte
6 Nordeste
7 Partenon
8 Restinga
9 Gloria
10 Cruzeiro
11 Cristal
12 Centro Sul
13 Extremo Sul
14 Eixo
15 Sul
16 Centro

Distribution of
population (%)

10-20
20-30
30-40
40-50
50-59
60-69

FIG. 3. Porto Alegre's districts and the distribution of poverty, 1996.
Adapted with permission from PROCEMPA

net formal jobs between 1986 and 1995, most of them in industry.[18] Like much of Brazil, the city also experienced an exacerbation of urban poverty and a relative decline in revenues during those years.[19] Porto Alegre's slum areas, or "irregular housing settlements," have grown since the mid 1960s (table 1).

Almost a quarter of Porto Alegre's population today lives in "irregular housing," such as slums or invaded areas, which fan outward from the city center, with the poorest districts generally the farthest from downtown. Figure 3 shows the city's districts and the levels of poverty in each of them, based on 1996 figures.

The districts closer to downtown tend to have larger numbers of middle- and working-class residents, while the districts on the periphery form a belt of poverty, mostly inhabited by those outside of the formal labor market. Illegal makeshift settlements are scattered through-out the city, but concentrated in peripheral districts, often as a result of forced removals.

Structural Transformations of the State

These social and economic changes have been accompanied by changes in the structure of the national state. After Brazil returned to formal democracy, large-scale municipal elections took place in 1985, and the "decentralization of government" was codified with the first post-dictatorship constitution, ratified in 1988. This signaled a broad shift from national to local state power, reversing the dictatorship-era pattern of centralization.[20] A coalition of actors, which included mod-ernizers within government, progressive politicians, and grassroot ac-tivists, formed the coalition behind the change.[21] Local governments were given more political autonomy from the federal state, and were free to develop "municipal organic laws," essentially municipal consti-tutions that could legislate on matters such as land-use policies. The new constitution also increased the taxes municipalities could raise, as well as the proportion of state and federal taxes passed directly to the city, such as vehicle, sales, and service taxes. The constitution decreed certain areas of service provision as "primarily" municipal domains, such as health, while establishing legal provisos for participatory mechanisms in municipal planning and in certain areas of service pro-vision.[22] Figure 4 summarizes the structure of Brazilian government and fiscal budgeting.

Over the course of the 1990s, municipalities became the principal providers of housing, education, cultural input, and health services.[23] So while the share of total social spending in Brazil by municipalities increased from 11 percent to 19 percent between 1987 and 1996, munic-ipalities have had increasingly to raise local revenues in order to meet demands for services.[24] Some cities, like Porto Alegre, have been fa-vored by rules that privilege the kinds of taxes that can be raised by large, rich cities, such as land-use taxes.[25] Although it exacerbated some inequalities and loaded new responsibilities onto municipalities, Bra-zil's decentralization created the institutional openings for actors with ties to civil society and social movements to carry out progressive ex-periments. By the late 1980s, many large city governments in Brazil be-gan to establish decentralization programs alongside participatory pro-

Brazil is a federal republic with three levels of government, federal, state, and municipal. Each level of government raises revenues and spends funds, and states and municipalities also depend on transfers from higher levels. Constitutionally, there are "concurrent responsibilities" for government functions among the three levels of government, but since the late 1980s, the country's more than 5,500 municipalities have become the de facto source for social spending and public investment, having assumed responsibility for health, primary education, social service provision, and transportation.

Municipal governments have an executive, headed by a mayor, elected for a four-year term; and a municipal legislature, composed of city councilors, also elected for four-year terms. The mayor appoints the heads of various municipal departments, such as the Planning Department and the Housing Department. There are some restrictions on municipal budgets, such as spending caps on personnel and minimum health expenditures, but municipal governments have significant leeway in setting the budget. The municipal budget is, by law, submitted by the executive branch to the municipal legislature for approval toward the end of the year. The Orçamento Participativo in Porto Alegre is not an official government institution, and it is the mayor who "officially" turns in the yearly budget to the legislature.

F I G . 4 . The structure of government and the budget in Brazil

grams. The capital cities of Curitiba, Rio de Janeiro, Recife, and Salvador had all developed participatory structures by 1985–88, with varying degrees of decision-making power.[26] There have also been local experiments in the areas of environmental action, health provision, poverty reduction, private-public partnerships, public transportation, and the use of computer resources at the municipal level.[27]

Brazil's Democracy: The New Citizenship, the Workers' Party, and the Orçamento Participativo

The transition to democracy in Brazil has juxtaposed a largely unresponsive, corrupt political system, dominated by patronage, particularly at the local and state levels, and an emergent civil society, based on social movements that since the mid 1980s have taken new stances on citizenship and public policy. Resolving this dichotomy is the fundamental challenge faced by Brazil today.[28]

Brazilian democracy's well-known ills have been labeled "social apartheid": many policies have carried over from the authoritarian period, and the majority of the country's citizens experience a disjuncture

between formal democracy and actual, lived democracy.[29] Notwithstanding the social mobilization to impeach the president in 1992,
Brazilian political life remains marked by patronage, as well as by a
weak and incoherent party system, defined by personalism, and an "ex-
cess of veto players" in a democratic system that is systematically biased toward pork-barrel politics.[30] Low civic engagement, a predatory
political culture, and a minimal state that is not responsive to the majority of the population persist.[31] Large numbers of blank or spoiled bal-
lots are cast in every election, and in surveys, large percentages of
Brazilians say that they would not vote if not required to do so.[32] According to studies like the Latinobarómetro and World Values Surveys,
Brazilians are dissatisfied with their democratic institutions, and support for democratic values has wavered in recent years.[33]

The 1970s and 1980s were also characterized, however, by the appearance of new civic associations and new urban social movements
making claims at the local level, often backed by ideologies of social
transformation and a break with the past. The "new unionism" around
São Paulo, the grassroots church activism (in the Ecclesiastic Base Communities), and the struggles for urban rights were all part of a diffuse
democratic movement that has been well described in the literature.[34]
These new movements politicized questions of access to services, coa-
lescing around nationally organized movements for urban rights such
as the Cost of Living Movement, the Housing Movement, and the Collective Transportation Movement, in the mid-to-late 1970s, which emphasized novel practices and values, including autonomy from manip-
ulative government agencies and patronage schemes, proceduralism
and democracy in decision making, and democratic access to urban services.[35]

What some have described as a decline in social movement activity
in the 1980s and 1990s in terms of contentious activity no doubt partially reflects the new practices of movements in the 1990s, some of
which have sought out more permanent institutionalization in the form
of NGOs and similar organizations.[36] With the transition to democracy,
social movements shifted practices and discourses toward demanding
a voice and participation in local governments and toward proposing
specific policies.[37] In 1989, for instance, the national meeting of the National Forum for Urban Reform concluded with a statement of principles that called for participation in the running of city affairs to be regarded as a basic right of citizenship.[38] These new propositional

practices of social movements were grounded in the ideologies of movements of the 1970s and 1980s, and while demanding dialogue with the state, they simultaneously challenged the limits of representative democracy by calling for participatory reforms and expanded versions of traditional rights.[39] Evelina Dagnino refers to this as "the new citizenship" that dominated Brazilian social movements in the 1980s and 1990s.[40] Its premise was "the right to have rights," and it lauded the invention of "new rights that emerge from specific struggles and concrete practices."[41] In demanding the recognition of new subjects, it proposed new forms of social relationships mediated by the state, as well as new relationships between civil society and the state.

The Workers' Party

The Workers' Party, or PT, emerged as one of the novelties of the post-authoritarian period as a political party with the explicit aspiration to translate civil society demands into party platforms.[42] The PT was founded in 1980 as a party where "social movements can speak," with an emphasis on internal democracy and openness, rejecting democratic centralism and vanguardist positions and aligning class struggle with citizenship.[43] The spectrum of founding members included, in addition to industrial union workers and leftist agitators, progressive Christian activists, representatives from an array of social movements, and intellectuals.[44]

Under strict rules, such as the absence of individual campaign funds, PT activists competed in the limited 1982 elections, but reaped only one victory, in São Paulo state.[45] The party built up support over the next several years and was a prominent player in the national movement for direct elections, winning two municipalities in the 1985 elections and some seats in congress in 1986, followed by a number of PT mayors in 1988, which brought roughly 10 percent of Brazilians under PT administrations. The party continued to grow in the 1990s, often experiencing electoral victories followed by setbacks, but nonetheless becoming a significant force in congress and senate.[46] And in 2002, the PT's candidate for president, Luís Ignácio da Silva, "Lula," was elected in a runoff contest with 61 percent of votes.

As the party grew in significance, it evolved ideologically. Throughout the 1980s and 1990s, the PT significantly broadened its discourse to a range of social issues, making broad alliances, and emphasizing democratic participation in government. At its Fifth National Meeting in

1987, the party renewed its positions on party liberty, civil liberties, and the right to association, criticizing the eastern European model of that era and calling for a "democratic popular" government, essentially a partly socialist state with democratic elections.[47] In 1991, at its First National Congress, the PT defined its program as democratic socialist, and in 1999, at its Second National Congress, it called for a two-stage "democratic revolution" anchored in broad and empowered popular participation. The rainbow of movements and social sectors represented within the PT also broadened, throughout the 1990s,[48] and the party started to win votes consistently in medium-sized and smaller cities throughout the country.[49]

The PT's experience in government and, in particular, its successful experiments, such as the OP in Porto Alegre, has been one of the driving forces behind these changes in the party. In many cases, despite the implementation of innovative social programs, many early administrations had trouble with intense factional disputes over the meaning of a PT administration.[50] On one hand, privileging the party's bases could jeopardize its reelection by narrowing the spectrum of potential supporters; on the other, broadening the range of social demands too much risked disfiguring the party's redistributive platform and alienating its traditional bases of support. The inability of various PT governments to effectively negotiate different societal demands was the source of many administrations' difficulties with both internal struggles and external pressures.

The learning experiences of early city administrations showed that devising appropriate political solutions would be as important as, if not more important than, good policies and programs.[51] Successful administrations were those that implemented participatory programs as a strategy for negotiation of demands and legitimation of platforms in ways that helped avert some of the conflicts. Broad-based participation provided political solutions: in terms of negotiating societal demands, it created settings where claimants were part of the negotiation of demands; in terms of governance, broad-based participation generated legitimacy for governance strategies, if not improving governance directly. Successful programs went beyond organized social movements, unions, and neighborhood associations to include unorganized sectors among the poor, working classes, and middle classes. By the mid 1990s, participatory programs had become standard in PT municipalities, and OP reforms were adopted in practically every PT local government from that time onward, not to mention the large number of municipalities not under PT control that have "copied" the OP.[52]

The Workers' Party in Porto Alegre

Porto Alegre figures centrally in the evolution of the PT, because its OP became the model for so many other administrations, and in time, the city also became the model administration and standard-bearer for the party. But the PT was not originally a strong party in Porto Alegre, then a stronghold of the Partido Trabalhista Brasileiro (PTB), or Brazilian Labor Party, since renamed the Partido Democrático Trabalhista (PDT), or Democratic Labor Party, which has a history of ties to the neighborhood association movement and unions in a few urban centers.[53] The populist PTB exerted enormous political influence on urban movements in Porto Alegre until the military coup of 1964, and as the PDT, it has continued to exert significant influence in local politics since the reinstatement of democracy, only declining in the course of the 1990s. The PDT today reflects a contradictory mix of economically progressive platforms, "family and country" discourses, and an allegiance to a few notable politicians. At the time of the first PT administration, the PDT was still very strong in Porto Alegre.

Only having elected one city councilor to the legislature between 1982 and 1988, and one federal deputy, the PT registered barely over 10 percent of votes in the 1985 municipal elections in Porto Alegre. In the 1989 presidential elections, the PDT candidate captured almost 70 percent of the votes in Porto Alegre, which was ten times higher than the PT vote, while in the 1990 gubernatorial race, the PT got only 10 percent of the vote in the city.[54] The PT would only become a significant electoral voice in the course of subsequent administrations, as the PDT became less important.[55] The PDT had influence in local neighborhood associations, in the directorate of the Union of Neighborhood Associations, and in the directorate of the Municipal Employees' Union.[56] Nonetheless, largely as a result of the OP, the PT has established itself as the dominant political party in town. It managed reelection with increasing support in 1992, 1996, and 2000, and among the one-third of Porto Alegre's citizens who have a party preference, two-thirds declare the PT to be their party of choice. Nonetheless, the PT continues to be a minority in the legislature, holding from nine to twelve seats, out of thirty-three, in the 1990s.[57]

The Orçamento Participativo

The OP was first introduced in 1989, and after trial and errors, succeeded by the mid 1990s in regularly drawing very large numbers of participants.[58] By 2000, upwards of 14,000 participants attended the first yearly OP assembly. Participation has been high, especially in the city's poorer districts, where, in practice, OP meetings are a key venue for meetings of community activists. The average participant in the OP today is poorer and less educated than the citywide average. In 2000, almost two-thirds of participants came from households with an income of four times the minimum wage (i.e., roughly U.S.$280 a month) or less, and 60 percent had no more than an eighth-grade education, against citywide averages of 45 percent and 55 percent, respectively.[59] Every year, a substantial portion of participants are first-timers, without any prior participation in civil society.[60] Table 2 profiles OP participants in 2000 in terms of income, race, gender, and education. As it starkly shows, OP participants at all levels are poorer, less educated, and more likely to be black than the city averages.[61]

The OP has provided for significant improvements in the city's poorer areas.[62] A significant portion of the yearly municipal budget (between 9 percent and 21 percent of a total budget that amounted to U.S.$610 million in 2000)[63] is dedicated to OP investments, systematically favoring poorer districts over wealthier ones.[64] The OP has approved hundreds of projects, including street paving, urban improvements in precarious areas, sewage, municipal public education, and health, with a completion rate of nearly 100 percent.[65] These projects have contributed to an increase to almost full coverage in sewage and water,[66] a threefold increase in the number of children in municipal schools,[67] and significant increases in the number of new housing units provided to needy families.[68] Porto Alegre's expenditures in certain areas, such as health and housing, are much higher than the national average,[69] and the municipality has tended over the years to spend less and less in administrative costs.[70] From the perspectives of governance and quantitative indicators, the OP has succeeded in attracting broad-based participation from the poorer strata of Porto Alegre's citizenry and in effectively linking that participation to redistributive outcomes.

The very successes of the OP raise several important questions about its participatory aspects. The literature on Porto Alegre has by now become quite extensive, and insightful case studies by Rebecca Abers, Lu-

TABLE 2

Profile of Orçamento Participativo Participants, 2000

	Citywide Average	All Participants	Delegates	Councilors
Women	55.4%	56.4%	55%	27%
Low income[a]	11.4%	30.3%	23.7%	21.4%
Black[b]	15.4%	28.1%	21%	22%
Low education[c]	15.8%	60.3%	39%	36%

SOURCE: CIDADE 2001; IBGE 2001.

[a] Low income here means household earnings below twice the minimum wage.

[b] Black here refers to the census categories *negro* (black) and *pardo* (brown).

[c] Low education means education up to completed primary (grade 8).

ciano Fedozzi, and Sérgio Baierle carefully address the OP's origins, unfolding, and impacts.[71] The city has also recently achieved "global status" for this participatory scheme, recognized by activists, international organizations, and policy makers from the North and South. It stands in contrast to the well-known electoral and institutional failures of leftist municipal administrations in Latin America and elsewhere.[72] Scholars have generally pointed to the novel institutional forms involved in participatory governance and to its governmental performance.[73]

The missing dimension of the research is a systematic examination of decision making and associative practices within and outside of the OP, and the relationships between them. While the participatory institutions in Porto Alegre have brought tens of thousands of participants to assemblies, discussion of the quality of democratic practice in those assemblies is still largely absent from academic discussion. High numbers of participants, which is often taken as prima facie evidence of democratic engagement in the OP, could mean that many of Porto Alegre's citizens engage in unfettered and reflexive discussions and contribute to the construction of a "collective will" (such as described for the Habermassian "public sphere"); but high numbers are also compatible with a system that simply generates legitimacy without actual input or discussion.[74] The difference between these two versions from the point of view of the democratic significance of the experiment is immense, but systematic qualitative evidence beyond selective interviews or the review of official figures is required. Advocates of Porto Alegre's experiment, such as its ex-mayor Tarso Genro, have described the OP as a "nonstate public sphere" but the question has not been empirically addressed.[75]

The challenge for social movements in Brazil in the 1990s and be-

F IG . 5 . A volunteer
registers participants
at an Orçamento
Participativo meeting

yond has been precisely how to convert its innovations into meaningful
state policies that promoted citizenship, rather than "re-clientilization"
given the conflict between movement practices and "the logic of political society in Brazil," according to Leonardo Avritzer. In reviewing the
results of a 2000 national study on the topic, Dagnino finds that the results of civil society participation in such public spaces is mixed. But if
the OP's inception indeed contributes to the formation of a genuine
Brazilian "public space," or, as I advance here, to an innovative
"state–civil society regime," then understanding these processes in
their day-to-day intricacies in and around this system becomes crucial
to theories of direct democracy and civil society far beyond Porto Alegre and Brazil.[76]

Toward a Relational Theory of Civil Society

The Porto Alegre story is the story of the mutual impact of participatory institutions and civil society on each other. The interest in the issue is not new. Earlier thinkers from Alexis de Tocqueville to Rosa Luxemburg and John Dewey concerned themselves with the conditions under which participation in governmental decision making could enhance public life, engage civil society, and contribute to the construction of genuinely democratic practices.[77] But when we turn to the current discussion, neither of the two main relevant traditions in sociology, the society-centered theory of democracy and the social movements approach, has a language for exposing relationships *across* society and the state, for which we have to turn to a relational approach.

The so-called social capital theories, in which the work of Robert Putnam and his collaborators is central, are the current focus of much of the society-centered discussion of democracy. In this approach, "networks of trust" in civil society, where norms of reciprocity and collaboration are taught and reinforced, are viewed as crucial to the health of democracy.[78] Bowling leagues, environmental groups, and all manner of civic associations contribute to the functioning of democracy and help keep the democratic state in check by fostering trust and discouraging clientelism and rent-seeking. This literature has sparked a vigorous debate about the origins of and preconditions for democracy, but what is of concern here is its underlying assumption, that civil society is by definition *autonomous and separate from the state*. This creates two problems for the discussion at hand; first, it obscures spaces *between* the state and civil society (such as the OP) as settings for civic action. Second, and more fundamentally, it does permit us to analyze the dynamic processes of interaction *across* state and civil society that constrain and enable both state and civil society. Neo-Tocquevillians like Putnam emphasize how a vibrant associational life contributes to honest and responsive political institutions. But they do not ask, conversely, how democratized political institutions influence associational life.

Social movement scholarship, particularly in its political opportunities (or "political process") guise, has offered much insight into the responsiveness of social movements to changes in the polity. While in recent times the literature has moved away from a purely state-centered orientation, the now classic formulation that has guided inquiries emphasizes that *political opportunities*, or signals from the state or from institutional actors, both encourage and discourage collective action from below.[79] As with society-centered theories of the democracy, the usefulness and assumptions of these social movements theories have been the subject of a lively debate.[80] From the point of view of the Porto Alegre story, however, this literature lacks an accounting of the processes by which social movements themselves can come to *change* the state, having little to say about the fact that the OP has its origins in social movement demands. This literature has too seldom asked what happens when social movements "win," which can affect "the rules of the game" in democratic polities.[81]

In contrast, a relational political sociology does provide a basis for thinking through the impact of participatory governance on civil society and vice versa. A central insight of relational sociologies in general is that traditional sociological categories like "class" or "social movements" ought to be disaggregated and understood as clusters of "people, power, and organizations," enabling us to see society as "patterned . . . relationships among cultural, economic, social, and political practices."[82] Relational political sociologists do not see civil society as a unitary entity separate from the state or the economy; rather, they reframe civil society as crisscrossing groups of people engaged in voluntary activities,[83] or as I propose here, the *institutions, practices, and networks of voluntary life*. Such an approach calls for the unpacking of the sometimes contradictory relationships between the state and voluntary associations and the way in which these shifting relationships both reflect societal social power and shape the functioning of the state and civil society.[84] The three central concepts here are state–civil society regimes, civic configurations, and civic practices.

Institutions: State–Civil Society Regimes

State–civil society regimes are the stable pattern of state–civil society interactions, whose defining feature is the way that societal demands are recognized. A regime includes all of the ways in which citizens interact with the state, as well as all of the ways in which the state might limit or enable the activities in civil society, and it is defined by the way these interactions constitute a pattern of recognition of societal demands. A relational sociology notes the way that distinctive, stable, regimes create specific logics for civic engagement that encourage or discourage particular kinds of practices in civil society, and pays attention to how the structured "turns" of state-society interactions at each round reflect the balance of power and legacies of previous turns, limiting some possibilities but also opening up other ones.[85] A regime also establishes a political logic that becomes the accepted way of resolving conflict between actors in society.[86]

In trying to understand the OP and its impact on civil society, a relational approach looks for how the OP is part of an overall pattern of recognition of societal demands by the state, and on *all* of the ways in which various segments in civil society (individuals, pressure groups, movements, civic organizations) interact with the state (formal, informal settings, meetings, protests, etc.), attempting to understand how it is that these interactions impinge on the functioning both of the state and of civil society.[87] Regimes vary from very open regimes to starkly authoritarian ones, and formal distinctions are possible along three possible axes: (1) the state's overall openness to societal demands; (2) the constraints the state places on civil society; and (3) the dominant institutional form of state-society interactions over societal demands. The broad family of regimes in which the state does not place significant constraints on civil society and is open to societal demands is composed of affirmative democratic regimes. Within that category, a division is possible between representative regimes and *empowered participatory regimes*. The OP is part of an empowered participatory regime marked by a high degree of openness to societal demands, few constraints on civil society, and bottom-up empowered participation as a way to process societal demands. Representative regimes rely instead on institutions like parliaments as the mechanism for input and processing of demands.[88]

TABLE 3

Comparison of Tutelage and Democratic Affirmative Regimes

| | State–Civil Society Regime | | |
| | | Democratic Affirmative Regimes | |
	Tutelage	Representative	Empowered participatory
Openness to societal demands	Yes	Yes	Yes
Constraints on civil society	High	Low	Low
Input and filtering of societal demands	Direct dialogue, state as ultimate arbiter	Representative institutions	Bottom-up participation

A regime of *tutelage*, in contrast, has as its principal characteristic the fact that the state places significant constraints on civil society in terms of demanding political allegiance in exchange for the recognition of societal demands. Tutelage regimes do not rely on democratic representative institutions so much as on direct dialogue between civil society claimants and the state,[89] but the state may impose constraints by selectively recognizing certain actors according to political allegiance.[90] The difference between tutelage and empowered participatory regimes is not whether there is or is not participation (and in fact, there may be significant participation as part of tutelage), but whether the participation on the part of civil society is politically constrained. In a tutelage regime, participation is always constrained, and the state retains final authority in decision making. Earlier periods of Porto Alegre's history characterized by tutelage regimes were followed by the installation of an empowered participatory regime, and in addition to a political logic, each type of regime established a logic of civic engagement.[91]

Civic Configurations and Practices

Within a particular regime, where there is a stable set of state-society interactions around societal demands that promote certain kinds of civic action, there may be local variation in the configuration of actors, organizations, and networks within civil society that position themselves vis-à-vis the regime. These *civic configurations* are shorthand for the local variation in the "interconnected, interdependent, and complementary set of actors" in civil society.[92] There can be variation in the levels of organization, as well as in the cohesiveness within these configurations. Attention to civic configurations also means paying attention to conflict and contestation within them, as well as attention to how different sites and organizations are connected together (how *brokerage* is performed), and how new actors are accepted as legitimate within a civic configuration (how *certification* is performed). In this book, I study three districts that have distinct configurations during the period of the empowered participatory regime—a highly organized and cohesive district, a highly organized and divided district, and a cohesive but weakly organized district. My argument is that each of these configurations sets the stage differently for civic practices within the overall empowered participatory regime.

Civic practices can be defined as a patterned set of day-to-day behaviors oriented toward associational life. When people engage in associational activity, they improvise, but they do so based on available scripts and in specific contexts that subtly constrain and enable action; moreover, they are bound by unspoken rules and assumptions.[93] In her study of meetings of volunteers, for example, Jane Mansbridge suggests that certain unspoken rules about appropriateness constrain behavior, thus promoting the avoidance of open conflict.[94] Attention to informal rules also means attention to the subtle ways in which actors present themselves in these settings and what may be at stake in doing so,[95] such as maintaining reputation and honor, particularly for those who have some standing in the community.[96]

The Study

This book is an "extended case study" that seeks to isolate the features of participatory reforms and the way they have impinged on civil society as a basis for a reconstruction of theories of civil society. Although it does not rely exclusively on participant observation, it was conceived very much in the spirit of the extended case method of Michael Burawoy and his students.[97] And in line with an earlier generation of classic urban case studies, such as Robert Dahl's 1961 study of New Haven, I have attempted to use the specifics of this case study to make larger theoretical arguments about civil society, politics, and participation.[98] More in line with classic studies such as Robert and Helen Lynd's *Middletown* (1929) and St. Clair Drake and Horace Cayton's *Black Metropolis* (1945) than with contemporary political sociology, however, I develop my account by relying on both evidence about change over time and ethnographic evidence, as well as aggregate indicators. The ethnography is based on two years of investigation in three districts of the city of Porto Alegre between 1997 and 1999 and in the municipal Conselho do Orçamento Participativo (COP), or Participatory Budget Council, as well as over 150 interviews, lasting from one to eight hours.

Relying on a variety of indicators, based on direct and indirect evidence gathered from interviews and archives, I analyze citywide changes, systematically compare different districts of the city, with different "starting points," and examine different associative outcomes in each of those districts. In line with the methodological belief implicit in relational arguments that the "quantitative-qualitative divide" is artificial, the aggregate evidence from the surveys is interspersed throughout the text, and the particulars of the research strategy and its guiding logic are both described in the Appendix, as are the potential sources of bias in this kind of research.

Although the city of Porto Alegre is treated as the "case" in this study, I focused my ethnographic investigation on district-level events rather than on city-based events, because it is at the level of the district that the most immediate interactions between civil society and municipal government take place. Treating districts separately also allows me to follow a "most variance strategy" in the case study,[99] because they make up highly differentiated social contexts and variation in terms of civic configurations.

I chose one very poor district without a significant associative tradition prior to the OP, and two largely working-class districts with divergent histories. The small (population 25,000) Nordeste district is one of the poorest and most remote districts of the city, with low rates of education and a median monthly household income for 1998 that was about half the city's average. This district was also chosen because of its lack of well-defined networks of citizens or of clear activist neighborhood traditions prior to the OP. Both the Partenon and Norte districts are larger (populations 114,000 and 86,000) and have a long history of neighborhood organizing, and both have significant working-class and lower-middle-class neighborhoods, in addition to slum areas. The Partenon district has a "militant" associative tradition tied to pro-democracy movements and the progressive church, and it has cohered around the OP. The Norte district has a history of conflict between neighborhood associations with connections to politicians of the PTB/PDT and insurgent activists with ties to progressive social movements, and these fissures have only been exacerbated during the establishment of the OP.

The Organization of the Book

The story I tell in this book includes the PT, innovative municipal administrative institutions, social movements, cadres of local administration officials, and church activists in Porto Alegre. But it is not a story primarily about any of these groups or institutions so much as a story of common citizens becoming involved with the day-to-day affairs of the community, developing ties, and becoming involved in pragmatic problem solving. The book traces these changing civic practices and networks in Porto Alegre in response to democratic innovations in the city's management, although not only through a historical narrative. The first part of the book provides the context and history of the experiment and its impact on civic practices in Chapter 2, starting with the neighborhood associations of the 1950s in Porto Alegre, before focusing on changes in the current period (1991–2000), while in Chapter 3, I tell the story of the OP's routinization from the bottom up in the three very different districts of the city I chose to study. The subsequent, ethnographic chapters discuss day-to-day practices in and around the district-level Budget Forum meetings. Chapter 4 discusses the "deliberativeness" of OP meetings, addressing how activists construct solutions to participatory dilemmas, while Chapter 5 describes the way activists make use of Budget Council meetings to conduct a variety of community activities beyond strictly budgeting matters, and create public-sphere–like interactions. Chapter 6 describes the day-to-day functioning of civil society in Porto Alegre and discusses sources of authority within it, and Chapter 7 offers some conclusions about the implications of this remarkable story.

CHAPTER TWO

A City Transformed

On the eve of the Partido dos Trabalhadores administration's in-auguration in Porto Alegre in late 1988, there was intense specu-lation about what it would mean for the community movement. One of the principal platforms on which its coalition partners in the Frente Popular (Popular Front) had been elected was the empowerment of the community movement; campaign materials promised to "create spaces of participation, monitoring, and popular control over the administra-tion," while supporting popular struggles and inverting municipal pri-orities.[1] The incumbent PDT mayor, Alceu Collares, called the PT's plans for popular empowerment "romantic" and unfeasible, declaring that his own administration had reflected the "best and most notable" aspects of popular participation in Brazil. The vice-mayor elect, Tarso Genro, like other *petistas* (PT members), resisted any comparison be-tween the previous populist PDT schemes and PT's proposals. Genro said that the PT intended citizens of all party affiliations to be able to participate in running the city, in contrast to what was perceived as PDT favoritism.[2]

The PT's project for participation and for the administration was anything but well defined at this early stage. In May 1989, the munici-pal branch of the PT defended the position that the administration ought to consider organized social movements and unions as "privi-leged" actors in its participatory schemes.[3] It also defended the position that the administration should directly stimulate forms of popular or-ganization, such as the popular councils. By 1993, at the start of the PT's second term in office, the resolutions were of a completely different na-

ture. Although they still defended a socialist and transformative project, these new resolutions called for increasing dialogue with all sectors
and broadening the base of support for the administration through participation and effective provision of services, deepening the processes
of decentralization, abandoning "sectarian disputes," and "increasing
popular control" of public investments.[4] In order to understand the
thorough shift in the party's understanding of participation, it is necessary to outline the changing dynamics between the state and civil society in the city in this period.

As discussed in Chapter 1, state–civil society regimes create distinct
logics of civic engagement, and Porto Alegre has had two types of
regime since the 1940s: a series of tutelage regimes and an empowered
participatory regime. Tutelage regimes have as their principal characteristic the fact that the state demands political allegiance in exchange
for recognition of societal demands, and the logic of civic engagement
that it creates is for individuals and organizations to choose between
acquiescence and opposition, with powerful incentives for individual
organizations to acquiesce and break ranks with the rest of the collective opposition. In empowered participatory regimes, the state is highly
open to societal demands via direct participation and without constraints, and the logic of civic engagement is to create incentives for collective engagement insofar as participation yields concrete results.
Since the 1940s, associations in Porto Alegre have cycled from opposition or acquiescence under a tutelage regime to a period of high civic
engagement and a transparent local state under an empowered participatory regime in the 1990s.[5]

The argument I make in this chapter is twofold. First, the creation
and eventual successes of the OP in the 1990s had to do with a particular set of legacies from previous tutelage regimes. In particular, they
grew out of a conjuncture of events that led to concrete proposals for
participatory reforms like the OP by community activists who were disappointed with the previous PDT administration's limited mandate.[6]
The eventual form and impact of the OP reflects the balance between
the demands of activists and the strategic concerns of a relatively politically weak administration, while concurrent fiscal reforms bolstered its
capacity to link tangible results to participation. Second, as the OP
eventually became successful in drawing participants and generating
legitimacy for the administration, it deeply transformed the associational landscape, fostering a cycle of collaborative state–civil society interactions with a responsive administration on one side and a denser, if

TABLE 4

State–Civil Society Regimes, 1945–2000

	1945–1977	1977–1985	1986–1988	1989–2000
State–civil society regime	Tutelage and authoritarian tutelage (post-1964)	Tutelage	Tutelage with participatory elements	Empowered Participatory post-1991
Formal institutions of civil society consultation	Some participatory instances through councils	Military-run *gaúcho* Community Council	"Self-help programs" and "consultative forums" for politically sympathetic associations	Establishment of OP and councils;
Informal interactions	Important	Important	Very important	Not important
Scaled-up groups and umbrella organizations	FRACAB (1959)	FRACAB, UAMPA (1983) and some *conselhos populares*	UAMPA and *conselhos populares*	City- and district-wide networks linked to state programs
Support organizations		Progressive clergy, NGOs, parties	NGOs, Parties	NGOs
Civil society practices	Participation in "social pact" with the state, occasional "anti-paternalist" opposition	New oppositions around pro-democracy movement, discourse of autonomy; some participation in programs	Cycles of acceptance and opposition; militant discourse of democracy, participation, and local demands	Broad participation in OP and similar fora; growth in new associations; discourse of citizenship, participation, and partnership; "militancy" and "citizenship" merged

less contentious, civil society deeply involved in city affairs on the other. Table 4 compares the regime established after 1991 with three prior periods of tutelage.

In Porto Alegre, a first period, marked by tutelage of associations in working-class neighborhoods to City Hall lasted from the municipal social programs of the 1950s through to the more constrained "participatory programs" in the deeply authoritarian years of the dictatorship in the 1970s. A second period, from 1977 until 1985, was marked by the emergence of increasingly politicized opposition movements in civil society in response to the relaxation of censorship by the military and the failure of urban improvement programs to deliver results on the city's peripheries. A third period refers to the Collares administration, when attempts at broader participatory reforms were stalled and more limited programs linked to political allegiance were instituted, replicating earlier tutelage regimes. Finally, in the 1990s, there was a rupture and transformation in the polity, with the creation and establishment of an empowered participatory regime.

From Tutelage to New Movements: Associations from 1945 to 1985

The populist Partido Trabalhista Brasileiro alternated rule in Porto Alegre with the more conservative Partido Democrático Social until 1964. Since the 1940s, Porto Alegre has been the PTB's power base because of support from the organized working-class communities in the city. Populism has been widely studied as a political form throughout Latin America and is generally understood to be a style of political leadership characterized by a top-heavy tutorial state under the rule of a charismatic leader with a professed commitment to the welfare of the masses. The result has often been a kind of class compromise, in which certain popular sectors—primarily organized labor—received some limited benefits and entitlements within the constraints of the political regime.[7] The "populist pact" was usually mediated through labor unions, however, and not through neighborhood associations. Nonetheless, politicians at times saw working-class neighborhood associations as important conduits between the state and the populace, and this accounted for strong ties between successive municipal administrations and those associations.

The first registered neighborhood associations in Porto Alegre's working-class neighborhoods date back to the 1940s, when they were seen as a means of dialogue with the local state, just as trade unions communicated with the national government, extending the national "populist pact" to where workers lived. This regime of tutelage of associations by the local state can be divided into two periods. The first, from 1945 to 1977, was relatively successful at drawing in civil society. During the second period, however, from 1977 to 1985, there were new demands and organized opposition by civil society to attempts at co-optation by government.

In the 1940s, the first municipal social service programs appeared, and by the 1950s, the municipal Social Services Department saw its mission as being to assist directly in the creation of neighborhood associations. Associations grew and were able to pressure municipal governments, achieving some of their demands around urban services under this regime. Populist mayors assured relatively comprehensive levels of urban services such as basic sanitation, primary schools, and public transportation for working-class neighborhoods, while validating some level of "popular consultancy" within the state in the form of consultative municipal councils, established in the mid 1950s.[8]

Throughout the 1950s, the municipal administration continued to engage neighborhood associations by sponsoring "municipal conferences," at which representatives from associations raised what were perceived as pressing issues. Some of the most important demands included primary schooling, ambulances, buildings for neighborhood associations, water and sewage, garbage collection, street lighting, public phones, post offices, and public parks. A statewide confederation of neighborhood associations, the Federação Rio-Grandense das Associações Comunitárias e de Bairros (FRACAB), was founded in 1959 at one such conference,[9] serving as a conduit for the demands submitted to the municipal and state governments.[10]

This dialogue between associations and government was curtailed by the military coup of 1964, which outlawed political parties and sent several of the PTB's leaders into exile, bringing FRACAB under the "intervention" (control) of the military regime.[11] Dictatorship-era laws limited associations to circumspect roles, but the military-appointed mayor carried out limited social service programs and attended to the demands of specific strategic communities. Meanwhile, the local administration dealt harshly with rapidly expanding "irregular" settlements—the encroaching favelas—forcibly relocating tens of thousands of settlers in the 1960s and 1970s.[12]

The state–civil society regime from the 1940s to the 1970s replicated the national government's strategy of populist tutelage. In the early years, the local state attended to societal demands but constrained civil society in significant ways, bringing pressure to bear on FRACAB and neighborhood associations, sponsoring municipal conferences, and only interacting with politically sympathetic associations. During the first years of the dictatorship in particular, the national state heavily, and directly, constrained civil society, among other tactics by jailing community activists suspected of subversive activities.

In the late 1970s, with the partial relaxation of martial law, neighborhood associations started to function more actively again, forcing the municipal administration to renew efforts at co-optation. Neighborhood associations regained control of FRACAB in 1977, and leaders opposed to the local administration elected to break away from City Hall shortly thereafter. From 1977 on, FRACAB addressed cost-of-living, housing, and wage issues in concert with national movements of the time.[13] It also sought out ties to progressive clergy, the growing student movement, and progressive sectors of the legally recognized opposition party, the Movimento Democrático Brasileiro. By 1979, FRACAB had sixty-five registered associations in Porto Alegre. The military-appointed municipal government responded by creating a parallel umbrella organization, under which politically sympathetic associations were offered privileged access to the state benefits, such as road improvements or food assistance programs in their neighborhoods. This program failed to attract many associations, so the municipal housing department stepped up its efforts to create new associations in the settlements, writing their statutes and picking their leaders, as well as providing funds for "self-help projects."[14]

Despite these efforts, independent associations continued to appear throughout the city as residents of the growing "irregular" settlements engaged in struggles to fight slum-clearance programs. In this period, associations engaged in both conciliatory and combative practices, vacillating between participation in government-sponsored "self-help" programs and promising allegiance to local politicians, but then turning to petitions and protests when the programs failed to deliver.[15] Between 1979 and 1984, protest activity was recorded in 61 of the 120 favelas in the city.[16]

Outside advisors, such as progressive clergy and members of NGOs, started to provide crucial assistance to associations, from mimeographing flyers to running "discussion circles."[17] As elsewhere in Brazil, these were often middle-class activists who moved into poor and working-class neighborhoods with the intent of supporting and politicizing local struggles.[18] In the words of one such advisor, they helped "involve residents in politics" and "foster[ed] ties to the labor movement."[19] Activists within the newly formed PT and other leftist parties started to recognize the importance of the "mass movement" and to develop influence within associations. For that reason, contested elections within the associations sometimes split along party lines, and party activists provided support to communities willing to contest what were seen as the co-optation strategies of City Hall.

With the transition to democracy on the horizon, the local administration worked hard to shore up its image as patron of the poor, including some well-publicized urban improvement projects in poor districts. But City Hall reacted to neighborhood demands for more improvements in contradictory ways, sometimes ceding improvements to politically sympathetic leaders and sometimes succumbing to pressure, although never fully meeting the demands of associations in the poorest areas. This behavior politicized and radicalized a generation of community activists, making them distrustful of government handouts, and significantly strengthening their beliefs in autonomy, rights, and entitlements.

After a citywide strike in 1983, in which neighborhood associations played important supporting roles, the União das Associações de Moradores de Porto Alegre (UAMPA), or Union of Neighborhood Associations of Porto Alegre, was founded to coordinate local demands and present a militant united front in dealing with municipal government. UAMPA was established in part because FRACAB was perceived as excessively friendly to the military-appointed administration. The autonomous UAMPA called for accountability, participation, and improved urban services,[20] but also sought to address broader social issues at the time, like the national debt, cost of living, urban reform, and even solidarity with activists in South Africa.[21] Among its principal activists were neighborhood cadres affiliated with a variety of the newly legal left-of-center parties, such as the PT and the reformed PDT. In this early period, UAMPA's board of directors always included representatives of different opposition parties.[22]

Another innovation of the period was the advent of neighborhood popular councils, created to "articulate the popular movement's demands" in permanent, autonomous fora.[23] The popular councils were supposed, not only to be a place to broaden the platforms of individual associations and movements, but also to serve as fora that would eventually be able to decide on policy matters. Similar councils had been formed with some success in other urban centers.[24] By 1986, there were four such popular councils in the city.

During the period of 1977 and 1985, the state–civil society regime was still one of tutelage, in which the local state selectively met social demands in exchange for allegiance, but in contrast to the previous period, this fostered not only acquiescence but increasingly contentious practices and novel organizations in civil society. In the late 1970s and 1980s, national politics had a considerable influence on the city. New national social movements exerted powerful influence, while advisors such as progressive clergy played increasingly important roles in community organization. Crucially, the prospect of the transition to democracy signaled to community activists that there was a political opening for new demands, not only for better services, but also for a voice in the new, democratically elected administration that came to power in 1986.

Participation with Constraints: The Collares Administration, 1986–88

Alceu Collares, an Afro-Brazilian professor of political science, was one of the first opposition mayors to be elected in Brazil. His 1986 victory came with a promise to institute popular participation, "ending unilateral decisions by the mayor." Collares pledged that "measures taken will be first approved by municipal councils" with popular participation.[25] The newly reformed PDT, which Collares represented, was heir to the old populist PTB, and its politicians still had significant legitimacy with Porto Alegre's population, particularly among its working classes. As a party with a formally socialist platform, it also had legitimacy with progressive activists within the community movement. But the PDT's vision of participation was, in effect, an attempt to recreate the populist pact that had been in place in Porto Alegre in the 1940s and 1950s, in which all of the community movement would be incorporated into the administration's structure. It proposed municipal councils to operate in tandem with city departments, allowing for formal consultation of community movements in city administration. These councils faced legal obstacles, and later in its term, the administration switched tactics to the selective recognition of demands by politically sympathetic associations.

Community leaders were already suspicious of these institutions, because they accorded little meaningful decision-making power to civil society and left final authority with municipal government,[26] limiting the role of community activists to "giving opinions, and making suggestions." UAMPA called instead for a participatory structure where the investment priorities of each district would be discussed with local community leaders.[27] Despite their misgivings, community activists did attend meetings called for by the Collares administration to discuss the new municipal councils in 1986.[28] The project for the councils was drawn up to include some community demands, but excluded the principal demand of devolving actual decision making to participants.[29] In 1987, the Collares administration sent its proposed project to the legislature, but it subsequently withdrew it in the face of likely rejection even by its own PDT legislators.[30]

The administration then went on to provide urban improvements and services through informal negotiations with politically sympathetic association presidents. This new mode of selective recognition was evident in the case of the neighboring *vilas* of União and Santa Rosa, two working-class neighborhoods with comparable demands for infrastructure improvements. Owing to ties between association officials and the PDT, União had its demands met, while Santa Rosa went without because of PT-affiliated clergy who served on its association's board.[31] In Vila Gleba, PDT-linked activists managed to introduce an urban improvements project, but on the day construction was about to begin, other community activists physically blocked it because of lack of community input into the nature of the project.[32] The administration went on to sponsor sporadic instances of participation, although still relying on sympathetic associations.

From late 1987 onwards, the Collares administration carried out a formal consultation with the popular council that had emerged in the Norte district, an area of traditional PDT support. In December of that year, activists complained that most planned projects, including some of the emergency sewage projects, were not yet under way.[33] The popular council quickly released a flyer expressing its dissatisfaction, and criticizing the administration: "Here come the [19]88 elections. There are people who are trying to present themselves as the 'savior[s] of the Norte district.' They just want votes. Do not fall for it."[34] Most projects were still pending by 1988.[35]

Unlike the tutelage regime during the last years of the military dictatorship, which had the effect of fostering increasingly contentious opposition in the community movement, tutelage under Collares sparked initial engagement, because activists assumed that the administration was receptive to their demands. The new PDT was, after all, a political party with ties to social movements. However, the many promises and few concrete gains in the city's working-class and poor neighborhoods during the Collares administration led to a demobilization of civil society. Broad-based instances of participation were clearly not established, and many who had supported the new PDT in 1986 felt that they had been co-opted in a familiar populist tradition. Numerous associations, as well as the autonomous umbrella organization, UAMPA, faced severe difficulties sustaining activity by the end of Collares's term.[36] Surveys from 1987 on found that the principal challenges facing neighbor-hood associations at the time were "difficulty sustaining long-term ac-tivity," "lack of information," "lack of resources," "lack of interconnec-tions with other associations," and "after a protest, the association empties out."[37] Another report cites the "lack of new leaders," "lack of a clear project," and "excessive clientelism and ties to political parties."[38]

Even with these shortcomings, the Collares administration did en-courage discussions about what participation in government would mean for the community movement at different points. Responding to these early possibilities of genuine reform, the community movement formulated its proposal for participation in the city's budget in 1986. This shift alone would foreshadow an important legacy of the Collares period for the future of participative budgeting in Porto Alegre. Com-munity involvement in city planning was coupled with a more skepti-cal attitude toward state-sponsored participatory programs, especially those endorsed by political parties claiming to represent the community.

The Frente Popular and Co-creation of Participatory Reforms, 1989–1990

Partially as a result of disappointment with the Collares administra-tion, but also because of the general discontentment with inflation and the national government, Olívio Dutra and the left-wing Frente Popu-lar won the municipal elections in late 1988 by a slim margin. Dutra, a founder of the PT active with the Bank Tellers' Union, staffed his mu-nicipal departments with PT activists without executive or legislative experience. At the time, administrators had many examples of what *not* to do, but knew little about *how to* democratize city government.[39]

There were disputes within the party about the role of a socialist party running a municipal government—would it be an administration for workers or for the whole city? Who would make decisions—the mayor, the party, or social movements? Should the PT administration's chief focus be managing the capitalist city or manning the trenches in the fight for socialism?[40] These choices were no different than the ones faced by the thirty-five other PT administrations elected in 1989 throughout Brazil, [41] but the political situation Porto Alegre *petistas* faced was unique. The participatory reforms that the administration ul-timately developed owe as much to the proposals and previous experi-ence of the community movement as to the administration's precarious political position and miscalculations during its first two years in power.

PT administrators envisioned participation as a dialogue with local popular councils—existing or in formation—in the districts where a standing general council with representatives from social movements would decide on policy matters.[42] Early on, administrators responded to calls by community activists to honor campaign promises and started discussions about participatory reforms. Activists once again brought to the table proposals for popular decision making in budgetary matters, which were incorporated into a government plan for participation.

The first round of participatory meetings on the budget took place in five places around the city in August 1989, with the unprecedented participation of almost a thousand people. These meetings generated tremendous "expectations," but "frustrations" followed.[43] Despite the number of participants, the meetings lacked transparency, as well as clear organization and adequate preparation. Participants were invited to submit proposals, but it was not clear how, if at all, these would translate into concrete projects. As a response to community criticisms, the administration then held a second round of meetings in September, this time in sixteen locations around the city, as demanded by UAMPA. There was the intention of involving participants in more stages of the process, and one representative per district was elected to a committee to select the actual projects for 1990. Because of miscalculations by the administration, few of the projects chosen by the communities in 1989 were actually initiated that year. Community activists who had been sympathetic to the PT felt betrayed, not only because their participation in the budget process had been limited, but also because it appeared to yield few results.

Disenchantment with the Organized

By mid 1990, "the administration was at the peak of its crisis."[44] A relatively weak party in Porto Alegre, the Workers' Party faced hostile local media, popular disenchantment, and a decline in support among organized sectors. It also faced opposition from the Municipal Employees' Union, which was then headed by PDT activists, as well as with some PT-linked unions, such as the Bus Drivers' and Conductors' Union. Believing that transportation was a priority issue for the city's workers in 1989, the administration had forced a confrontation with local transportation companies that led to a municipal takeover of local bus companies. Seeking much needed revenue, the administration had raised bus fares, alienating neighborhood activists without increasing wages for unionized bus drivers. The PT's strategy of state ownership of the transportation sector—which it had hoped would rally support, given that the vast majority of the city's residents rely on public transportation—resulted in failure. The PT-friendly national labor federation that controlled the bus drivers' and conductors' unions, the CUT, severed its ties with the administration in a harshly worded public statement and eventually led a strike.[45]

The administration also faced new problems with UAMPA and with some organized community activists in areas where the OP meetings were already being held. In the Norte district, for example, where one of the 1989 plenary meetings was held, activists came with an agenda and a prepared list of demands for urban improvements beyond what the administration considered the limits of the discussion. Those activists took a hostile stand toward the administration's attempts to run the meetings. They walked out of the meeting, taking a third of the participants with them. In addition, the administration's attempts at directly "stimulating" activism in an acceptable form also failed. For example, in the remote Ilhas district, administrators attempted to create a *conselho* that would represent civil society as a whole in negotiations with City Hall. According to administrators, "community activists replicated clientelistic patterns" by electing one of the local "bosses" to head the *conselho*.[46]

In the end, organized groups like unions and neighborhood associations did not prove to be a reliable source of political support for the administration, as many had hoped. Instead, administrators found the movements too combative and their demands (such as calls for lower bus fares and urban improvements) excessive and too focused on immediate goals. Participants in the 1989 OP protested in front of City Hall, demanding the construction of slated projects and the resignation of officials associated with the OP.[47] These events led many in the PT to conclude that the administration had failed to engage potentially sympathetic movements constructively in reshaping its participatory scheme, and they also surely led many in the administration to view social movements in a negative light.[48]

Community Demands

Among the most hostile to the administration were organized groups in civil society that had bet on the previous Collares administration and lost. Autonomous neighborhood association leaders who had proposed a form of participatory budgeting to the Collares team in 1986 were disappointed by the failure of his administration to introduce it. These and other groups, such as the Fundação de Assistência Social Educativa (FASE), or Foundation for Social and Educational Services, an advisory NGO that provided technical support to neighborhood associations, approached the new PT administration with varying degrees of suspicion. Despite their skepticism, they nonetheless made concrete proposals for reforming the OP.

According to Benjamin Goldfrank, the demands of community activists included (1) greater voice in and broader scope for collective decision making, (2) greater transparency of OP proceedings, and (3) an assurance that investments through the OP would be decentralized.[49] Criticisms of the OP's previous design included holding a single meeting per district without preparatory sessions. To activists, this restricted participation to simply raising demands. Those who had participated proposed several specific changes, such as starting the process earlier in the year, holding a yearly meeting to offer an accounting of ongoing projects, and explanations of the yearly budgeting cycle. Similarly, they criticized the administration for not allowing decision making on the city's overall investment priorities and fiscal and personnel policies.[50] Community activists also demanded a binding "Plan of Investments" listing the projects chosen, so that their actual implementation could subsequently be compared.[51]

In response, the PT administration made several changes. For example, in 1990, the administration introduced a "municipal day of accounting," which later became a regular feature of the yearly OP cycle. In 1991, administrators introduced a document that listed all of the administration's planned investments for the following year, and rules for apportioning investments to districts were also then crafted.[52] Administrators originally proposed directing investments to a few neighborhoods in order to create visible results; community activists instead wanted investments distributed all over the city. The compromise that emerged was that 65 percent of investments would go to five priority districts, according to a mathematical score based on each district's (1) population, (2) overall need, (3) level of participation in the OP, and (4) "strategic" importance, a technical criterion devised by the administration. Administrators rejected the proposal that participation be organized around existing neighborhood associations in favor of an open system in which any citizen could participate. As explained by an activist, "the participatory budget is for citizens, not for associations . . . we work with direct citizenship and not associations."[53]

Changing Course

From 1990 to 1991, the administration changed course on several fronts, altering its perspective on privileging organized groups, abandoning attempts at direct organizing, and shifting its views on the proper format for a participatory program.[54] The position of "a city for workers" gave way to a "city for all" that communicated with a broad section of the population in government-assisted *fora* highlighting transparency, training, and individual participation.[55] Publicity materials promised that "popular participation will be perfected each time."[56] An internal document from April 1990, "The Hour of Strategic Definitions," defined a five-point plan calling for a change in the relationship between the population and the executive, involving participants in all stages of the budgetary process, from demands and overall priorities to monitoring outcomes.[57]

A new administrative structure was developed to coordinate participation. A new agency, Coordenação de Relações com a Comunidade (CRC), or Office of Community Relations, was assigned to oversee the OP, and a new planning agency, Gabinete de Planejamento (GAPLAN), was put in charge of the urban planning that emerged from the OP. Facilitators were assigned to each district who were responsible for attracting new participants, helping to run meetings, and facilitating the discussions.[58] In line with the principles of participatory democracy, these facilitators were to help form discussions on priorities and projects, but not to direct or control the agenda. An important function of facilitators was didactic: "increasing the discussion of concepts of budget policy," "challenging citizens to think of problems of their district as a whole," and "establishing relationships based on values of cooperation and solidarity."[59]

The process now took place in institutional settings rather than relying on organized civil society to take care of those meetings and "bring demands" to an assembly, as had been the case in some of the districts in the 1989 and 1990 meetings. From 1990 onwards, there were two plenary meetings per district, interspersed with intermediary meetings for delegates, which civil society groups could help coordinate. All of these meetings were institutionally assisted by the government and formally autonomous from civil society organizations, in order to foster participation by those outside organized movements. Representatives from each district continued to push the administration to bring more and more issues under the scope of collective decision making, including the proportions of sectoral investments, personnel expenditures, and permitting participants to change the rules of the OP.

In 1991, the administration formally created the Conselho do Orçamento Participativo (COP), or Budget Council, with two representatives from each district, as well as one each from UAMPA and the municipal employees' union. The administration empowered the Budget Council to make final decisions over the year's budget, including the right to revise the rules of the OP. The elected councilors of the new Budget Council promptly revised the rules for the allocations of funds, removing the criterion of "strategic importance." The new criteria for allocating funds across districts were a district's (1) need for a particular service, (2) population in needy areas, (3) overall population, and (4) ranking of priorities.

Also in 1991, fiscal reforms based primarily on raising land-use taxes put municipal finances in order. The PT had assumed a municipal administration in deep deficit in 1989; personnel commitment alone amounted to almost all of the projected budget. But by 1991, the administration's budget for investments amounted to 16 percent of the total, allowing for many more projects negotiated through the OP.[60]

These changes cemented a reformed participatory budget process. With funds available for investment, clear rules, and a substantially larger civil society input into overall investment priorities and district allocations, many of the demands of community activists for participation in government had been met. But there were other changes that showed an evolution in the administration's position on organized civil society. The decision to stop relying exclusively on organized groups, including unions and social movements, and instead to create open meetings with City Hall facilitators was a final move away from the PT's original perception of its administration as an "organic whole," in which party, movement, and government were complementary. Remarking on the historic rupture with previous PT thinking on the question of governance, Mayor Dutra recalled: "The project of establishing

popular councils is not a job for the administration. This is a party political question. Even if the popular councils are not instruments of political parties, and much less of the PT, they [the parties] have to have a
project to stimulate the organization of the popular councils."[61] The separation between popular councils and the institutions of participatory
governance thus became formal.[62]

Rather than relying on "the force of ideology" or "the voluntary will
of the masses," administrators now came to believe that societal needs
had to be mediated and that the contexts in which participation took
place should be run and coordinated by the administration.[63] More important, administrators also learned that they could not necessarily in-
tuit the demands of the masses, as many had at first assumed. This signaled a rupture with any remnants of a vision of tutelage of civil society
carried over from previous regimes. The administration was not to
serve as ultimate arbiter of societal demands, and neither was it to directly organize civil society or privilege political allies. Rather, in the
new regime, societal demands would be made through broad participation that did not distinguish between the organized and the unorganized, and participants themselves would be the arbiters of demands.
Once this regime became routinized, it would have a profound impact
on associational life in Porto Alegre.

Routinizing the Orçamento Participativo, 1991–2000

In 1991, participants started to see returns from 1990 on a much
larger scale than had been visible in the first year of PT administration.
First, with the changes in rules, participation more than doubled to
over 3,000 for 1991, and again to over 6,000 in 1992. The majority of participants were poor residents from the city's favelas or from one of the
vilas, or working-class neighborhoods. Most participants in these early
years were linked to neighborhood associations, and had learned about
the OP through these groups.[64] But participation quickly expanded beyond organized groups. In the first year, rates of participation per district were related to the presence of organized networks, but for every
year after that, district-level poverty and the amount of resources directed at each district predicted participation.[65] Remarkably, some of the
poorest districts without vigorous associational activity eventually reported the greatest rates of participation.[66]

This relatively broad participation helped pass the OP budget in the

municipal legislature, despite the fact that the PT did not have a majority in that body. In late 1991, the OP budget was threatened when the
municipal legislature held an emergency meeting to reverse the land-
tax increases, in effect threatening to eliminate most of the OP projects.
OP participants organized a mobilization of hundreds to attend the legislative hearings and monitor the voting on this regressive taxing measure. A letter to the legislators warned that changing tax policies would
in effect preclude new investments in the city's periphery and be contrary to the popular mandate established after a year of discussion in
"meetings held in all the neighborhoods and *vilas* of the city."[67] The tax
changes were not approved, and since 1992, the OP budget has been
approved every year without major alterations, as have most of the requests to raise taxes, despite the fact that PT has remained a minority in
the legislature.[68]

The administration was also able to avert some of the difficulties
with its own employees' union via the OP. In his final days in office,
Collares had given a raise to municipal employees, which the incoming
PT administration did not honor, although sympathetic to the municipal employees' demands, because it was seen as a move by Collares to
destabilize it. The PT administration was able to end a sixteen-day
strike over wages in 1991 by bringing the municipal employees directly
to the Budget Council to debate their demands.[69] A member of the Budget Council who was present at the negotiations recalled that "the municipal employees had to come and defend their proposal with us, and
they had to defend how much they wanted, and we said, 'But we want
this road and want schools,' and they ended the strike." By the time of
the second PT administration, municipal employees had only carried
out one strike, with a relatively low turnout.[70]

The PT was reelected in 1992, with the OP as its "central axis" of governance, with high approval ratings.[71] Under Tarso Genro, the administration sought to expand the basis of participation to the middle classes,
many of whom had supported the PT in its early years but did not necessarily feel compelled to participate in fora dedicated to urban infrastructure needs.[72] It also sought to bring in NGOs, unions, and social
movements whose "organizational features, demands, and concerns
with the city did not coincide with the structure . . . of the actual OP."[73]
At the newly established thematic meetings on "Transportation,"
"Health and Social Services," "Education and Culture," "Economic Development," and "Urban Planning," and longer-term citywide concerns

were addressed that could not be effectively addressed at the district-level meetings. The "Education and Culture" thematic meetings, for example, were intended to "affect the day-to-day functioning" of the Education and Culture departments, rather than purely "concentrating on investments in these areas," as was perceived to happen in the OP.[74] At the same time, the administration introduced a format of citywide conferences to discuss broader visions around specific areas of concern. Participation in these conferences was also impressive, as evident in the city congress of 1995, for example, which had 2,600 participants, representing over 200 associations and groups.[75]

Participation continued to grow, reaching 7,600 participants in 1996, and the PT was once again reelected, with Genro's vice-mayor, Raul Pont, as the new mayor. Pont's administration sought to move decision making away from strictly local and immediate demands to longer-range, broader concerns, such as social services and job training. The city's multiyear plan was debated in the 1997 OP, and the administration emphasized participation in institutional councils, such as those established on the rights of children and adolescents, and on the environment, as a means of extending participatory decision making away from the capital investment projects of the OP. Participation in the OP and various councils continued to expand during this period, as new groups continued to join, such as cultural groups and groups representing homeless persons. The investment priorities chosen by OP participants also appeared to shift at this time, with marked increases in preferences for education, health, and social services.[76]

Civil Society and the Orçamento Participativo, 1991–2000

The routinization of the OP deeply altered the fabric of associational life in Porto Alegre. The democratization of the state opened up new avenues for civil society to shape forms of governance directly, as well as to make binding decisions on the direction of the city's investments and the rules of the process itself. Unlike previous experiences, the recognition of these demands was not tied to political allegiance, instead relying on massive participation from the city's poorer districts. Under tutelage regimes, so-called "popular sectors" were represented, but the privileged representatives were politically sympathetic working-class associations. This generated discontentment and protest, be-

TABLE 5

Transformations of Civil Society in Porto Alegre, 1986–2000

Year	Neighborhood Associations[a]	Housing Cooperatives[b]	District-Level Popular Councils[c]
1986	240		2
1988	300		4
1990	380		6
1994	450	11	8
1996	500	32	11
1998	540	51	11
2000	600	71	12

SOURCES: Various.
   [a] Functioning neighborhood associations, estimated from unpublished documents from UAMPA, CRC, and Baierle 1992.
   [b] Estimated number of housing cooperatives from interviews.
   [c] Popular councils are district-level voluntary entities that coordinate neighborhood associations.

cause activists within associations became critical of such schemes. As-sociations had vacillated between acquiescing and protesting, however, because under tutelage, there are incentives for individual associations to pursue individual demands and gain favor with the administration. Under empowered participation, not only was the spectrum of partici-pants much broader, reaching into the ranks of the poor and unorga-nized, but the recognition of their demands and the resolution of con-flict took place under a different logic. The recognition of demands was not conditioned on political sympathy or even on whether associations were formally organized, and claimants negotiated among themselves within participatory institutions. Owing to this new logic, civil society transformed itself in terms of numbers of associations and practices.

It is difficult to estimate the scope of these changes with precision, but as Table 5 shows, the number of active neighborhood associations roughly doubled in this period.[77] The data in the table also show that the number of housing cooperatives, organizations of residents in squatter settlements who collectively own land, and active popular councils have increased substantially. Neighborhood associations are often a principal reference point for social activities among community residents, for mutual assistance, for intermediation with authorities, and for resolving conflicts in the neighborhood. Although there are other types of local organizations (such as cultural groups and mothers' groups), these often revolve around the neighborhood association, making it a good proxy for the overall density of civil society.

Table 5 reflects the fact that the Collares period also fostered many

new associations in response to the perceived opportunities for participation early on in his administration. But the calculus for participating
in and forming associations changed in the 1990s. Earlier, in a context of
uncertain returns from municipal government, neighborhood activists
had difficulty attracting participants to meetings on a regular basis.
Now, there were incentives for extended collective work through the
OP, which translated into new associations or the reactivating of inactive associations. Individuals concerned with a particular issue began
to attend OP meetings and eventually mobilized a number of equally
concerned neighbors, who later formed a more permanent association.
Similarly, there are many stories about the creation of new associations
when an existing association was not willing to take up the cause of the
poorest residents of an area.[78] Because the OP addresses issues central
to the concerns of poorer residents, the impact has been greatest in poor
neighborhoods. The three poorest districts of the city, Nordeste, Lomba
do Pinheiro, and Restinga, were among those districts that experienced
the most pronounced changes.[79] The OP itself has helped spark growth
in civil society, serving as sort of an incubator to new organizations.

In the OP, participants acquire not only the specific competencies related to budgeting but also skills in debating and mobilizing resources
for collective goals. Evidence about patterns of participation support
this contention. As described earlier, participation in the OP has different tiers. General participants attend plenary meetings; from among
them, delegates are chosen to deliberate in the districts, and from
among the delegates, councilors are chosen to deliberate at the Budget
Council. Each year, between 15 and 20 percent of participants had no
previous OP experience and no ties to organized sectors like neighborhood associations. Many of these previously uninvolved citizens go on
to become delegates and councilors in the OP and in associations. Survey results also show that among general participants of the OP, 10 percent reported that their participation in civil society had declined after
they started to attend OP meetings, 27 percent said their participation
had remained the same, and 27 percent said it had increased. As a previously uninvolved participant who eventually became a councilor put
it: "I had to learn about the process as the meetings took place. The first
time I participated, I was unsure, because there were people there with
college degrees, and I don't [have one]. But in time I learned."

This renewal of civil society is also evident from patterns among delegates and councilors. According to survey data, while almost all dele-

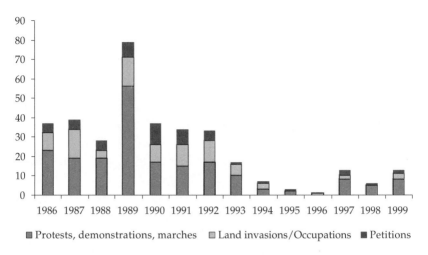

FIG. 6. Contentious activity by community-based movements, 1986–99

gates participated in a regular neighborhood forum like an association, half of them had got their start in a neighborhood association via the OP, and not the other way around.[80] Among councilors, about one-third had got their start through the OP. In another survey, approximately 40 percent of neighborhood association presidents reported that they had been introduced to associational life by the OP. As a community activist described it, "new leaders appear with new ideas every year," in his district, and "many of the *vilas* now have developed associations to fight through the OP, and old ones are reopening to make demands in the OP."

This increased density and renewal has been accompanied by a decline in contentious activity such as protests, petitions, and land occupations. As seen in Figure 6, the number of more controversial activities aimed at City Hall declined over the years in Porto Alegre, from a high point early in the PT administration prior to the routinization of the OP. They occurred one-third less frequently in 1996–98 than in 1986–88.[81] As a community leader noted, "before the [PT] administration, we would go and discuss something with the government, give them a deadline, actually demand a deadline, and if it wasn't met we would go to the media, mobilize the population, and go after them. With the PT administration, this does not occur anymore, or hardly occurs."[82]

While the early protests against the administration were in part a response to the perceived political opening a leftist administration would provide to popular demands, they also reflected discontentment with the failures of the first versions of the OP. However, by 1990, a UAMPA director presciently noted:

> [The administration] now privileges a certain type of participation other than that of the barricade, the banners, and the protests, but pressure through participation in the various open channels. The pressure will take place within these channels. It is removing the movement from the streets and giving us a chance to organize within these channels [such as the OP] . . . which does not mean that the classic forms of pressure cannot be exercised. But [these forms of pressure] are being emptied out for the better or for the worse, but I think for the better.[83]

Looking back over the 1990s, a longtime PT activist recalled, "[T]hat old militancy of going door to door to confront the government is gone. Now the OP is everything," while another said that "the era of the mass protest [has] ended in Porto Alegre." Despite diminished frequency, protests have not in fact completely disappeared, however, sometimes even emerging within OP meetings, as described in the next chapters.

And while it is even more difficult to gauge trends in personal mediation, such as promises of favor-trading with politicians or calling on influential people in government to expedite a project, evidence suggests that it has also dramatically declined. Community activists often recalled stories about how in the past, "when you had to get something done, you had to go and sit in [a politician's] waiting area, and when you saw him, you told him why you needed this street or materials for the association." Among neighborhood association presidents interviewed, only 2 percent of those who had started their civic engagement through the OP in the past five years admitted to engaging in an exchange of benefits for political support, while among those whose civic careers predated the OP, 18 percent admitted to participating in client-patron exchanges, most of them in the past.[84] A 2001 survey by Avritzer also revealed that personal mediation had declined. Whereas 41 percent of associations had looked to politicians for benefits before the OP, none relied on politicians for benefits after the OP.[85] Even some of the OP's most vocal critics, such as city councilors from other political parties, agree that clientelism has declined in Porto Alegre in the 1990s, according to the research by Goldfrank.[86] This contention was also supported by a prominent community activist who campaigns against the PT at election time, who noted, "[O]ne thing the PT fellows are correct about is that favors from politicians don't count for anything now." Indirect evidence of clientelism, such as requests by city councilors for executive projects and the concentration of support of individual politicians in specific areas, is also lower in Porto Alegre than other cities in Brazil.[87] Because of the transparent nature of OP projects, it is practically impossible for city councilors to offer specific urban improvements in exchange for support.[88]

Instead of combativeness or personal mediation, new practices in civil society now involve proposing and evaluating justification of public policies through participatory channels. Even a cursory reading of association newsletters reveals an evolution throughout the 1990s toward a language where the meaning of popular struggles is equated with participating in the OP, in contrast to earlier conceptions of popular struggle as confrontational politics against the state. Central to this kind of practice are the reinvigorated popular councils, umbrella organizations that became active in eleven of the city's districts by the late 1990s, many as response to the OP. The popular councils reflect both the new practices and the increasingly interconnected civic life of the districts. In the Leste district, for example, the council developed in 1991 as a function of OP activities, and in 1992, its leaders split into two groups: one that was developing its knowledge of health policy, and one that was dedicated to land-use policy, with the intent to influence both kinds of policies in the district.[89] Writings from the popular council of the Glória district claim that it is an umbrella organization to "fight together for issues for the whole district and make decisions that will benefit the greatest number of people, not just one association."[90] It is clear from its founding statutes that the council itself is principally aimed at OP proceedings:

WHAT DOES A POPULAR COUNCIL DO?
Pressure the Administration and the Legislature for works and laws.
Define priorities for the Participatory Budget.
Monitor the works and projects of the Administration.
Speak for the whole district.[91]

Just as community activism has refocused toward the district, as opposed to the neighborhood, activists have also crafted new citywide networks in the years since the OP reforms. Observers of the process note that the OP has become a new "network of conversations. Many people do not realize that we have created the capacity for dialogue every week as a result of the OP."[92] Since many participants in the district-level and municipal OP meetings have ties to disparate home associations, it has served as a vehicle for communication and interconnection across civil society.[93] UAMPA has been in crisis, with declining participation, since it disengaged from the OP in the early 1990s, but it has been supplanted by many other municipal networks, such as the municipal fora for cooperatives and various new councils.[94] In the 1990s, there have been numerous municipal mobilizations, often sponsored by the administration directly or indirectly, but eliciting broad participation. These include a citywide effort against "hunger and misery" in 1991, a citywide mobilization against unemployment in 1991 and 1992, and municipal efforts to promote human rights and fight discrimination.[95]

Enabling and Constraining Relationships

As Vice-Mayor Genro had predicted, the regime of state–civil society relations under the OP was different from anything that had been seen before in Porto Alegre. But while it is tempting to read its history as solely a result of the considerable foresight of *petistas*, its appearance and evolution reflect a particular conjuncture. The PT, a politically weak party with a commitment to participation, restructured its position vis-à-vis participatory democracy and social movements over the first two years of trial and error. Activists in civil society greeted the incoming administration with high expectations and specific proposals, but also with a skepticism based on experiences with previous participatory attempts. Their insistence on broad-based decision making, transparency, and clear rules helped shape the OP as much as the administration's search for legitimacy beyond organized groups in civil society. In fact, administrators quickly found that the PT in power could not "organically" reflect the wishes of social movements—the demands of movements in many ways frustrated the ability of administrators to meet them, which quickly caused friction between organized movements and administrators. The OP became the central axis for interfacing with civil society and a means to mediate different demands. Rather than there being strikes by municipal employees and land invasions by community activists, these two sectors and the unorganized negotiated in the OP. Owing to a fiscal reorganization, the administration was able to link participation in the OP to actual projects over a short time frame. Once community activists saw that participation in the OP yielded results, it became routine.

The result was the establishment of a new state–civil society regime in which the recognition of societal demands and the resolution of conflicting demands took place under a radically different logic than in previous tutelage regimes. Instead of selectively recognizing claimants in civil society, as had been the case under tutelage, the administration in the empowered participatory regime opened participatory avenues to all of Porto Alegre's citizens. And instead of reserving the power to arbitrate among different claims for itself, under the new regime, the state empowered participants themselves to negotiate over demands. For the PT, this proved to be a successful strategy, earning it legitimacy and avoiding potentially damaging conflicts.

And the impact of this newly empowered participatory regime and of the routinization of the OP also occasioned a profound transformation in civil society itself. Several new organizations and new activists were brought into active participation in civil society as a response to this new associational environment, although this also transformed practices in civil society itself. These changes raise a number of questions about this participatory institution and the quality of its meetings and procedures. How did this regime interact with different local config urations? What is decision making within the OP like? How do participants interact in this participatory setting? What is the role of "politics" in OP meetings? How important is the participatory budgeting process to community life? What is this new political culture that evolved from "the old militancy"? The rest of this book takes up these questions in turn, using ethnography to show "structures as they happen."[96]

CHAPTER THREE

New Actors and New Competencies

We used to trade favors, now we trade work. Things have changed.
—Magda, interview

Everything is through the OP now. It is obvious that some would be unhappy about that.
—Marcos, interview

The Chico Mendes municipal school stands out from the surrounding buildings in the Nordeste district of Porto Alegre. The school is a few meters away from the district's only thoroughfare, Rubem Berta, and during the week, teachers who live in other parts of town park their cars in the school's dusty parking lot. On Saturday afternoons, however, when representatives of the various municipal departments trek from downtown to meet with OP delegates, Volkswagen Kombi vans belonging to the city administration occupy the small lot. The school itself is a product of OP deliberations, and the decision to name it after the Amazonian environmental activist Chico Mendes was made in the forum of delegates of the Nordeste district when it was being built. The structure, like that of the others built by the administration, is inspired by the writings of the Swiss educational psychologist Jean Piaget: the environment inside is open and evokes space by avoiding corners and long corridors. On most Saturdays, participants from the district's eighteen *vilas* make the long walk—sometimes almost an hour—to sit in the child-sized seats in the school's main dining room. They are among Porto Alegre's poorest citizens—practically all of the *vilas* of the Nordeste district are land occupations or the result of the removal of such occupations from elsewhere in the city. Most of these delegates are employed, but the majority work in the so-called "informal economy," ironing clothes or doing stints in construction. Few of the delegates have any education past primary schooling, and most have recently become involved in civic life as a result of the OP, although a handful of long-term participants have previous activist experience.

The traditional sociological expectation, particularly among society-centered theorists of democracy, is that establishing participation and the development of new associations here would be the hardest among the three districts in the study. Table 6 provides some demographic and associational detail on the three districts. Not only are participants in Nordeste in the direst straits, but they are also the least educated, and collectively had the least experience in associations and social movements when the OP began. Unlike the two other districts' rich histories of involvement in social movements and associations of the 1970s and 1980s, there was little organization at the neighborhood or district level prior to the OP. For society-centered explanations of democratic evolution, not only are societal legacies the most important factor, but these legacies were built over many generations and not prone to rapid change.

But in fact, participation in Nordeste has been numerically and proportionally higher than in the other two districts in this study and is among the highest in the city, and it is here that rapid expansion in new associations has occurred. In the Norte district, in sharp contrast, despite highly organized civil society in 1988, establishing the OP has at times been very difficult. The district's OP forum has been a site of divisive community contestations, and many of the district's community activists still block the process. Partenon's highly organized civic networks have made the adoption of the OP a relatively smooth process, with active involvement of organizations, although never reaching as many participants as in Nordeste. The comparison between the three districts forms the basis of this chapter.

Each district is composed of a number of neighborhoods. In Nordeste, most of these are slum settlements, made up of substandard,

TABLE 6

The Districts of the Study

	Population (1996)	Percentage of Poor Households (1996)	Active Associations (1988)	Active Associations (2000)	OP Participants (2000)[a]	Conselho
Nordeste	24,261	61%	4	28	1571	No
Partenon	114,127	38%	20	27	613	1988/89
Norte	88,614	50%	22	30	605	1986/87

SOURCES: FESC 1999; interviews.
[a] First plenary participants.

self-constructed housing, much of it precarious, and most of its residents are in the informal market. Prior to the OP, most of these residents were politically disenfranchised. In Norte, there are working-class neighborhoods with paved roads next to slum settlements, and prior to the OP, there were conflicts between these relatively privileged workers and the slum dwellers. Finally, in the Partenon, there are a range of neighborhoods, including slum dwellings, working-class neighborhoods, and middle-class neighborhoods.

Against society-centered arguments, which would focus solely on the legacies in each district, I propose in this chapter that a relational argument better captures the dynamics of the routinization of the OP, because it highlights political contestation. As noted in Chapter 2, the OP transformed the abilities of civil society to organize itself. I argue in this chapter that in the districts, two features of the OP are seen as having the greatest impact on the "rules of the game" of civic life, (1) the way it connects previously unconnected settings, or the brokerage it occasions, and (2) the way it legitimizes the involvement of new entrants in civil society, or the certification of new actors. This has upset some established relationships in which certain activists and organizations previously dominated both brokerage and certification. I argue, therefore, that it is not the simple presence of established civil society as much as the absence of actors who feel their influence diminishing that accounts for the successful establishment of the OP. Three paths to the routinization of the OP and their consequences are described below: (1) "government-induced activism" in Nordeste, where there was little prior civic engagement; (2) "scaled-up networks" in Partenon, where established activists and organizations blended with the new structures of the OP; and (3) "competing allegiances" in Norte, where established networks were threatened by the new structures of power.

The Nordeste District:
Government-Induced Activism

The Nordeste district is among the most remote districts of the city. Bordering the municipality of Viamão, the district is sparsely populated and linked to downtown by only one main road, Rubem Berta. Much of the district is made up of undeveloped land, and residents often remark that in the evening, it is as quiet as the countryside "where they are from," with the lights of downtown Porto Alegre flickering in the dis-

FIG. 7. Recently
paved road in the
Nordeste district
(2000)

tance. The quiet of the evening is often interrupted by gunshots, however, because the district has the dubious distinction of being the most
violent part of the city, with murder rates comparable to the most violent urban areas in Brazil.[1] Although some of the residents trace their
origins to rural Rio Grande do Sul, most came to this remote area of the
city from other central parts of Porto Alegre. Several of the eighteen settlements that make up the district are results of "relocation" efforts
from downtown districts in previous years.

Home to almost 25,000 residents, Nordeste remains one of the poorest and least well served districts of the city. Although there is piped
water in all the settlements today, one-sixth of individual homes are
without running water, and one-third of homes are not properly connected to the sewer system. According to official figures, one-fourth of

the homes in the district are without adequate infrastructure, with some 60 percent of households considered poor. Median monthly household income in Nordeste in 1999 was about U.S.$220,[2] less than half of the Porto Alegre median household income. Furthermore, the proportion of adults with up to three years of schooling is twice as high as the city average.

The introduction of the OP fostered a great deal of new activism in the district, which had had only four functioning (and three inactive) neighborhood associations in 1989. By 2001, there were twenty-eight different neighborhood associations participating in the OP; twenty-five of these were "registered" at a Civil Registry Office, which gave them the status of nonprofit organizations with statutes and bylaws. Of the twenty-eight, fifteen held at least one meeting every month, and the remainder met at least once every month. The district's Budget Forum functions regularly, drawing between thirty and fifty participants per meeting, and the district also has regular meetings of the institutional councils on health, social services, and on economic cooperatives, among other issues. The district-level activist network that has formed around the OP has become Nordeste's chief nexus, mediating between City Hall and the district's residents.

Two of the four earlier active neighborhood associations were formed in 1987, one in 1983, and one as long ago as 1960.[3] The oldest, in Safira Velha, which originated as a remote squatter settlement in the 1950s, was eventually given a building for its association by the municipal authorities during the dictatorship. Its longtime president boasted a positive relationship with City Hall throughout the 1970s, when he "brought running water, street lights, the playground for the children, and managed to establish the police station in the district."[4]

The other three associations emerged from more recent relocations from the wealthier neighborhoods of Porto Alegre. The Collares administration designated portions of public land for the communities of the landless, supporting the growth of these three associations. In 1987, in Chácara da Fumaça, activists launched a neighborhood association as a way to give voice to the demands of this growing community, and in the following year, the Collares administration opened a small school there. In Residencial Machado, responding to incentives from the Collares administration, community activists formed an association with the help of UAMPA in 1987, which participated in the federal milk ticket distribution program, carried out social activities, and sent petitions to municipal authorities.

In 1988, all four associations were generally engaged in different forms of personal mediation between association presidents and the Collares administration. There was also little district-level activism or substantive involvement between neighborhoods. Although some active participants in these three neighborhoods attempted to create alternate associations in the various settlements in the district, "difficult life conditions" were cited as impediments to actually getting new associations off the ground. Several settlements, for example, relied on dangerous illegal supplies of electricity clandestinely siphoned from power lines by residents. Others had problems during the rainy months, when shacks often washed away. A pamphlet put out by an ad hoc coordinating committee in one of the settlements provides an evocative picture of the restrictive conditions of everyday life in these areas in this period:

Come to the meetings.
Do not walk around armed.
Do not sell alcoholic beverages.
Try to create good relationships with your neighbors.
Do not steal electricity from nearby posts.
Do not make large investments in your house (the land is not yet ours).[5]

In sum, the Nordeste district was one where associational life was not very developed. As a geographically remote district, it seldom attracted outside advisors to help organize movements and associations. The exceptionally insecure daily life of its residents also inhibited higher levels of organization. The associations that did exist occasionally managed to get sympathetic City Hall officials to make improvements, but they did so largely through personal mediation by their presidents. But because these four separate associations had little to do with one another, the district did not have established actors to serve as brokers between settlements and who could certify new organizations as new legitimate associations.

Orçamento Participativo Projects and the Routinization of Participation

Even though participants eventually warmed to the idea of working with City Hall and one another, they initially regarded the OP meetings with suspicion, manifested in limited regular attendance until the 1993 rounds. Participants from Nordeste were largely absent from the meetings in 1989 and 1990; the first meetings drew only five participants. Over three hundred participants came for the second meeting in 1991, however, responding to the successful construction of 650 new homes in the neighborhood in 1990. The number of participants fell again in 1992, but according to activists, "things really started to happen in late 1992." Several projects that year, including the school, and over 1,500 new homes brought the number up to almost 700 participants in the first meeting of 1993. Other noticeable projects, such as a health clinic built in 1994, stimulated steady growing participation. By the late 1990s, participation rates in this neighborhood were among the highest in the city.

There has never really been opposition to the OP in Nordeste. Although some presidents from the older neighborhood associations openly claimed to have ties to political parties like the populist PDT, this never translated into overt opposition to the OP. One reason for this absence is that there simply was little organized political activity here in the first place. The first political party organization of any kind in the neighborhood was the PT *núcleo,* founded in 1998 and essentially disbanded by 1999. The other reason is that the OP here did not threaten the position of any established activists, because there were no preexisting organized districtwide networks to disrupt. Neighborhood association presidents in many cases could still exert leadership in their specific areas and maintain respect in the community through the OP. As a functionary from the *prefeitura* put it, there "are personal problems here but there is no political opposition. . . . The supposed political opponents have participated since the very beginning. People are more practical than that."[6] Pragmatic calculations on the part of activists from other parties also help explain the lack of opposition to the OP.

The Impact on Associational Life

The greatest impact of these changes in Nordeste has been the explosion of new neighborhood associations. Most community activists in the district today trace their history in community involvement to the OP. One activist who would become a district councilor, who came from one of the land invasions that had formed a new association, recalled:

> It was 1993, and there was the OP and we were in this strange situation; there were more than fifty families with us, and we didn't know what was

going to happen to this piece of land. One of us went to the OP meeting and we formed a committee . . . and then we found out that the land belonged to the *prefeitura* (City Hall), started to make demands in the OP, and began to take part in the meetings with the other associations.[7]

This story is typical, and versions of it are repeated at the over two dozen new associations throughout the neighborhood.

By virtue of the sheer number of new participants in the OP and the new connections between previously unconnected sites and groups, the OP has had its greatest impact on associational life in places like Nordeste. What activists have not been able to accomplish, however, has been to establish a permanent district-level popular council like those found throughout the rest of the city. There were failed attempts to do so in 1992, 1993, and 1999. Arnaldo, who had participated in an attempt to start a popular council in Nordeste, recalled: "[W]e proposed that we develop a popular council, a forum outside of the OP with representation by people involved in neighborhood associations, charity groups, day care centers, and so on, and it would be a popular council. But it never took hold and doesn't exist today." Several interviewees did not in fact distinguish between the OP and the nonexistent popular council, using the terms interchangeably. Arnaldo went on to explain that whenever the idea of a popular council was brought up, "people would respond, 'But I already participate in the popular council every Saturday.'"

Despite the blurring of lines between the OP and civil society, the impact of the participatory budget process on associative life here is evident. Today's twenty-seven neighborhood associations, of which twenty-five held at least one meeting a month during my research, embody this fact. Although no popular council has been established to serve as a forum outside the purview of the OP, institutional councils linked to the OP meet on a regular basis. Most notably, although participants from this neighborhood are the least experienced, their level of participation in the OP has been higher than anywhere else in the city.

The Partenon District: Scaled-Up Activism

The name Partenon, which derives from a literary club that existed around 1900, is indicative of how this neighborhood is distinct from the rest of the city of Porto Alegre. Today, what is especially noteworthy about this district is the well-functioning popular council, an autonomous and permanent forum in which activists from various neighborhoods participate. The popular council, which became much more active as a result of the OP, not only coordinates the demands of individual neighborhoods but also mediates with the city's administration.

Partenon was a well-organized district prior to the introduction of the OP, with social movements, an incipient popular council, and twenty functioning associations in 1989. Accordingly, the changes resulting from the OP process are less obvious in quantitative terms here than in Nordeste, because the number of neighborhood associations over the ten years in question has only increased from twenty to twenty-seven. The greater shift has been in terms of the scaling-up of district civic life, with much more focus now on district-level activities as opposed to individual neighborhood associations. The existence of the popular council and of active connections between neighborhoods meant that when the OP was established, there was already a tradition of brokerage between neighborhoods. The OP did not upset this preexisting relationship, because it was able to absorb these previous networks into the new organization.

This district is the most diverse and encompasses ten neighborhoods, which vary in composition from the largest, "Partenon proper," with a mix of working-class and lower-middle-class homes, to Azenha, a small neighborhood that is one of the city's richest communities, to the neighborhoods of João Pessoa and São José, which are among the city's poorest. The median monthly household income for the district is U.S.$390, and about one-sixth of adults fall into the lowest education bracket. In all, about 10 percent of homes in the district are officially inadequate in terms of access to infrastructure, and one-fifth of the homes do not have adequate sewage connections. Approximately 30 percent of households are poor, a figure above the city's average, but below those for Norte and Nordeste.[8]

Although precise data do not exist, the district was known as a hotbed of urban activism and of PT sympathizers prior to the election victory of the PT in 1988. In addition to the work of liberation theology activists here, the Movimento Negro (Black Movement), and various other prodemocracy movements were active in the neighborhoods. The district had two principal areas of activism throughout the 1980s. The first emerged in the militant Campo da Tuca neighborhood, already described by the researcher Pedrinho Guareschi in 1985 as having been embroiled in fights with the municipal government since the 1970s, and the other surfaced in Morro da Cruz, which had competing neighbor-hood associations throughout the period.[9]

In Campo da Tuca, residents managed to achieve some urban im-provements in the mid-1970s, but this was shortly followed by dissatis-faction with government officials' failure to follow through on all promises. The presence of political party activists and progressive clergy radicalized the stance of the association over time and led to a state of open conflict with City Hall. In Morro da Cruz, in contrast, un-der the dictatorship in the mid 1970s, the city administration helped es-tablish a neighborhood association, which initially received relatively positive treatment from the military-appointed mayor. By the late 1970s, however, the association began to demand that the administra-tion make more improvements in its neighborhood. There was tension, but owing to the lack of a critical mass of party or church activists, no open conflict developed as in the case of Campo da Tuca.[10]

Coordinating demands from both Campo da Tuca and Morro da Cruz, activists attempted to form a united front to deal with the city ad-ministration. At several points in the 1980s, a group of Partenon ac-tivists joined forces owing to the efforts of progressive priests who me-diated contact between the two associations. In 1984, participants tried to create a "Democratic Council of the Partenon" to unite the disparate groups in the struggle and create a semi-permanent, democratic forum to debate overall urban needs. A network of progressive clergy in about ten parishes throughout the district played a central role in organizing between the different associations, combining "faith with the popular struggle."[11]

Organizers proposed an "emergency program" to be taken to the au-thorities as a list of demands that included the cancellation of Interna-tional Monetary Fund (IMF) payments and a freeze on the price of util-ities and medications. A letter was sent out to a dozen neighborhood associations in the district inviting their participation in a meeting to form this new council, calling on residents to "form the DEMOCRATIC COUNCIL OF THE PARTENON. . . . Its objective: to mobilize and orga-nize the population in the defense of its interests."[12] Although the coun-cil never functioned on a regular basis, it successfully mobilized resi-dents around issues like unemployment, which led to an occupation of the state government for ten days in 1984.

The Partenon district also provided a solid voting block for the pop-ulist PDT in the first democratic elections of 1985. The voting district

FIG. 8. Logo of the Conselho Popular do Partenon, ca. 1991

with the highest vote for Collares was Zonal 113 in Partenon.[13] Documents from the Collares administration show that Partenon activists and its eighteen associations featured prominently among those selected for the administration's participation program in 1986. The administration clearly considered the district a potential basis of support for its participatory plans, but the presence of radical clergy and other oppositional social movements in the district eventually generated discontent with the administration's inability to fulfill its campaign promises. By 1987–88, the Collares administration had abandoned Partenon. As one activist explained, "my neighborhood used to be the 'headquarters' of the PDT, but the popular council that Collares was supposed to create never materialized and a lot of us switched over to the PT in 1988."[14]

The PT Administration and the Orçamento Participativo

The Conselho Popular do Partenon (CPP), the district's popular council, was created by a coalition of activists in 1988 as an expression of collective frustration after three years of false starts by the Collares administration. Most of the activists involved in the CPP were sympathetic to the PT,[15] and the frustration with the Collares administration in the incipient *conselho* was replaced by hopeful expectations about popular participation in the PT administration. The Partenon district was one of the first to consolidate the OP. As early as 1989, popular council activists began organizing meetings regularly at the Nossa Senhora das Graças church and helped formulate the participatory structure of the OP meetings in the district, with high participation from the start.

Partenon community activists were also involved in shaping the OP as the process took hold.

The actual amount of resources directed to Partenon initially was relatively low in comparison to other districts, but the visible completion of projects increased participation in 1990 and 1991. Among the district's first demands was a set of steps going up a hill next to Vila Vargas. Two long-standing demands, a new bus line to Morro da Cruz and garbage collection on the hill, helped bring in more participants in 1991. Functioning sewage projects and the paving of almost two kilometers of a crucial road linking some of the poorer *vilas* to main thoroughfares in 1992 were widely praised in the community, with the number of OP participants once again multiplying in 1993 and 1994.

The popular council became increasingly active in those years, because its role in running the OP brought it increased visibility in the district. Nevertheless, the question of how to integrate with the OP created ambiguity for many participants. Activists on the popular council recognized the OP as an important advance for their communities and sought to play a supporting role, but for some this fact nurtured an "overidentification" with the PT administration.[16] "Independence from the wealthy" and "autonomy from political parties and other institutions" were among the "founding principles" of the CPP.[17] In contrast to movements that only pressured existing administrations for specific demands, the CPP saw itself as a forum that would propose policies and take a proactive role in governance.[18] In March 1991, in its first official statutes, it announced that it would "monitor the government" and "propose policies for the administration,"[19] clearly maintaining a position independent of the party in power.

In 1991, when a full-time facilitator from the administration assumed responsibility for the OP, the CPP moved to a more auxiliary role in running the OP. From then on, the popular council assumed a semi-official role as intermediary with the municipal administration. Requests for municipal services, such as fixing a broken streetlight or street paving, were directed at the CPP, which passed them on to the administration.[20] Records show that the popular council dutifully followed up on most of such requests.

Even so, dissatisfaction was growing among CPP activists who were beginning to feel that they were too "tied to the administration" and "doing its job."[21] Discussions ensued about their appropriate role. A flyer from the time asked, "The CPP, is it part of City Hall, an organization of the PT, or is it [an instance of] Popular Power?" and answered that activists within the CPP "don't want to be activists of a public administration or of a political party."[22] From then on, the CPP sought to establish a more independent identity, holding its meetings on a different night of the week, but continuing to play many important roles within the OP.

New associations have been formed in Partenon, particularly among the district's outlying *vilas*, but the increase in numbers is relatively small when compared to a district like Nordeste. The greater shift for Partenon since the establishment of the OP has been the increased visibility of the CPP, whose brokerage role between neighborhoods increased as the council itself became institutionally integrated into the OP. Partenon is also the district where participation has been among the strongest at the level of institutional councils (such as the councils on health, social services, and the environment). Today, the district also has a large number of street committees—ad hoc groups formed to discuss OP priorities and other community problems that do not go on to become formal neighborhood associations. According to one activist, the CPP "no longer encourages the formation of new associations. The era of the association is over. This is the era of the OP and of the council."

The Norte District: Competing Allegiances

The Norte district, home to about 90,000 people, is like much of Porto Alegre in that it is made up of striking contrasts. Half of the households are poor, and 13 percent of homes are considered to have inadequate infrastructure; 27 percent of heads of household have only three years' education or less.[23] A densely populated district, Norte is today divided between established neighborhoods and about nineteen settlements. Many of these are known as traditional sites of Porto Alegre's industrial working class, such as the Sarandí neighborhood. The district is divided by Sarandí river, the banks of which are dotted with small, irregular settlements. During the winter, the river often floods, sweeping away homes in the more precarious areas, which causes recurrent housing problems. Many of these working-class neighborhoods have provided support for populist PDT politicians. Voting Subdistrict 158, or Zonal 158,[24] which overlaps with much of the district, is one of the PDT's traditional bases of support, and it has backed PDT mayors, members of city council, and members of the state congress. The PDT's share of the vote in the district was among the highest in the city in 1985 and 1988.

Before the introduction of the OP, there were twenty-two active neighborhood associations and a popular council, and civic life was already divided, with tensions between PT-linked activists and those with ties to populist PDT politicians. These tensions have become even more intense with the introduction of the OP, principally between activists in the popular council and participants in the OP. When the OP was introduced, it became an alternate route to brokerage between neighborhoods, threatening the privileged position of the popular council. Activists within the popular council for a time controlled OP proceedings, but they severely limited real participation, in essence blocking the certification of a wider range of organizations and participants as legitimate claimants.

"Good Communities" and Their "Antlike" Opponents

At least since the 1950s, the Norte district's working classes were relatively privileged beneficiaries of the attention of populist mayors and governors. From the 1970s on, middle-class advisory NGOs like FASE, progressive clergy, and, later, PT activists helped foster oppositional activism within the same neighborhoods, encouraging the radicalization of demands and the democratization of existing associations. The conflict between the two kinds of activists—those who defended traditional associations based in "good communities" and those who believed in linking neighborhood associations to larger political struggles—defines much of the history of Norte until the late 1980s.

These associations were often social clubs that limited membership to dues-paying residents, but that remained the privileged institutional voice for the district in terms of access to public authorities. The presidents of these associations sometimes received additional benefits, and some remained in their roles for over a decade. For instance, according to an activist from the 1970s, the streets of the Santa Rosa neighborhood were completely paved in 1976 and 1977 as a result of its allegiance to the military-appointed mayor. Activists from these types of neighborhoods sometimes expressed resentment at the "land invaders" and "slum dwellers," or *vileiros*, who settled near their "good communities."[25]

In the 1970s and 1980s, community activists, often with the help of progressive clergy or outside advisors, worked to "open up" existing

F I G . 9. Norte
neighborhood

neighborhood associations. This included loosening the restrictions on membership and attempting to relate to the concerns of the "irregular" favelas in the district. As an activist put it, "the PT was a party that came from below, like ants, [and] entered one association, then another, winning some."[26] Activists attempted to train new leaders in those neighborhoods to run for the presidency and transform the association's rules to make it more democratic and more politically engaged. These attempts resulted in a coalition for free public education in 1984,[27] which despite some early victories, was not able to maintain steady participation as its leaders had hoped.[28]

The Popular Council in 1987 and 1988

The impetus for organizing a districtwide forum came from the populist Collares administration. The Norte district was central to the Collares administration's plans to establish municipal councils.[29] In 1986, meetings were held in the district to discuss and define the rules for the proposed municipal councils.[30] Neighborhood associations listed demands and priorities, and since the Collares administration's municipal councils did not materialize, local activists attempted to form an autonomous organization, with assistance from NGOs and the citywide autonomous umbrella neighborhood organization. Their common platform demanded improvements in the sewage service in the district and a call to create a popular council that would have a voice in the municipal administration.[31] In the course of discussions for the creation of the popular council, activists submitted lists of demands to the administration, which promised that the projects would in fact materialize.

In February 1988, another large meeting was held to establish a permanent forum. This time, participants demanded access to the city's investment plans for the year and decided that they would explicitly avoid being taken in by electoral promises in the November elections. The proposal was to carry out a study in each *vila* to ascertain residents' needs and to contrast these with the candidates' specific proposals.[32] In May, an agenda was defined to pursue demands to improve the services of the administration, increase access to investment plans, further decentralize the provision of services, and increase local participation in the 1989 budget.[33] The popular council's directorate was made up of a coalition of neighborhood association presidents, of whom six were populist PDT activists; four, PT activists; and two, activists without party affiliations.[34] Only formally registered associations would be represented on the popular council.[35] Despite having both PDT and PT activists as regular participants, the popular council continually voiced its disapproval of the PDT's Collares administration.[36] By the end of 1988, residents of several of the Norte district's neighborhoods were strikingly disillusioned with the Collares administration, and in the Santa Rosa neighborhood, they burned an effigy of Collares.[37]

The Partido dos Trabalhadores Administration and the Orçamento Participativo

In November 1988, the PT won City Hall, aided in no small part by the growing dissatisfaction with the PDT administration. However, the popular council in the Norte district remained under the control of both PDT and PT activists for the next few months. Leaders of the popular council believed that the PT administration would allow the council to control the administration's activities directly. One of the resolutions from a meeting in March of that year was that the popular council should remain "independent, autonomous, and combative" vis-à-vis the administration, while seeking "real power" within it. The popular council developed a number of committees around specific concerns, such as housing and health, and devised proposals that it would forward to the new administration.[38] On its own initiative, it put together working groups to propose solutions to the district's social problems, calling for the administration to build housing for all residents of irregular *vilas* in the district and for extending urban services to all residents, including the construction of a public clinic, a school, day care centers, a meeting hall, and a soccer field.[39] It also assembled a list of overall priorities, with demands for sewage service, street paving, and other emergency projects topping the list.[40] Finally, it asked that City Hall permit neighborhood associations help determine "which items will be answered this year, and which will be in next year's budget."[41]

The first actual meeting of the district OP began with a fight between the popular council and the PT administration. Leaders of the popular council left the premises in the middle of the discussion, taking one-third of the participants with them, "because we understood that the group that should run the local meetings should be the organized movement."[42] It is noteworthy that PT activists on the popular council were among the most vocal critics of the administration and encouraged others to challenge it more openly.[43] In preparing the next year's budget, the mayor and his team responded to criticisms of exclusion by meeting with the popular council to discuss the proceedings for the 1990 rounds.[44] The administration then effectively ceded control of the process to the popular council for the 1990 rounds, and the popular council organized the OP meetings in the district from then on, deciding on criteria for district-level priorities and on the meetings' format.

Unlike in Partenon, the OP was seen as a threat to preexisting networks and relationships of brokerage between neighborhoods. For a time in Norte, community activists mobilized against the OP, attempting to delegitimize it and to establish parallel networks of linking neighborhoods. This included a group whose slogan was "Bringing together all that unites the people," which met regularly through 1990–91 as the "Independent Popular Council of Norte" and established a small newspaper and an AM radio show.[45] The radio program featured participants discussing community affairs and announcing social events in the district, while generating trenchant criticism of the PT and the OP process, such as claiming that the OP was a fraud and that no actual projects would come of it.

These charges against the PT administration and the OP process became difficult to sustain once projects actually began to materialize in neighborhoods. These included a large sewage project, primary schools, and legalization of the land titles of three former land occupations. Prior to these projects, some OP advocates in the district claimed that credibility was difficult to muster under constant criticism, because they "were criticized for being brown-nosers [*puxa-saco*] of the administration." One PT advocate said that he "used to pray for the day that they would tell me that the construction of the project is beginning on such-and-such day, so that we could show the community that the process really worked. And one day I got that call, and from [19]92 onward, the process took off."

Over 1991 and 1992, the administration made a number of bureaucratic changes, including instituting new facilitator positions for the OP, which were usually filled by community activists. Many of these posts were filled by activists from the Norte district, and some were on the board of the popular council. The PT presence then declined in associations and in the popular council. PT activists recalled that, "we came to work for the administration, but later realized this was a mistake, because then the PDT became hegemonic in some districts."[46] Eventually, "most longtime PT people left."[47] By 1993, a number of key PT activists had left local activism for positions in the administration, among them some of the popular council's directors, paving the way for the control of that organization by the populist PDT. As a result, the latter now controlled the way the OP operated.

One rule in place in Norte (and nowhere else in Porto Alegre) between 1990 and 1994 was that each neighborhood association would have three delegates to the OP, and that one of them would be the association president. This made it difficult for new participants to get involved, and there were regular complaints from would-be participants. The popular council continued to control the OP and prevent new collectives of citizens from participating other than through already existing associations, many of which were once again under the control of the PDT. In effect, the popular council attempted to block the certification of new actors by limiting the process to previously established associations.

In 1995, however, when there were enough sympathetic participants from within associations to constitute a quorum, a number of participants working alongside the organizer from City Hall staged a "coup" and changed the rules of the popular council. They thus created an independent forum of delegates that opened up participation to all, making rules identical to those in other districts: participation was now open to any individual citizen or group of citizens, thus allowing less formal street committees to participate and ultimately fostering more civic engagement in civil society.

After 1995, when the OP became separate from the popular council, the process took the form that it has today, and participation increased substantially. The number of participants and the number of groups attending expanded, since it was no longer a requisite that a specific neighborhood association had to represent any given area. Conflict between groups continues today, but the new participants represent a wider array of people from outside formal neighborhood associations. As a result of these changes, participation has flourished, and many new associations and autonomous groups have emerged parallel to existing associations. These include neighborhood associations in areas where an existing working-class association refused to take the demands of slum areas seriously, and a number of work cooperatives. Whereas in the past, PT activists attempted to win over and democratize existing associations, the OP has made it possible for new players to enter the civic arena. One of the greatest sources of dissatisfaction for some neighborhood association activists is, in fact, the appearance of so many new activists. According to one such activist, "[N]ow anyone shows up in the OP and thinks that he has leadership, but in reality most of these new people don't have the experience in the community movement." The popular council once again started to oppose the OP process, instituting a policy of boycotting most OP meetings.

When rules for participation changed in Norte, not only did participation take off, the proportion of participants from outside of neighborhood associations expanded. In 1998, for example, 79 percent of participants in the Norte OP were not linked to a neighborhood association, compared to 36 percent in 1995 (as against 54 and 52 percent in Nordeste). The number of new associations in Norte emerged mostly after 1995, when the OP started to include broad segments of participants, creating connections among them, and recognizing them as legitimate claimants in the OP.

New Configurations in Civil Society

The OP has become routinized, with broad participation, in all three districts discussed above. Aggregate participation figures do not reveal much about the quality of participation, but do indicate larger trends.

TABLE 7

Participants in the Orçamento Participativo as a Percentage of Total Population

	1990	1991	1992	1993	1994	1995
Nordeste	0.14%	1.50%	1.14%	5.24%	2.93%	3.17%
Partenon	0.07%	0.30%	0.96%	0.68%	0.96%	0.70%
Norte	0.09%	0.16%	0.68%	0.49%	0.39%	0.70%
Citywide	0.08%	0.28%	0.59%	0.83%	0.74%	0.91%
	1996	1997	1998	1999	2000	
Nordeste	2.81%	2.94%	3.73%	7.80%	7.11%	
Partenon	0.71%	0.63%	0.71%	1.02%	0.75%	
Norte	0.56%	0.93%	1.04%	0.69%	1.01%	
Citywide	0.78%	0.92%	1.05%	1.29%	1.18%	

SOURCES: PMPA, various.
NOTE: Percentages reflect the sum of first and second plenary meetings.

Table 7 shows that participation has been high in the Nordeste district since 1993, and that a significant proportion of the population attends meetings, especially considering that the total population figures include all residents, not only those who are over sixteen and eligible participants. Norte and Partenon have had lower proportional participation. In Norte, it declined between the first plenary of 1992 and the second plenary of 1994, only to begin to increase again in 1995. Because of the popular council's oppositional stance toward the Orçamento Participativo, organized civil society here has at times posed obstacles to the establishment of the process, including restricting participation until 1995.

The configuration of civil society networks in relation to the OP and the roles that different organizations have assumed in each district is also different. Nordeste had the least associational traditions and has seen the greatest growth in neighborhood associations. District-level organizations, such as a popular council, are absent in Nordeste, and the OP is in essence the main meeting place and conduit for all district-level activity. In Partenon, activist networks seem to have deepened along the original lines of neighborhood activist networks and expanded as a district-level process. Organized district-level civil society in the guise of the popular council performs significant coordinating functions for the OP, organizing meetings and coordinating demands. The popular council also acts as an additional conduit for connecting with the municipal state. In Norte, the new activism that has occurred has often been in parallel to existing associations. There is a popular council as well, but its main activists are conspicuously absent from meetings, and it forms a parallel network.

The expectations that the poorest and least organized district, Nordeste, would be the least likely to have active participation in the OP is reversed in the comparison of the three districts. Its residents, who were previously the most disenfranchised and without access to networks of power, have become the most enthusiastic participants. In Partenon, the popular council essentially merged with the OP, and community activists did not block the OP. In Norte, where not only were there organized networks but also a politically enfranchised working-class base, the process proved most difficult. The allegiance of these working-class neighborhood activists to previous schemes such as the tutelage programs that benefited them, combined with the fact that PT activists from Norte left organizations for the administration, made for a very difficult routinization of the OP. Popular council activists in Norte perceived the brokerage and certification of new actors as a threat.

Each of these resulting configurations—where the OP itself is the main meeting place for the district (Nordeste), where the OP and district networks are intermeshed (Partenon), and where the OP and district networks are distinct (Norte)—implies different sorts of relationships, which bear upon the kinds of interactions that take place in and around the OP, as described in later chapters. There are appreciable differences in the profiles of the elected delegates from each district that support these assertions.

As Table 8 shows, delegates in Norte and Partenon have appreciably longer experience in both civil society and the OP, and these districts have larger groups of veteran community activists with ten or more

TABLE 8

Profile of Delegates in Each District

	Nordeste	Partenon	Norte
Years of Experience in the Orçamento Participativo	3	6	3
. . . for five or more years	19%	38%	31%
Years of experience in civil society	4	10	8
Started in civil society with or after the Orçamento Participativo	50%	43%	44%
Has ten or more years of civil society experience	8%	19%	15%
Average number of outside settings regularly participates	3	4	2
Participates in another district-level setting	10%	70%	45%

SOURCE: Author's survey of delegates, 1999.

years of experience. It also shows that most delegates in the Partenon district are involved in another districtwide setting, be it the autonomous popular council or an institutional council, whereas only a fraction of Nordeste delegates are so involved.

It could be said that in the case of Nordeste, the OP is central—if it weren't for the OP, disparate associations would not come into contact with one another. In Partenon, the OP is central to the district's civic life, but in its absence, associations would still be in contact via the popular council. In Norte, the OP and the popular council are divided—while all associations participate in the OP, some gravitate to the popular council and some gravitate to OP-related settings with no ties between the popular council and the OP. In the following chapters, I examine the impact of each of these configurations on deliberation and open-ended discussion with the OP.

CHAPTER FOUR

Deliberative Repertoires

> . . . this communal interest does not exist merely in the imagination, as the "general interest," but first of all in reality, as the mutual interdependence of the individuals among whom the labor is divided.
> —Karl Marx and Frederick Engels, *The German Ideology*

Constructing the "Common Interest": Deliberation and Conflict in the Orçamento Participativo

The Commercial Club of Sarandi, a Rotary International affiliate, is located in an unremarkable building dating from the 1950s, which serves as one of the traditional middle-class meeting places in the district. In March each year, the club's ballroom is rented to the Workers' Party city administration for the Orçamento Participativo's first plenary assembly, which attracts upwards of a thousand people. For that evening at least, the ballroom is filled with residents from very different neighborhoods than those that usually attend the functions of the club. Here, as in the city's fifteen other districts and in the five municipal thematic meetings (which became six in 2000), a festive ritual takes place to launch the year's proceedings. Beginning at 7 P.M., in each of the similar assemblies around the city, for almost a month, administrators put on a highly structured meeting that opens with music or theater by notable local artists. An accounting of the previous year's projects and demands follows, culminating with the mayor and vice-mayor replying to community questions and criticisms. Child care is provided (the "little OP").

In March 1998, the first plenary meeting for the OP in the Norte district was about to begin. Outside the meeting hall, the busy confluence of participants registering seemed to be a state of general confusion. Whole neighborhoods sometimes arrive together with banners and noisemakers, and people often come dressed in costume: Rio Grande do Sul *gaúcho* cowboy outfits or *capoeira* (Afro-Brazilian martial art) garb that identify them as part of a cultural group that will make demands during the year. Barbara, a newly elected neighborhood association leader, was anxious about who would show up, because fewer than half of those she'd expected from her neighborhood were at the bus stop as planned. The number of people from any one self-identified group determines its number of delegates, according to a measure of diminishing returns; registered participants may choose to participate as unaffiliated individuals or declare membership in a group in civil society.[1] Neighborhood activists like Barbara would walk people through the registration line to make sure that they were counted correctly in order to "get the delegates." Barbara told me that she hoped she had "brought at least fifty, because that would ensure at least three delegates." Almost a hundred people at a meeting earlier in the week had told her they would come, but she realized that "people are tired after a long day of work," she said, and she would be happy if fifty showed up.

After this first plenary meeting, the process draws out for much of the year. Delegates like the ones from Barbara's neighborhood will meet weekly in the Norte district to discuss priorities and projects, and will then elect two councilors to serve on the citywide Budget Council which finalizes the municipal investment plan and reviews the procedures for the following year. The institutional design of the OP includes combinations of types of decision making, including deliberative discussion followed by voting. This chapter asks whether, and how, that discussion comes to meet a norm of "deliberation" in which there is inclusive discussion, reasons are given, and justification is sought.

Deliberative Moments

Theorists of deliberative democracy such as Joshua Cohen, Jane Mansbridge, and Amy Gutman have, in recent writings, put forward sophisticated accounts of deliberation as a democratic decision-making process superior on normative and practical grounds to constitutionalism, adversary democracy, representative democracy, and other aggregative collective decision-making procedures.[2] Simply put, these theorists argue that democratic deliberation is able to provide meaningful solutions to the inevitable, intractable difficulties that arise in modern polities, including the deep moral disagreements that erupt among reasonable people and choices over the allocation of limited collective resources.

Deliberation implies discussion among "equal, free, and reasonable" participants as part of the decision-making process. A truly deliberative discussion is one in which all participants are considered equal and are equally free to intervene and to question the topics of debate.[3] It is important that interventions appeal to "reasons acceptable to others."[4] Participation in deliberation must, moreover, be inclusive of all those affected by the collective decision. Theorists of deliberative democracy count on the "transformation of individual preferences" as a result of deliberation. In principle, in truly deliberative decision making, then, participants will come to accept collective decisions as fair and justified, and as Mansbridge writes, "either find or create common interests among them that will have priority over their conflicts."[5]

Scholars who have studied deliberation have often addressed the obviously important question of the inclusiveness of meetings, but inclusivity is not the primary issue in the OP, which is by any standards a highly inclusive institution. This ethnography did not find any pattern of systematic exclusion, and aggregate evidence shows there is parity or near-parity of participation in terms of education, income, gender, and race. That is, participants and their elected representatives (delegates and councilors) essentially mirror the less-privileged citizens of Porto Alegre, as well as some of the inequalities among them.[6] Among delegates, women and the less-educated (as well as the highly educated) face slightly lower chances of being elected, although statistical analyses, not reported here, show that this partly has to do with the availability of time and connections in civil society.[7] When the composition of the OP is compared to, say, Porto Alegre's city council, it becomes clear that it is a highly inclusive setting.[8]

The challenge here is whether such an inclusive setting can actually be said to be deliberative and to meet the qualitative criteria for democratic procedure. Assessing whether discussions become "deliberative" implies differentiating between different sorts of discussions and actual deliberation by questioning the content as well as the conditions under which the discussion takes place. Although decision making in the OP does approach normative ideals of deliberation, it is neither free of conflict nor automatic. Rather, participants face the recurring dilemmas, inherent in deliberation, of representation, coordination, and power mobilization, which put pressure on them to opt out of deliberation in some way, such as by derailing the meeting or simply leaving. But deliberation can be facilitated by the presence of well-connected activists, often working on the margins of official meetings, who coordinate solutions and generate trust in the process. The importance of these difficulties to deliberation and of civil society networks have seldom been addressed with regard to empirical examples.

The Orçamento Participativo as a Deliberative Setting

The OP has evolved over the years to encompass wider areas of municipal budgeting, giving citizens' forums more power. For example, the introduction of thematic meetings organized on a citywide basis in 1994 and 1995 expanded decision making to include longer-range decisions about priorities for health and education. Participatory decision making on school curricula and the like has also considerably expanded citizen decision making and participation in government beyond the OP. Even so, the OP meetings still capture the bulk of participation and remain the model for other participatory mechanisms in Porto Alegre.

OP decisions are taken in forums structured in two tiers, where citizens participate respectively as individuals and as representatives of various groups of civil society, such as neighborhood associations, cultural groups, and special interest groups. They meet throughout the year, first to deliberate and decide on projects for specific districts and on municipal investment priorities and then to monitor the outcome of these projects. The yearly cycle is composed of a first plenary meeting, intermediate meetings, a second plenary meeting, and the Budget Council's meetings, as shown in Figure 10.

The OP process begins festively, as we have seen, with the first plenary meeting in March. The first collective decision of the year is the choice of delegates for the local Budget Forum. This includes two decisions: how many delegates per group will be allocated, based on a mathematical formula of decreasing returns, and who those delegates will be.[9] The choice of delegates for the neighborhood or group is made outside of the OP proceedings and is not subject to formal checks.[10] In Barbara's case, her informal association only had twenty-two people in attendance, which meant two delegates. Only one other person besides Barbara was available and willing to serve as the second delegate for her group. As she explained, in practice, "it's not really [just] a matter of electing somebody, because it has to be somebody with time and commitment."

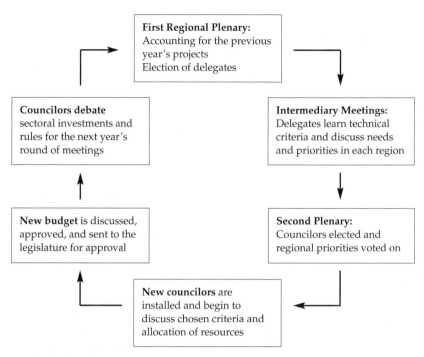

F IG . 10 . The yearly cycle of decision making in participatory budgeting (1990–2000). Adapted with permission from CIDADE.

The other function of the plenary meetings is to give citizens the opportunity to question the mayor and his staff, and they eventually line up at the microphone to do so. There is little real deliberation, but this "accounting" provides transparency and legitimacy, and participants repeatedly highlighted the importance of this part of the process. Owing to the fact that participants were vested with the power to demand accountability, it was impossible for the mayor's team to avoid having to answer for a range of governmental actions, much beyond the participatory budgeting.

The next set of decisions to be made, and probably the most important ones as far as participants are concerned, is the selection of projects and priorities at intermediate OP meetings, which take place from March to June or July. Forty to sixty delegates meet in each of the districts and in the parallel thematic OP meetings on a weekly or biweekly basis to acquaint themselves with these technical criteria and to deliberate, formally and informally, about the district's needs. The meetings' agenda usually involves the discussion of technical criteria for specific

FIG. 11. Budget
Forum meeting, Norte

areas of investments. Although these meetings were meant as technical discussions, it was in these forums that deliberative discussions actually took place, with participants debating principles of distribution, sometimes shifting preferences and signaling these preferences in their questions and concerns.

At the end of the four-month period, delegates come to a vote on priorities and specific projects and select their two councilors to the Budget Council at a large second plenary meeting.[11] By the second plenary meeting, delegates usually come with a clear idea of the kinds of projects and priorities on which they will vote, and they have often already made deals with other delegates or tried to persuade them to vote a certain way, since a single neighborhood usually is not able to decide on a project or priority on its own. As experienced participants have learned, the general excitement of this voting assembly sometimes means that, without previous discussion, "there are inevitably surprises." Accordingly, seasoned participants ensure that a broader range of delegates have previously discussed the possible outcome of the votes.[12]

From then on, most of the decision making happens at the Budget

Council, where councilors from each district and thematic area meet with the administration's representatives to reconcile the demands from each district with the available resources and then to propose and approve a municipal budget. For several months, the forty-two budget councilors meet twice weekly with representatives from different municipal departments, like the planning departments. Councilors, who are held to a maximum term of two years and who are subject to instant recall, maintain links with the budget forums that elected them throughout the process, particularly as projects make, or fail to make, the final budget. From figures given by the administration about funds available for investment, and given the overall priorities chosen by each of the districts, councilors divide the budget first among broad investment priorities, then among districts, and finally decide on individual projects. After a specific amount of money is allotted to street paving, for instance, street-paving funds are divided among each of the districts based on a formula that considers the district's level of need, population, and how it ranked that particular priority.[13] Extensive discussions of individual projects then follow, since the funds allotted to each district will not quite match its preferred projects. For example, in late 1997, several districts had small surpluses for paving projects, and councilors vigorously debated whether to bank the funds for the following year, return them to a general fund, or to cede them to other districts. In that year, councilors decided to cede the funds to one particularly economically disadvantaged district.

After approving a budget and sending it to the municipal legislature, councilors then spend time revising the rules of the whole budgeting process. These are also clearly deliberative discussions examining the abstract principles of redistribution, fair decision making, and their relative merits. In recent years, significant changes to the rules have included broadening the Budget Council's powers to cover the administration's personnel expenditures, changing the criteria for assessing how resources are to be allocated to each of the districts, and altering recall procedures for councilors, in effect, continually revising the rules of deliberation themselves.

Deliberative Breakdowns and Participants' Dilemmas

Although the OP relies on deliberation at several meetings throughout the year, democratic theorists warn that these types of discussions often fail to meet democratic deliberative standards. To be considered "democratic deliberation," a discussion must meet the criteria of inclusiveness, be procedurally "free and equal," and rely on appeals to reason. Far from being a seamless process of consensus formation, however, OP meetings can often be deeply conflictual, with participants occasionally deploying pressure tactics and other strategies for opting out of deliberation. In fact, participants may feel they have no choice but to impede deliberation, because they feel they are being co-opted by the participatory process, or because they then have to return to their district or neighborhood to explain why their preferences in the discussion shifted from the constituency's priorities.

At higher levels of decision making, the interests represented become increasingly complex, as do the issues discussed, adding to the growing tension. At the Budget Council, for instance, representatives may come to discussions from districts that are poles apart, sometimes with each district potentially representing "popular mandates" of 100,000 people or more, creating dilemmas between deliberation and representation. These dilemmas are inherent in complex combinations of decision making, such as those established by the OP. Yet when participants perceive a sense of trust in the process and are assured of its continuity year after year, they might be willing to agree to have their own specific neighborhood's demands listed as a lower priority in *this* year's plan in favor of a districtwide project, although this is seemingly at odds with their self-interest.

The Power Mobilization Dilemma

OP meetings take place in what is, invariably, a politically charged context. The PT was elected in 1988 largely by protest votes, and many activists who originally persuaded their neighbors to attend meetings were involved in militant opposition to the previous municipal government. Because the OP is the main interface between public authority and civil society, it is here that broad oppositions and conflicts with public authority take place. This poses another dilemma for activists in the context of discussion and deliberation; sometimes, as they lose ground on a stated position, deliberation becomes less appealing than the threat or even actual practice of opposition to the process.

In the Partenon district, the favela next to the Catholic University had requested but was not granted a stoplight by the OP for its street corner next to the university in 1995. Ipiranga Avenue is a very busy thoroughfare, with speeding cars, and more than one child from this favela had been badly injured just trying to cross the street. The technical criteria established by the federal government, which found too many other traffic lights in close proximity to the corner in question, were the difficulty. Despite their knowledge of this technical restriction, activists from the favela again demanded the traffic light in 1997, and this time the district chose the project, but it was rejected by City Hall engineers on technical grounds. Several times at meetings in 1998, this issue was brought to the attention of the administration's members, and at a meeting late in the year, when one of the top administrators from the Public Transportation Department was present, Jairo, a neighborhood activist in his twenties, threatened to disrupt traffic if nothing was done:

> Jairo: I am glad you are here today, because I hope you are ready to admit your mistake in turning down our demand, because since we made the demand, there have been three accidents on our street corner, all involving children from our favela who were trying to cross Ipiranga Avenue.
>
> Administrator [taken aback]: Look, we can schedule a meeting in your favela to discuss this criterion, but you can't just demand traffic lights anywhere you want, there are criteria, and maybe other things you can demand, like speed bumps.
>
> Jairo: I am here to announce that we are going to stop traffic on Ipiranga Avenue for one hour during rush hour this week. We are going to call the press, and we will do this until you decide to approve our project.

Applause and confusion ensued, and other activists from the district tried to dissuade Jairo. Later on that week, there was a traffic stoppage during rush hour, which was described in the local newspapers as a protest against the administration's failure to control traffic problems. Activists from the Popular Council were on hand at the time to dissuade the residents from holding up traffic for too long, and, after a few minutes, traffic resumed. At a meeting a few days later, the topic was taken up again during the announcements:

> Jairo: I want to announce that last week we stopped traffic because we never received an adequate explanation for why we didn't have the traffic light put in place for us last year. I want to let everyone know that we will do it again next week if we have to and the week after that.
>
> Edílson [OP councilor for the district]: Just to let everyone know, the Popular Council has started to investigate the matter, and the Municipal Government has said that it will schedule a meeting to discuss different options if the traffic light can't be put up.
>
> Marcos [an activist with the district's popular council]: I hope that the *companheiro* will call the Popular Council before anyone decides to stop traffic again. (December 1998 field notes)

The matter was not immediately resolved. A number of meetings were scheduled in the favela, and other options, like speed bumps, were discussed. Yet residents remained hostile to the alternate proposals and justification for the restriction. No other traffic stoppages took place, but the issue remained a point of contention for residents in plenary meetings in 1999 and 2000. The district's popular council worked actively to prevent further traffic disruptions and to foster dialogue between the administration and the activists from the favela. For Jairo, whether to continue with traffic stoppages would depend on the results of the following year's discussions. If, as he told me, "the issue is not addressed early next year and we don't see results, we'll go back to doing the same thing."

Self-Interest and Collective Interests: The Coordination Dilemma

Participants also had to contend with how to weigh the interests of others in deliberations. When the decision at hand involved a project in their obvious immediate interest, such as voting for the paving of a street in their neighborhood, the calculus was fairly clear. It was also apparent when a "trade" had taken place, when, for example, delegates from one neighborhood would vote for a sewage project in another neighborhood in exchange for its delegates' votes for paving their streets. Prioritizing an issue meant countless discussions, a great deal of convincing, and ongoing negotiations outside of the formal meetings. According to an activist, their neighborhood's project had been chosen because of persistence in convincing nearby neighborhoods. "Before the meeting, we went from neighborhood to neighborhood to see who could vote for our project. That's what you have to do." On other occasions, it was promises to vote for someone else's project. Yolanda, a neighborhood activist in the Norte district, told me that she relied on a lot of explicit bargaining for a sewage project in her neighborhood, and an association leader nearby told her to "get your people to vote for my crèche, and we'll vote for whatever you want."

Many similar decisions required a different kind of logic altogether. In all three districts, the sheer number of neighborhoods and delegates made it unlikely that simply arriving and voting for a project would automatically put it on the list of approved projects. And bargaining was often not an option, since there was no exact equivalent project that would allow a comparable "trade." Even if there were two analogous demands in two neighborhoods, street paving in one, and sewage in another, it was unlikely that in practice both would be funded, since one would be prioritized over the other. Sometimes, it was necessary to coordinate several individual neighborhoods to vote on a single collective project. In the Nordeste district, a long-standing demand had been for a new school in the area. But given the high costs of new educational projects of that magnitude, many participants felt that prioritizing education would be a waste of time, while they could instead ask for the more realistic objective of paved roads. At a meeting in 1998, the City Hall facilitator proposed that if the district chose to make the area of education its first priority, it would likely receive a large project by virtue of being a needy district:

> Facilitator: Look, people, I have a suggestion about the education demands that are causing us so many problems in the area. If we decide to coordinate demands and make education one of our top priorities this year, we'll probably be able to demand a new school. We need to talk, but if we don't put it among our top priorities, we won't be able to get it, because it is an expensive project.
>
> Jonas [OP councilor]: I think that he is right, we need to talk to everyone about putting education first; we always complain that we don't get anything, but we don't put it among our priorities.

A number of activists then worked "behind the scenes" to make sure enough people voted for education at the next meeting. The district did finally prioritize education for that specific year, and as a needy district, it received one of the single largest endowments for a project from the following year's budget, funds of over a million reais (roughly U.S. $500,000) to build a new school. Some, like Jonas, who had gone from favela to favela to discuss the importance of collectively prioritizing education for the year described it as a lengthy process of trying to "convince people that voting for education doesn't mean that we won't get other projects also for the same reason."

But negotiations were not all as easy as this one. Occasionally in the Nordeste and Norte districts, participants claimed they were disadvantaged as a result of being from a small favela and not having enough votes to trade. Another participant said that since her favela only "had two delegates last year; it is not worth going to meetings." Others claimed that small neighborhoods do have a chance, as long as they come to meetings and make their case. One activist in Norte said: "Small favelas have a chance. The opportunity is the same. But people have to get organized. Sometimes they can find other people with the

F IG . 12. Budget Forum meeting, Nordeste

same priorities and vote together. Sometimes they just have to tell everyone how important their situation is."

In fact, in my fieldwork, there were instances where small favelas managed to get votes for their project by convincing everyone else of their difficulties. The ongoing nature of the process and the assurance that one's projects would be considered the following year made these sorts of resolutions possible. In the Norte district, the Favela Beco 1, a small neighborhood with about twenty family shacks, was able to win 180 meters of basic sewage pipe and had its project voted in first place. The neighborhood association president explained their success:

> We won our project, for basic sewage, as first priority for the district for 1999. Look, there are several streets in Norte that need sewage, and ours is small. Everyone from the favela was there on the day of the vote, and I made an appeal to everyone to vote for our street. It is a small project, but the open sewage was visible to everyone and clearly brings sickness. And so other people voted for our project first because our situation was so dire.
> Q: Other delegates voted for you?
> A: Lots. We had eight delegates, and we got over a hundred votes for our project. People really helped us out.

Of the three districts, it was in Partenon where small favelas were systematically assured projects, despite their size. Here, the popular council served as an important parallel meeting site that allowed seasoned activists to coordinate the complexity of competing demands in order to protect small neighborhoods and reward activists who came year after year. In the other two districts, the roles of community activists were more circumspect, precisely because a parallel meeting site like the popular council was not viable. Several activists in the Partenon district described this process of organizing demands ahead of time with satisfaction. As one activist recounted about a specific instance in which five different small neighborhoods each wanted a street paved: "If you imagine that each neighborhood has twenty votes that they can use for one street, none of them will get anything. If you put them together, that's one hundred votes and one street in first place and one in second."

One participant described how "it was OK" that his demand for street pavement had yet to materialize, despite his having actively participated for three years. He explained that he "started to participate out of curiosity a few years ago; I came to a meeting, and after a couple of meetings, there was a vote for streets. Vargas Street got thirty votes, another street forty votes, and I voted for my street, so we got one vote! Then they explained to me how it worked, how Vargas Street had been waiting for four years, the other street had been participating for a long time, and like that I am sure my street will get it this year; if not, for sure, the year following."

Here, the popular council plays a pivotal role in dividing up and ordering projects to make sure various sizes of neighborhoods are given a chance, in effect extending participants' time horizons. A popular council member explained: "[T]he way it works, the popular council tries to resolve all fights between streets over projects, and we try to make sure everyone gets a chance; and if people come for the first time, they have to wait, because others have been participating for years voting for other streets. We also try to divide the paving kilometers as much as we can, 20 meters here, 70 meters there, so even small projects get a chance." In fact, street-paving demands were divided among numerous streets in the Partenon district, more than in other districts. In 1999, Partenon won 1.5 kilometers of road paving, which it split among ten streets, some projects being as small as 90 meters. Several other districts, in contrast, implemented larger individual paving projects. For example, Nordeste won 3 kilometers, which it split among only three projects.

Coordination dilemmas are inherent in decision-making arrangements such as this one. In the context of scarce resources, some collective decisions require that participants give up individual demands in order to make a collective demand. Deliberative democrats count on the transformation of individual preferences as the solution to this dilemma, but, as we shall see, this is not an automatic process and depends on the strategic intervention of activists.

The Representation Dilemma

A final dilemma pertains to difficulties that representation poses to deliberation and vice versa. Participants' roles as deliberators sometimes conflicted with their roles as representatives. It was not uncommon for delegates to complain in meetings that "they were losing face in the community" when projects did not materialize, or that they "had to answer back to their neighborhood" for certain results. But this dilemma presented much more of a challenge in the citywide Budget Council than in the district-based forum of delegates. Councilors claimed that they faced greater pressure than delegates who represented individual neighborhoods, because they represented wider interests, across entire districts, constraining their position as deliberators. It was also often difficult to keep different constituents within their districts informed:

> It is difficult; there are a lot of things we talk about, and although we try to bring everything back to the district and keep everyone up to date, it is difficult. (Marcos, councilor, interview)

> You cover a lot of information in the [Budget Council] meetings, and it is complicated to go to explain it back to the districts. (Mara, councilor, interview)

> A good councilor is someone who goes and defends the interests of the district up there in the Budget Council and always brings back the information. (Gerson, delegate, interview)

One of the recurring complaints by delegates in the district forums was that councilors failed to maintain adequate communication with neighborhood associations about citywide Budget Council decisions.

At one meeting in May 1997, confusion ensued because of procedural misunderstandings between councilors from three districts and the rest of the citywide Budget Council. One of the administration's long-standing municipal policies has been to form partnerships with activists who want to run community-based day care centers. Since 1996, the decision about approving particular day care centers has been decided by the citywide Budget Council. In 1997, three districts chose to delay turning in their list of proposed day care centers to the Budget Council on time because of the insufficient resources allocated to funding the centers. The councilors from the three districts understood that their roles as deliberators conflicted with their roles as representatives. In their function as representatives, they felt they had to defend their community's needs for more resources, although this meant that as representatives, they were in effect asking to postpone the discussion at the citywide council, thereby obstructing an already agreed-upon process. In this case, the three budget councilors attempted to close discussions by leaving the meeting and lowering the number of participants below the required quorum.

The meeting was packed with activists from the three districts in addition to the regular councilors. The decision about day care centers was second on the agenda, and when they reached the item, community activists started to yell from the floor that their districts' concerns about resources had been ignored. The councilor from one of the three districts in question (Glória) opened the floor to one of the activists to ask for a delay in the discussion "because we did not have time to prepare our projects for the Budget Council; we were going by the old rules. We have come here to protest that this way, three districts are going to lose out on day care centers!"

Several councilors from other districts complained about this intervention and argued that only councilors from the district were supposed to speak in this venue. Other councilors complained that the three districts in question had chosen not to present projects as a protest and were now paying the price for their procedural obstinacy. One such councilor said: "I want to remind everyone that people from the Cruzeiro and Glória districts are not organized, do not come to meetings, just sign their names, and leave. I am against delaying the discussion." The Glória activist spoke up again, saying: "We have a history of struggle and hard work in the district. The government is at fault here and not us, and we demand that the discussion be halted!" This outburst was followed by applause from the Glória activists in attendance, but when the vote took place, the citywide councilors voted by a wide margin not to delay the discussion. The councilors from the three districts in questions had already left in an attempt to undermine the quorum, but the discussion about the day care centers proceeded without them. In the end, the vocal community activists left the meeting calling the other councilors "doormats" *(capachos)* of the administration.

At another Budget Council meeting in 1997, councilors from poorer districts brought a proposal to change the system of weighting to make it difficult for some of the wealthier districts to obtain infrastructure services. Having extensively discussed the proposal with their districts, the councilors brought the proposal before the Budget Council. Heated discussions ensued, with some councilors defending overall fairness (against the proposal) and others arguing that this was the legitimate position of the city's poor (for the proposal). In these discussions, and others like them, councilors drafted proposals in their districts and were then charged with "defending" the proposals before the citywide Budget Council. At the Budget Council, deliberation required maintaining certain norms of discussion, including procedural consistency and a process through which individual councilors are open to changing their preferences as a result of discussion and debate. This is in sharp contrast to the intransigent defense of individual positions or deploying disruptive tactics such as strategically attempting to prevent a quorum before a binding vote. These two roles—representative of the district and deliberator—conflicted, and this was most apparent at the level of the citywide Budget Council, where the negotiations over district-level interests were the most complex and potentially conflictual.

Civil Society Networks

It should be clear by now that deliberation over priorities and projects is not a discrete event that takes place as meetings begin and end. Rather, there is a great deal of work at the edges of the meetings that help official deliberations function smoothly; these include informal discussions and negotiations, the recruitment of new participants, and the coordination of activities between neighborhoods. Many of these transactions helped overcome the inherent dilemmas of official deliberation I have discussed. If district-level delegates are well informed about the situation in other neighborhoods, for example, it is easier to come to a collective decision about a larger project and coordinate demands. Well-connected community activists who serve as delegates make a significant difference in the deliberativeness of discussions and whether breakdowns happen frequently or not.

As noted in Chapter 3, however, each district was differently endowed with civil society organizations, and these were configured differently vis-à-vis the OP. The Partenon district had a highly developed autonomous network in civil society, and one of its key organizations, the Popular Council, played a crucial role in coordinating demands, protecting smaller neighborhoods, and "working behind the scenes" to prevent conflicts. As a City Hall employee put it, "[T]hey [the Popular Council] run everything; you show up, and they have already scheduled all the municipal departments, dates, and meetings." In Nordeste, in contrast, individual neighborhood activists have far fewer district-level networks and no parallel venue like the Popular Council to coordinate interests between neighborhoods outside of the OP. While there are many new neighborhood associations in Nordeste, there is relatively little networking between them, and as a delegate put it, "the OP is the only place in the district where everyone meets." In Norte, developed district-level networks of neighborhood activists do exist. However, here, because of their political ties to other parties, these civil society actors are more often than not in direct conflict with the OP. An activist from the Popular Council in Norte contended that the "Popular Council is separate from the OP. It is not the function of the Popular Council to run the OP; our meetings are different than in some other parts [of the city] where the Popular Council is tied to the administration."

Partenon clearly stands out from the other two districts that I studied because of the Popular Council's autonomous but constructive engagement in the OP process. One City Hall facilitator remarked, "[W]orking in the Partenon was very easy," because they "set everything up and offer a lot of help with the meetings." Another facilitator mentioned that "a lot of these guys have many years of experience, and they have the whole process coordinated at the district-level, which avoids problems." One of the Popular Council's functions in this regard is to improve the quality of discussions in the OP by increasing awareness of the needs and issues of the whole district. A widely distributed pamphlet that the Popular Council put together to help educate participants stated:

> The resources destined for our district, as well as for the other fifteen districts, are not sufficient to attend to all of the demands . . . therefore, we need

to define which of the demands will really attend to the principal needs of our residents, that is, works that have a social interest, such as: streets that lead to a school, hospitals. . . . We shall only reach agreement about the priorities of the Partenon district with broad and democratic discussions. Talk to your neighbors, find your neighborhood association, participate in the meetings of the popular council, form a street committee, and let's clear up our doubts.[14]

Respected activists also monitored meetings, with the objective of improving the quality of discussion and allowing the meetings to run more smoothly. This included keeping discussions on topic, reminding participants of the rules, and proposing compromises between different positions. For instance, when a discussion about technical criteria turned to general complaints about City Hall, these activists would immediately intervene and steer the discussion back on "topic." It was almost impossible for outside City Hall facilitators to rein in these discussions; yet activists from the Popular Council commanded a certain degree of respect and were able to perform this seemingly awkward function in an open deliberative setting. At a meeting in 1999, for example, the agenda included putting together a commission to follow up and monitor the projects in the district for the year. One of the participants raised his hand to speak and gave a long speech about why his neighborhood was being deprived in the process of the OP. He was interrupted by Marcos, a veteran activist of the Popular Council, who broke in to say: "Look, I don't want to disrespect the *companheiro*, but this is not the time to do this. There are meetings to discuss projects for the year, and if you have a specific problem, there is a meeting of the popular council where you can address this. But this meeting, right now, is about putting together the 'works commissions.'" The man who interrupted the discussion immediately changed his approach, wanting now to find out what he could do about bringing projects to his favela.

In the other two districts, the situation was rather different. In Nordeste, there were fewer district-level networks and no organized district-level civil society body like the Popular Council. In the district-level Budget Forum, councilors and delegates do play an auxiliary role by, for example, submitting items for the agenda. However City Hall facilitators do most of the work done by Popular Council activists in Partenon. After the first plenary meeting of 1998, for instance, the initial number of participants determined the number of overall delegates for the year. Because of the low showing from some small neighborhoods, half a dozen neighborhoods would have no delegates unless they formed broader alliances with other neighborhoods. There was much anticipation as neighborhood activists tried to estimate how many delegates there would be and how they would be distributed by neighborhood. The meeting facilitator from City Hall listed the number of delegates per neighborhood, then proposed a series of compromises that would allow for the six small neighborhoods to pool their representation in order to ensure at least two delegates to represent their interests.

There were more frequent breakdowns in Nordeste's meetings than in Partenon's, and delegates had a more difficult time coordinating demands between neighborhoods. But there were conscious efforts by community activists to improve the quality of meetings in their district. In 1998, the district's two budget councilors asked an NGO that specialized in technical assistance for community organizations to run a training meeting on participative budgeting. Delegates were concerned about a number of projects having been rejected at the citywide council because they had failed to meet technical criteria. Additionally, many delegates did not fully understand the yearly meeting cycle. The lively training session attracted sixty of the district's seventy delegates.

Unlike Nordeste, Norte had a Popular Council in place, but one that maintained an oppositional stance toward the OP, having little to do with the budget meetings. As in Nordeste, the district's two OP councilors and district-level delegates performed the auxiliary roles of the budgeting process, such as going "from favela to favela" to "let people know about the process." However, in this district, because of the explicit opposition from the Popular Council, deliberation was often rife with mistrust and accusations, a clear example of the power mobilization dilemma. Because the district-level budgeting meetings are open to everyone and City Hall facilitators are vigilant about letting known political opponents speak, breakdowns in the Norte district meeting occurred regularly. More than once, participants from the Popular Council came to OP meetings and interrupted the discussion with the explicit purpose of derailing deliberations. At the Norte district's first plenary meeting of 1998, for example, almost the entire question-and-answer period was dedicated to broad criticisms of municipal government policy. Popular Council leaders have the right to criticize the OP process without any obligations of constructive participation and their criticism thus generally polarized meetings. In spite of the fact that

Norte was one of the districts that received the most municipal investment, Popular Council critics leveled attacks alleging the administration's lack of concern for the district. For instance, one critic implicated
the administration for its failure to act on health hazards involving a
river running through the district. One of the first people to speak at the
meeting in question was Edith, a Popular Council activist, who said: "I
want to raise the problem of the Sarandí river. We are facing a huge
problem with it again. The old part of the river is starting to flood and
causing all kinds of problems. My husband has gone home to fetch pic-
tures for the mayor to show the kinds of problems this is causing. I
don't know why the administration chooses to ignore it."

This was greeted with thunderous applause, and several other
speakers from the Popular Council went on in the same vein. Forty-five
minutes later, the mayor and his staff offered detailed answers. The
mayor addressed the fact that the community had chosen a project in
the area to drain the river, but that a previous project of a bridge was
still being completed. The meeting had become visibly polarized, however, and audible hissing followed his response.

Because Edith chose not to participate in OP meetings, it was possible for her to make these comments, claiming "not to know" whether
OP delegates were dealing with a problem, but, as she later confided,
she did know "that there is a problem that the administration is not
solving." Her criticisms were cited several times in subsequent meetings following the plenary meeting, with similar breakdowns in deliberation as delegates swayed by the Popular Council activists adopted
inflexible and oppositional stances against the administration. Edith
had only attended OP meetings once or twice during the year, each
time to raise the issue of the polluted river in a similar way (regardless
of the agenda) in order to derail discussions.

Conclusion

Aggregate level evidence about trust in the process based on a survey of participants conducted in 1998 supports the above analysis of
the three districts (see Table 9). Participants in Partenon and Nordeste
were more trusting of the process than those in Norte, notwithstanding
that residents of Norte were slightly more likely to have directly benefited from the OP and that this was the district that received the most
funds.

Ethnography in Norte showed that participation is often conflictual and full of mistrust, and that it was in this setting that deliberative breakdowns happened most frequently. Instead of promoting coordination within the OP, respected Popular Council activists from organized civil society networks created mistrust by derailing OP meetings. Overall, Norte participants tended to be more skeptical of the performance of City Hall personnel, the process as a whole, and even of their own delegates.

On the other hand, the research also shows that a district that has received relatively low investments, such as Partenon, can register higher levels of engagement and trust in the process as a result of the high involvement of organized civil society. The presence of organized networks of activists in the body of the Popular Council actually helped coordinate demands between neighborhoods and helped assure the quality of the deliberative process at OP meetings. In Nordeste, despite the lack of preexisting networks and the absence of a popular council, the OP functions relatively well. City Hall personnel played an important role in creating solutions to deliberative dilemmas, which led to more deliberative discussion in Nordeste compared to Norte. This fact suggests, again, that while civil society networks are important for democratic deliberation, the absence of organized opposition is even more important.

Comparing the OP to any ideal type of deliberative discussion, it is apparent that a crucial part of democratic decision making combines

TABLE 9

District-level Trust in the Orçamento Participativo

	Nordeste	Partenon	Norte
Proportion of total OP investments invested in the district, 1990–1998	1.9%	2 %	3%
Per capita average investment of OP projects per district, 1990–1998 (U.S.$)	$286	$64	$121
Has had OP projects in own community.	60%	67%	70%
Participants who were informed of OP meeting by organization or activist in civil society.	55%	53%	25%
Participants who believe that population "always or almost always" makes the decisions in the Orçamento Participativo	74%	71%	63%
Believes delegates and councilors in the Orçamento Participativo "always or almost always" bring communications back to the community	67%	71%	58%

SOURCE: 1998 Survey of Participants. Calculated from Marquetti 2001 and GAPLAN, various years.

aggregation (how participants "weigh" resources and consider districts' preferences) and deliberation (how councilors and delegates debate this weighting system). Although most decisions were reached by putting the question to a vote, significant deliberation, both in meetings and "at the edges" of official forums, literally paves the way for these votes. The complex process is spread out over a calendar year, and the dilemmas of participation are resolved through the efforts of civil society in some districts and by municipal administrators in others. Civil society, and in particular, its positioning vis-à-vis the OP, has proven very important. Yet the district with the least organized preexisting networks, Nordeste, is the one where the process functions relatively well, in comparison to Norte, where organized civil society is politically positioned against the process.

Deliberating about collective decisions and projects was not, however, the only objective accomplished at these meetings. Fostering other meaningful forms of collective action and discussion is an indispensable aspect of the OP as a forum for discussing community problems and priorities. I address these as forms of emergent public spheres in the next chapter.

CHAPTER FIVE

Emergent Public Spheres

A t a Wednesday night meeting of the Partenon Budget Council, with about fifty delegates participating, the agenda focused on the discussion of technical criteria in the selection of environmental projects for the district. During the early part of the meeting, however, which was usually dedicated to announcements, two activists took over the floor in a heated discussion. Marcos and Claudio argued about the location of a new public clinic in the district. Claudio had worked on petitions asking for the clinic for the past few years. It served a needy part of the district and had recently been built as a "special project" sponsored by a state congressman who was opposed to the PT, and now Claudio sought to invite people to its opening. The clinic, however, had been built on property that was designated for a street-paving project chosen by the district through the OP the year before. Claudio argued that a public clinic brought a needed service to the area and was more important than the street project. Marcos maintained that the public clinic had come as "a favor," and that it was not fair that the people's decision on the street be disrespected.

The activists and City Hall facilitator running the meeting had a difficult time calling the meeting to order, as representatives from several different neighborhoods became involved in the shouting match. Others rebuffed accusations of favor trading with accusations of partisan bias. This dragged on for several weeks, continuing to play out over several OP meetings and meetings of various neighborhood associations in the area. Discussions filtered down to the press, with both Claudio and Marcos giving statements to newspapers. Civic life in the district became polarized over this issue; some activists claimed that because a project financed by an opposition party had become prominent in the district, the PT wished to undermine it. Others believed the public clinic had deliberately been built where it was to thwart OP projects. And not a few participants in the Budget Forum expressed discontentment with the suddenly overtly politicized nature of its meetings.

Two months after the original fight, community activists created a commission to meet after the OP meetings to resolve the matter. The commission was composed of several different activists, including people with ties to different political parties, among them Claudio and Marcos. The commission contacted the municipal public health department and invited doctors and public health officials to visit the clinic and offer their opinions; activists also acquired figures about public health coverage throughout the district. Within a few weeks, the commission had reached a consensus that the clinic did not offer sufficient benefits to justify overturning the collective decision about street paving, and it was closed shortly afterwards. The clinic had had precarious funding from a grant from the state government, with a small staff working irregular hours, and had been built on property that belonged to the city. Rather than face a legal challenge from the municipal government, the state government abandoned it. Concurring with the final commission report, Claudio no longer raised the issue at meetings, and the OP road project went ahead. In the many discussions that took place, activists like Claudio debated not only the actual need for the clinic but the overall needs of the district and the proper way for the population to make demands of the government. One of the debates was a complicated ethical discussion about whether the fact that the district had been given a clinic overshadowed the fact that the funders of the clinic had been motivated by opposition to the OP.

This was one of many examples in my fieldwork of meetings becoming sites for open-ended discussion of community problems over and above the stated agenda and the allocation of budgeting priorities. Understanding this apparent puzzle requires an appreciation of the importance of the OP in the districts and its distinct features. In addition to the flexible agenda and the presence of civic activists, the OP fostered a sense of the "public," defining "needs" as collective problems and creating a common language in which to discuss them. OP meetings in the three districts came to accommodate what I term "emergent public spheres": open-ended debate about issues of collective concern and community problem solving. The Budget Council became a place in which citizens could discuss community affairs, plan and coordinate political and civic actions, debate district-level and national political events, demand justification of government, and ultimately create lasting bonds with other activists.

The Budget Forum became a site for emergent public spheres because of the overlap of networks there, while the transformation of "needs" into "public problems" helped create a language of public interest and responsibility, and the logic of justification fostered a "language of rights." This process occurred differently in each of the districts, however. Experienced activists made a difference in assuring the quality of the discussion, and in Nordeste, the overwhelming importance of the OP meetings created additional difficulties.

Public Spheres and Popular Sovereignty

Examining how events like the discussion over the health clinic emerged and were sustained offers us insight into the impact of the OP on civic life. Unlike a union hall or neighborhood association, the state-sponsored OP is not the type of "free space" in which scholars imagine community discussion happens.[1] With the specific agenda of deciding on budgeting priorities and high levels of community engagement, it would not be unreasonable to think that OP meetings actually took something *away* from community life. In fact, there is a tradition in social theory that worries precisely about the "bureaucratization" of social movements, or the "colonization" of their worlds by governmental logic.[2]

The public sphere, as articulated by Jürgen Habermas, which refers to those spaces of "rational deliberation" and opinion formation where citizens debate common problems, is at the center of recent sociological debates on civic participation.[3] In the public sphere, citizens engage in open-ended conversations on issues, conversations that are, in principle, not strategic or purposive. For Habermas, the public sphere is located in the "life-world through the associational networks of civil society."[4] As valuable as these insights have been for social analysts, a relational sociological approach would call into question the assumption that it is only in "the lifeworld" that such debates take place, instead asking when and how people act and communicate in this way, regardless of the specific site or sites where this takes place. Accordingly, I treat the public sphere as neither a particular place nor a particular institution, but rather as the actual conversations between people that meet the standards of open-endedness and public-mindedness.[5]

The issue for ethnographic investigation is to develop criteria for assessing the quality of these communicative interactions. Does any kind of off-topic discussion or collective action in the OP qualify as part of the "public sphere"? In order to proceed with the analysis, I offer an empirical definition: I define "public sphere" as an instance of public-spirited communication, something that "comes into being when people speak public-spiritedly."[6] (Individuals may, however, be present and involved in the discussions and not engage in these public-spirited discussions. Theorists of deliberative democracy define participation in terms of an individual's ability to intervene in and affect the decision-making process. Someone present but excluded from decision making would not be a participant, for example.)[7] Specifically, I include as part of the public sphere only those discussions framed in terms that consider broad ranges of interests and do not regard any individual or group interest as more or less worthy.[8] To determine whether a public sphere is present requires attention to the course, subtleties, and inflections of these open-ended discussions—whether they veer from certain topics, or whether they remain public-spirited, and whether disagreements degenerate into personal conflicts. Issues of collective concern, or those that are framed as public issues, are important parts of public sphere discussions, even if these public issues originate in the "private realm."[9] For example, a discussion about a shooting in a neighborhood is not necessarily public-minded, but when the discussion turns to problems of the neighborhoods in the district in general, it becomes a public-spirited discussion.

In looking at the emergence of the public sphere within the OP, I focus on two factors: the presence or absence of social networks at the meetings and the language deployed. A particularly salient factor is the role played by the social networks of civil society in democratic communication.[10] Although for most sociologists the conversations of the public sphere take place within the "lifeworld," an established civil society is more likely to foster regular conversations that are based on common trust and better information.[11] Robert Putnam's well-known investigations of what makes democracy work have noted the importance of civic networks in making possible cooperation and collective behavior around common goals, and in "turning an I into a we."[12]

The other factor worth paying attention to is what language participants deploy in order to carry out these conversations. Habermas, for
instance, intimates that the public sphere "can only emerge in the context of a liberal political culture and corresponding patterns of socialization."[13] Brazil does not have the tradition of "social responsibility
and practices of commitment to the public good" noted in the case of
the United States or a long-standing "civil religion" of the kind understood to be a prerequisite to democracy.[14]

The Meeting Takeover

Budget Forum meetings took place weekly or semimonthly in a central public setting in all three districts, drawing an average of fifty participants for each meeting much of the year. These assemblies lasted up
to two hours, and for several months, the agenda included the technicalities and relative merits of certain projects for the district. In both
Nordeste and Norte, they were held in a school on a weekend afternoon, while in Partenon, meetings were held on a weeknight in a
church hall. In all three districts, participants tended to come from a
range of neighborhoods within the district. The agenda for the meetings was usually drawn up in advance by the facilitator and the district's councilors, and time was allotted at the start of each meeting for
announcements. A typical meeting might also include presentations by
technical experts from each of the various municipal departments, followed by discussions in which participants could ask questions or com-
ment on the topic. The facilitator was responsible for keeping to the
agenda and calling on participants, who signed up for a turn to speak.

It became clear in the course of my fieldwork that OP meetings were
important sites for wider community discussions than simply deliberating on the city budget. Although nongovernmental community items
of common interest were not part of the scheduled agenda, "meeting
takeovers" frequently occurred similarly in all three districts. The discussion of the day's events and news and the participants' opinions
about these events often featured an ongoing discussion interspersed
with the scheduled discussion. Often, while announcements were
made during the meetings, participants would ask to discuss a news
item.

In Partenon, participants made it a habit of bringing news clippings,
which often led to discussions that had to be closed off to keep to the

agenda. A typical occurrence took place at a meeting at Partenon, when a number of activists, as usual, had announcements. Laura announced that on Thursday, the Porto Alegre City Council would vote on the approval of ten more community-run day care centers, and encouraged activists to pressure city councilors. Edilson chimed in to mention that there would be now be 110 community-run day care centers for the whole city. Marcia followed with an announcement that Porto Alegre's gay rights group would be celebrating its tenth anniversary the following week and gave the address for the party. Walter followed with a long announcement that sparked several minutes of discussion:

> Walter: Greetings to all of you tonight, especially those of you who are here for the first time. To those of you who have just arrived, you should know that even we who have been here a long time are always learning something new. This is the essence of community life. [Pulling out a newspaper clipping] I wanted to share with you a news story in today's newspaper about Ford and General Motors. Ford has had 122 percent growth this last year in Brazil, but they are firing workers in São Paulo. They want to pay less and less taxes to the government, and the workers still cannot afford to buy the cars. It says here that they are making more profits in Brazil than in the past.
>
> Gilson: Walter is right, our governor is in discussion with Ford and General Motors, two of the richest companies in the world, and they want our poor state government to give them an interest-free loan.

Several activists followed up with comments and discussion until the meeting was called to order again several minutes later. Open-ended interventions like these were acceptable in this context, and activists quite often took the opportunity to share news, events, and anything else deemed relevant to community life. When asked about it, Walter, who always brought news clippings, told me, "[Y]ou are always learning something," because otherwise "people are in the dark about injustice." For Walter, whose civic engagement dates to prodemocracy social movements in the 1970s, the assemblies were a forum to discuss news in order to foster the "critical consciousness" prized by liberation theology activists.[15] Other participants, many of whom were newer participants in civic life, also made it a point to discuss news events in these assemblies because of the perceived worth of discussing items that impinged on the community.

While participants seldom seemed to mind these "interruptions," facilitators sometimes described them as disruptive: "Some of these interruptions are childish; people just want to create problems." But the facilitators did not prevent interruptions, so as "to avoid creating a bigger problem." The discussion of a specific "news" issue sometimes became a discussion of politics and economics, government policy, or macroeconomic problems, not to mention specific community problems, and a meeting would sometimes be taken over by talk of problems that might embarrass the administration or the Workers' Party.

Such was the case in Nordeste, where a school shooting had taken place a few days prior to the OP meeting.[16] The agenda of this particular meeting was to discuss education projects for the next year, but participants kept returning to the shooting. Early on in the meeting, Carla used the announcements period to begin a long discussion about having received an inadequate response from the police about future safety in schools. Then, throughout the meeting, participants repeatedly raised the issue with a representative of the Education Department, who dismissed their advances, remarking that it was a police issue. Carla spent most of the meeting in the back of the room discussing school safety with several other women, and toward the end of the meeting, she asked to make an announcement. First, she apologized for interrupting the meeting, saying, "I have an announcement. Tomorrow we will have a demonstration to protest the lack of respect for human rights in this city and this district. I know lots of you are with the Workers' Party, but it needs to respect workers, and tomorrow we are calling on all mothers to march all the way to the police station to demand a police officer at the school."

Her announcement was applauded, and the following day, fifty mothers marched to the police station, where they were greeted by the press, as well as by city councilors representing the Workers' Party and other parties. Carla made a statement to the press that appeared in the newspaper, and a police officer was then assigned to the school. Although Carla's topic was more instrumental than Walter's "newspaper clipping reading," it was clearly a public-spirited presentation on a collective problem. Implicit in Carla's action was the understanding that these assemblies had become one of the central settings for engaging with others in civil society. Her presentation also illustrates that there was no censure of participants for discussing issues that, in principle, might hurt the administration, while showing that community activists like Carla knew the strategic importance of these settings.

Carla realized that meetings often had broad ranges of participants with diverse ties throughout the district. The Budget Forum therefore

TABLE 10

Community-Oriented Discussion in Ten Orçamento Participativo Meetings, 1998

	Nordeste	Partenon	Norte
News items[a]	6	47	9
Other events[b] in the district	45	67	21
Other events in the city	8	14	8
Community problems[d]	45	51	31
Protests organized[c]	3	2	1
Petitions or similar	2	1	0

SOURCE: Author's own count at meetings.
NOTE: The count included events at ten meetings in each of the districts in 1998.
[a] News Items included newspaper and TV news discussed.
[b] Other events included announcements for community events and meetings.
[c] Protests were counted if they were organized at the meetings.
[d] Community problems were nonbudget items discussed.

assumes a central place in coordinating collective action and has symbolic importance as the place where "the whole community" is present. Among neighborhood associations in the 2001 survey, virtually 100 percent had been represented in the OP, and all had had at least one person participate in the previous year, even if as representative of another group, a figure much higher than the number of associations represented in local popular councils or in the citywide union of associations.[17] Surveys of delegates revealed that they participated in an average of 1.4 settings in civil society outside of the OP, attending an average of two additional meetings a week, meaning that a very broad range of neighborhoods and associations was represented in one way or another at the OP. In 1998, I recorded how often these interruptions took place. Table 10 shows the count for a sample of ten meetings in each district.

The count includes several types of community-oriented activities that take place during OP meetings. The category "News items" includes the number of news items or newspaper clippings discussed in the early part of meetings. Often these were politically charged stories or items having to do with the economy. At the time of my research, currency fluctuation and corruption in the banking sector were favorite topics of discussion. "Other events in the district" include announcements of events, such as fund-raising barbecues, cultural celebrations, or elections in neighborhood associations. The category "Other events in the city" encompasses meetings of the citywide league of neighborhood associations, events like a human rights conference, or a meeting of the cooperative association. Actions such as "Protests organized" at the meetings were less frequent, but they included mobilizations against the police or against the municipal housing agency. The meetings served as sites for announcements about and discussions of the protests in question, although they often were not formally where the protests were organized. The category "Petitions or similar" includes a number of petitions signed and passed on to agencies such the Municipal Health Agency and the Municipal Education Secretariat. "Community problems" includes denouncements of faulty government services, such as a rude doctor at a public clinic, as well as events like open sewers or a broken streetlight. This count does not include events taking place "backstage," such as discussions in the hallway, during a break, or otherwise held outside of the official meeting time.[18]

Speaking as Mothers and Workers:
A Public-Minded Language

The overlap of groups of people with different ties and the institutional setting that permits interventions do not, however, fully account for the language of public interest and public goods or the collective orientation of these actions. As has been discussed by a number of scholars, the fragmentation of social life is the norm on urban peripheries like these in Porto Alegre. Life in each district does not escape this pattern, which is exemplified by the violence and fear that made it difficult for residents to circulate freely between homes at night. The transience of those who reside in squatter settlements and the economic unpredictability of their lives also contributed to this fragmentation.

What, then, are the symbolic conditions that make a language of citizenship possible in this context? Democratic thinkers from John Dewey to Hannah Arendt to Jürgen Habermas all emphasize, in one way or another, that a collective understanding of "public" is a necessary precondition to democratic discourse.[19] In this context, there is no widely regarded national language of "public goods" or "public interest." But as "needs" become "public problems" of concern to a wide group of people, they provide a language of democratic motivation and responsibility.

This language of citizenship, however, was not based on the abstract rights and duties of citizenship but on sharing common problems and working toward common solutions at the meetings. It also was not a language explicitly based on religious notions of social justice, as might be expected given the historical importance of liberation theology in social movements in Brazil. Nor was it based on a socialist discourse of class empowerment, such as might accompany a Workers' Party experiment. Rather, this language of citizenship emphasized (1) "the good of the community," and (2) the struggle to improve things for the community, which it defined as the group of persons with similar problems and living situations. It defined the struggle as collective and pragmatic problem solving, and not necessarily contentious activity. Good citizens were those who "worked for the community" by attending meetings, who did not seek personal gain from meetings, and who avoided divisive language, which was actively discouraged by more respected activists. For example, at one meeting in Norte, a longtime participant tried to motivate a group of new participants to stay at the meeting after an hour by saying, "For ten years many people have come here to solve problems. We fought for it, mobilized for it, and achieved it. We focused on the closed sewer because we got together with our neighbors and fought for it. And after that, we learned that we have to fight for larger things. We have many problems we need to still solve."

This language was often deployed in discussions when participants wished to persuade other participants to become more involved in the process, or to persuade others of the value of a certain position. Discussions about the "hows" and "whys" of social problems emerged in conversations this way, just as discussion of specific needs and issues led to discussions of broader issues. During the course of my research, the discussion of a specific technical issue sometimes spilled over into free-flowing discussions of politics and economics, government policy, macroeconomic problems, and specific community problems. Participatory governance is thus not functionally specific; that is, the realm of issues addressed was not limited to education or health, and the types of social issues touched by municipal budgeting ranged from human rights to sewage service. It was not uncommon for a discussion about funding a cooperative to lead to a discussion of unemployment, or for a discussion about a park to lead to a discussion of the environment, while a discussion about building up a slum might lead to discussion of land tenure and migration. Some participants described this as a particularly enriching aspect of the process, claiming to have acquired "political consciousness" as a result of active participation in the OP. As a relatively new participant put it, "You learn a lot in the OP. You learn about what part of municipal government does what . . . you begin to ask questions, like, why doesn't the city government have more money for health and housing?"

Often, the discussion of a social problem implicit in an investment project became a discussion about the limits of municipal government. In Norte, for example, an agenda on social service projects for the district was limited to a small number of projects for senior citizens, prompting a participant to attempt to create an ad hoc committee to coordinate the provision of social services generally. Laura signed up to ask a question of the technical expert from City Hall, but when her turn came to speak, she decided instead to make a plea for the creation of a social services committee for problems with children. She addressed the whole group present, arguing: "We have at least 500 children in the district needing day care. Without day care and without schools, we are bringing up violence in the district, but by then it's too late. We need to bring the community to debate these issues and participate." The discussion momentarily turned to violence and crime in the district, with several people sharing stories about a wave of violent robberies. In this discussion, people's private needs for day care and stories of being robbed were linked to the public problems of crime and a lack of social services. Josué collected the names and addresses of volunteers for a committee. Participants often mentioned a sense of belonging to a larger community of citizens who are facing problems together as a result of having worked together over the year to decide on projects. A relatively new participant, Ana, described how the sense of sharing common problems was important: "You participate and you realize that your problems are the same as everyone else's problems, and you work because your problems are the same."

For Ana, whose participation in these assemblies is her only involvement in civic affairs, the sense of the "public" comes from having worked collectively to make decisions throughout the year and from developing a sense of belonging to a community of others with similar needs or problems. Her vocabulary was not an explicit vocabulary of social justice based on religious or political ideologies, however. This fact bothered older community activists linked to social movements, one of whom found that people "these days only talk about projects and not enough about the big questions." The language deployed by participants was based on needs and common problems and was used to create a sense of the public and public-minded speech.

Demanding Justification: The Impetus for Open-Ended Discussion

Budget Forum meetings also facilitated open-ended discussion and civic involvement by conveying a sense of empowerment to participants that came from being able to demand justification. OP meetings were empowered fora, and municipal authorities were bound by their decisions. They had to account for the progress of projects demanded by participants, which helped provide a common language of rights. Citizens were entitled to justification throughout the yearly OP cycle, able to demand accounting from the government and from one another. This permeated the discussions that took place in and out of the OP. The examples of civic actions I have discussed so far all involve demands for justification: that mothers can demand justification from the police, for instance, and that activists can demand justification from one another, as in the case of the clinic discussion.

This important event in the OP process is the first yearly meeting when municipal government teams, including the mayor and vice-mayor, visit each of the districts and account for the progress of projects demanded by the districts. As has been noted, not much real deliberation goes on during these large meetings, but this "accounting for" fulfills an important function. Activists use these fora to demand justification for government actions in general, and rarely do so of specific OP projects alone.

Because the regular district-level meetings were vested with the power to demand justification, it was practically impossible for government agencies to present specific projects or discuss technical criteria without having to account for actions or projects in the district if participants felt that there was a problem.

One agency usually involved in tense discussions was the Municipal Housing Department. For example, at a meeting in the Norte district, word had gotten out that housing officials were going to come to the OP meeting to explain technical criteria for new projects for the year. The meeting hall was completely full of residents from two different squatter settlements who wished to contest a recent policy decision to eliminate the slums. The government representatives tried in vain to postpone the discussion, but were unsuccessful and were forced to provide accountability. The meeting became quite heated, as activists from different neighborhoods began to chime in about the decision:

> Adalmir: What about the Renascer neighborhood? We have been fighting for twelve years for the government to allow us to stay on this land, and the

community has always been behind the fight. Our people are suffering and the Municipal Housing Agency has always ignored our request! (Applause)

Pedro: (attempting to call the meeting to order) People, people, these are not part of the agenda; today we are discussing technical criteria.

Arno: (interrupting) We of the Dique neighborhood are worried that we are going to be moved. We think the agency needs to worry about the dignity and living conditions of the people! (Applause)

The meeting did not come to its actual agenda for an hour. Representatives of the Municipal Housing Agency debated with activists and an agreement was reached to schedule meetings the following week to address the issues at each of the slums in question.

These examples were not unusual, and despite the best efforts of activists and facilitators to follow the agenda, government agencies came to expect to have to account for any number of actions at OP meetings. These district-level meetings were known in the community at large as places where citizens can have direct access to government. In an important sense, the principles of transparency and accountability extended to other discussions. Together, these two aspects of participatory governance made open-ended discussion and action possible.

Moral Authority and the Quality of Discussion

Thus far I have discussed emergent public spheres as being similar in all three districts. In fact, in all three districts, such interruptions were common occurrences.

As Table 10 shows, these interruptions were most common in Partenon, followed by Nordeste, and then Norte. This section discusses the impact of the configuration of social networks around the OP on the open-ended communication of the emergent public spheres. Much as an active and respected group of activists helped create the collective decisions characteristic of deliberation, these same activists helped foster, and contain, emergent public sphere discussions.

In the Partenon district, the existence of denser social networks and the presence of experienced activists meant that informal rules of conduct were enforced so that interruptions of meetings occurred within certain topical and behavioral boundaries. Experienced participants worked in the background to resolve conflicts and create compromises, and they enforced certain unspoken rules to prevent interruptions that might otherwise have derailed meetings. As one of these experienced participants explained to me, if it were not for people "like her" in the background, "meetings would be much more full of conflict. We try to discuss issues ahead of time and find compromises." In addition to "working in the background," these experienced participants also actively curtailed certain kinds of interventions.

Partenon had a number of functioning neighborhood associations and other civic organizations, and evidence suggested that there were significant connections among them. Three-fourths of the participants of the assemblies in Partenon, for example, participated in one of these other associations, and over half of them participated in an organization beyond their neighborhood. It was common for participants to meet one another at other meetings throughout the week. Participants had significant experience with the assemblies and civic life in general; on average, participants in Partenon had six years of experience with the assemblies and had been participating in civic associations for ten years. Out of the forty-odd regular participants, almost one-fourth had been participating in associations of one kind or another since the 1970s, according to my survey. A number of incidents during my fieldwork confirmed that it was experienced participants, not the official facilitator, who commanded the respect to keep meetings in line.

Several times during my fieldwork, these experienced community activists enforced informal rules of participation, which included avoiding personal attacks and allowing only certain kinds of interruptions. At a meeting, during a discussion about the agenda, Marcos claimed that the next agenda ought to include an item to prevent Cláudio from making comments, saying, "He talks too much" and "is always trying to show off." These two men had had disagreements in the past and often clashed over issues, such as the health clinic described at the beginning of this chapter. To other participants, their disagreements now seemed personal. Both men were community activists with long histories in their respective communities; they were known throughout the district. Since the clinic incident, they now appeared to contradict each other at almost every turn. This time, however, others vocally interfered, coming to the defense of Cláudio and telling Marcos, "You can disagree, but this is not how you do it." At other times, similar potential conflicts were diffused, and certain types of behavior were criticized as inappropriate for "people who work for the community."

Activists enforced other informal rules preventing certain kinds of open-ended discussions deemed to be occurring "at the wrong place."

Discussions that were deemed "overly personal," such as those having to do with particular complaints or personal intrigue, were usually interrupted. During the OP meeting's announcements, if a participant tried to start a conversation about a broken pipe in front of her house or on the rudeness of a bus driver, it would likely be curtailed by one of the more experienced participants with a suggestion of where to deal with this problem, telling the person, "This is not the place for this. We can try to figure out where to go with this problem, but right now the agenda is something else." Similarly, complaints about other participants or accusations of improprieties in a neighborhood association were also often stopped.

While these activists curtailed certain discussions and activities, there was little evidence that they tried to dominate other participants. While these activists commanded significant respect from others, nothing indicated that they used this respect to advance a particular agenda or to gain particular benefits. And although these activists limited certain discussions, they did not do so on the basis of political allegiances, as might have been expected.[20] Rather, the standard seemed to be that if a certain issue was framed as a "public issue"—such as involving an impropriety at a neighborhood association, a broken pipe that represented a problem for the community, or the national economy—discussions on that issue were much more likely to be allowed to run their course.

Norte was something of a special case. Although I witnessed open-ended discussion there several times in the course of my fieldwork, participants rarely took the time to coordinate outside activities. Moreover, the noticeable absence of key local activists meant that the forum did not always assume the character of a "master public" for the district and that participants did not use it to coordinate activities and protests as effectively as in other districts. Nonparticipants also sometimes appeared at meetings in order to derail discussions. "Our community movement meets in the popular council, and not in the OP," one of the Norte neighborhood activists who did not participate in the OP told me. "Those of us with experience know that the real community work does not take place there."

The "Only Place in the Community"—A Drawback

Although participants intentionally manipulated OP meetings to steer deliberations in the direction of socially salient issues such as education and day care, sometimes these interventions took on a personal dimension. A few times, in all three districts, participants interrupted meetings for discussions that were not public-minded and sometimes "staged" them for a private purpose rather than for public-minded discussion. These events took place most often in the Nordeste district, where there were no other places where the district as a whole could come together. There was little evidence in the assemblies of the drawbacks of participation most often noted by scholars, such as the domination of the less eloquent by the culturally better-equipped or the emergence of an oligarchy of movement experts who retained social power by controlling meetings.[21] In fact, meetings were often unruly and sometimes difficult to call to order. Nevertheless, the evidence points to this specific disadvantage to participation in the Nordeste district assemblies. The fact that the OP was "the only place in the community" for people to assemble made it a setting of great importance to local activists. It was there that it was thought appropriate to air grievances and there that individuals' reputations in the community were determined. A number of conflicts between municipal bureaucrats and participants took place during fieldwork, and a Nordeste participant described his district as one that "was not intimidated by administrators with college degrees and was not afraid of fighting with them."

While theorists of the public sphere might find conflict and disagreement to be fundamental, not all disagreements and conflicts here were public-spirited ones. Without a core of experienced and respected activists to manage these conflicts, the interruptions in Nordeste took over meetings, created personal conflicts between activists, and at times caused other participants to leave feeling that these meetings "were pointless" or "too disorderly." These kinds of interruptions were at odds with the public-spiritedness of other interruptions and sometimes completely derailed the agendas of the meetings.

My survey evidence shows that in Nordeste, the district assemblies were meeting places for networks that would otherwise have had little contact, although there were informal settings where activists from different neighborhoods might meet. For over half of the participants at Nordeste assemblies, the assemblies were the only meeting they participated in during an average week. For most of the other half, the other main forum in which they participated was in their home neighborhood. Fewer than 10 percent of participants at the assemblies participated in any kind of regular meeting outside of their neighborhood other than the OP. In Latin American urban peripheries, calculations of honor, reputation, and respect are important, and people used the OP as a stepping-stone to a higher profile in community politics.[22] Interruptions were staged at OP meetings both by participants who were vigilant about protecting their reputations and by people seeking to question someone else's reputation and honesty.

One of these interruptions took place at a meeting that was slated to discuss the year's budgeting process. About forty delegates were present, and the meeting was just starting when a conflict broke out between two participants, who accused each other of having accepted donations from a political party in exchange for votes in their neighborhoods. One of the two, Maurício, who was to assist in running the meeting, was visibly angry and said: "I am sorry, but I think we need to take time out from the meeting to discuss. . . . I won't have my name used like this without having a chance to challenge my accuser. I want a show of hands to see who agrees to discuss this before discussing budget projects." The City Hall facilitator attempted in vain to bring the meeting to order. Confusion ensued, and the meeting continued, leaving the heated discussion between activists unresolved. Almost an hour was devoted to the discussion of the accusations, with several participants leaving without retracting or apologizing. Activists like Maurício understood that OP meetings were a place where issues concerning the community at large ought to be resolved. It is not clear, of course, that coming before the community and facing accusers (and exchanging accusations) are necessarily public-spirited or collectively oriented activities. But because this district lacked any other regular setting for significant interaction between these individuals, it was here that these issues were resolved. When I asked Maurício why he had chosen to interrupt the meeting in this way, he replied that it was because this "is where the community meets. There is no other place in our district. What happens here is important for the whole district."

Another example occurred a few weeks later. A shouting match broke out in Nordeste, again over someone's reputation. This time it almost led to a physical fight. There had been a disagreement between two participants, with one man claiming that the other had tried to make him "look stupid" in front of the whole community in the rounds of questions and answers before the municipal education representative. In the absence of more experienced community activists to stop the shouting from escalating, each accused the other of trying to make him "look bad," and the OP meeting degenerated into general confusion as one of the men made his way toward the other. The men were separated by other participants before blows were exchanged, and the meeting was postponed to another week. The facilitator strongly admonished the participants at the following meeting, but it was not clear that the facilitator had the moral authority to prevent such altercations from taking place again. Although no other incidents quite like this one occurred during my fieldwork, significant interruptions for private purposes and personal conflicts took place with regularity.

Not all the participants I interviewed were happy with the overwhelming importance of the OP meetings in community life. Some expressed a wish for a greater separation between participatory budget activities and neighborhood associations. One person told me that because Nordeste does not have any other meeting place as a district, "there is a lot of confusion about what we're supposed to do." Instead of public investments, "all kinds of topics are discussed," which often caused the meeting "to serve no real purpose." In fact, meetings did serve a purpose for some participants, although not a publicly oriented one. It was here that people developed and maintained reputations, resolved disputes, and jockeyed for prestige. Without a significant number of experienced participants to curtail these interruptions, they continued to occur. In Nordeste, in contrast to other districts, activists have tried several times over the years to try to create a popular council, but unlike in several of the city's other districts, they have never succeeded. Paulo, a Nordeste activist, said in an interview:

> Our district . . . does not have an independent forum like a popular council for community discussions. There is confusion between the OP meetings and a popular council. There is confusion among people. People who participate in the OP think they are participating in a popular council. In the OP where public investments are supposed to be discussed, all kinds of topics are discussed, like safety and crime, that are not subject to municipal investments. But neighborhood associations participate in meetings of the OP, and all of these questions therefore become part of OP meetings.
>
> Q: But why is there no independent forum?
>
> Paulo: You know, our district is very poor, people have difficulty, they don't have experience, and then after working the whole week, they don't want to go to another meeting. But we are trying to start it again.

Conclusion

Ethnographic evidence quite clearly shows OP meetings to be occasions for community-oriented collective action, problem solving, and open-ended civic discourse. Government-sponsored meetings on the technicalities of street-paving projects would seem at first glance to be unlikely places for public spheres to emerge, especially considering the setting of poor urban peripheries. Yet participants in them regularly carve out space for civic discourse and deliberation, which is possible because the discussions of needs and the power to demand accountability at these meetings constitute a language of common interest and rights, for which the OP serves as an intermediary.

This chapter clearly shows that public sphere–type discussions can and do take place in settings sponsored by the municipal government, and that despite the different trajectories of the three districts, they took place often in each of them. Nonetheless, the evidence illustrates that civic configurations are important. In Norte, the fact that certain key activists did not participate in it meant that the forum was not always a venue where "all of civil society" was represented. Conversely, in Nordeste, the fact that the OP was the district's only public forum sometimes led to activists disrupting meetings for purposes of self-aggrandizement. Without a core of experienced activists to rein in meetings, discussions sometimes moved away from public-minded concerns.

CHAPTER SIX

Militants and Citizens

"No Place for Politics"

Antônio Girard, a City Hall OP facilitator in Nordeste, followed a ritual on Sundays when there was no OP meeting scheduled in the district. Without a driver for the day, he started in the late morning and took a carefully planned series of buses throughout the district to visit neighborhood associations that were having an event that day. By four in the afternoon, he would have visited three or four associations, some that had their own building and some that met in a borrowed place like a school or day care center, or even in a backyard. Because Antônio visited on Sundays, the events often were barbecues, followed by a round of beer and informal soccer games late into the early evening. Occasionally, his reception was muted, depending on what had taken place at the previous day's OP meeting. Eventually he would be asked to buy a raffle ticket for three or four reais (then around U.S.$2) to support local activities. Antônio considered this ritual an important part of his work; he was "gaining the trust of the community" and "showing respect to the associations" through his presence. He felt that the informality of the weekend visit would not be mistaken for meddling, as opposed to dropping by on a weeknight in the midst of the associations' "business" discussion.

These association barbecues were very much like typical Sunday afternoon gatherings across the city; people would be asked to make sure there was enough beer and soda, others would be in charge of the fire and ensuring that the right person barbecued the meat. All afternoon long, neighbors sat around, gossiped, played loud music, and ran after their children until enough people were ready to go home to watch the soccer game or one of the popular Sunday evening television programs. One of the only differences from other similar barbecues was that conduct like public drunkenness was curtailed on the grounds of "disrespect to the association" or "disrespect to the community."

The OP meetings and specific community projects were frequent topics of discussion, as was talk about "the movement"—the organized activities of associations. Discussion of politics in the broader sense was more complicated in this setting. While neighbors with known political affinities would talk politely, and even discuss international affairs or national politics, certain kinds of political talk were generally understood to be off-limits here, such as discussions about local political campaigns, political party recruitment, or internal party business. As I was more than once reminded when I asked about these topics, "This is the association—this is not the place for politics."

This strict silence about specific kinds of politics seemed peculiar given that Porto Alegre is a city with a highly engaged civil society, with intense discussion among "average citizens" about seemingly "political" topics, such as inequality in service provision, public policy choices, and the state of the national economy. And community activists often freely told long and complicated stories about party political intrigue or speculated about the strategic reasons for the votes of certain city councilors on specific pieces of legislation. Nonetheless, the neighborhood association and any OP meetings were seen as settings where it was absolutely unacceptable to talk politics.

Associative activity is a highly codified world, with very specific rules that govern what is considered appropriate. Specific values and traits are alternately valued and devalued. "Avoiding politics" is an actively policed rule and not an accidental outcome, and this distinction is a central part of the way in which community activists make sense of associational activity in Porto Alegre. I argue that in Porto Alegre's political culture, one in which much of civil society's activity revolves around the OP, community activists understand there to be three "worlds": those of "the government," "the community," and "political parties." The borders dividing government and community are blurry but are clearly understood to be sites "separate from politics." Although most activists do not distinguish the "community movement" from participating in the OP and therefore in government, they also paradoxically treat "politics" as a separate realm, even if some commu-

nity leaders have ties to specific political parties. Neither is any distinction made between "social movement militancy" and "civic participation" in this political culture. This chapter traces the implications of
these political cultural codes for the way associations operate, their relationships with political parties, and conflicts over styles of leadership.

Principles of Vision and Division

Political culture within a relational framework has been defined as
"the accepted and legitimate way of doing politics," and scholars
within this tradition have been attentive to "the principles of vision and
division that actors apply" to the social world.[1] That is, attention to the
way that actors view and divide the social world tells us something
about the way that political culture operates to orient action. In Porto
Alegre, a political culture has emerged in civil society that reflects two
shifts in terms of principles from previous times. The empowered participatory regime has blurred the boundaries between the "world of
government" and "the world of the community," and "militancy" has
merged with the concept of "citizenship."

In the talk of community activists, it is possible to distinguish three
separate sets of values, operating in the three worlds—government,
community, and politics. Rules of expertise and specific knowledge
bind the world of government, rules of solidarity and honor bind the
world of community, and strategic rules and calculations bind the
world of parties and party activists. With the OP, the blurry boundaries
between government and community have meant new forms of mediation and access open to "average people." In contrast, activists still see
and actively protect a meaningful divide between party politics and
community associationalism.

In the past, associations in Porto Alegre could be divided by whether
they were "more combative" or "more social."[2] Some associations were
known as more "social," and certain kinds of organizations, like the
popular councils, were understood to be "militant." Today this distinction is no longer meaningful. The role of community leaders has similarly changed. In the past, some were defined as "militants" allying
themselves with political parties to fight against or to gain favor with
government in order to benefit the community. Neighborhood association presidents who were not "militant" were long-term community
leaders who fostered close ties with specific politicians. The effectiveness of their leadership depended on the projects they brought to the

neighborhood and the power of their "patrons" in municipal government. It was not uncommon for these "brokers" to campaign for candidates directly, to work as consultants for campaigns, or even to work
directly for the municipal government.

In the past, it was often necessary to turn to political party activity of
some kind to benefit the community. Today, one can easily access government via the OP, and community leaders establish and maintain
their respect in the community through this form of participation. The
role and place of political parties in this landscape is also transformed,
as the locus of politics has shifted outside of the associations themselves. Many community activists have a "practical relationship" to political parties, but even those who have ideological commitments to the
PT "leave political party activity" at the door of both the association
and the OP.

"Militancy" has evolved and merged with a conception of "citizenship" borne of the "new citizenship" social movements of the 1980s
and 1990s. When asked to describe their participation in community
groups, many activists use words and expressions related to both contention (such as "fighting for," "militancy," and "the struggle") and cooperation ("the community," "citizenship," and "trust"). Carlos, a rep-
utable community leader in Norte active in health issues, described the
beginnings of his civic involvement. As a teenager, he had been part of
a Catholic youth group. He and his fellow catechism students went to
support a bus strike by hurling rocks from behind bushes at "scab" bus
drivers. For Carlos, this was his first act of citizenship and civic engagement, and it is consistent with his view that "community" and
"movement" are essentially interchangeable.

These two faces of the world of community described by activists,
those of cooperation and citizenship, on the one hand, and contention
and militancy, on the other, are described as civil society's "two faces."[3]
The features of civil society in Porto Alegre thus differ from those in
other cities in Brazil. As I argue in this chapter, the "division of worlds"
is central to how activists understand community life, as are popular
conceptions of both "government" and "politics."

The World of the Community

Neighborhood associations are at the center of the world of the community, because they are pivotal to collective claim making, interfacing
with authorities, and offering crucial social support to residents. The

practice of associations is essentially homogeneous today, with little meaningful difference between "militant" associations and others.

One of the associations that Antônio might regularly drop in on every Sunday was the Chácara da Fumaça Neighborhood Association. Founded in 1986, the association has recently distinguished itself by regularly bringing participants to OP meetings, and serving as an important "node" in OP negotiations, such as when delegates voted for a school in the neighborhood at the expense of other projects. Not far down the road from Chácara da Fumaça is Parque das Orquídeas, a slum settlement on land illegally occupied by squatters. The squatters formed a formal committee in order to participate in the OP and subsequently an association with statutes, a charter, and very active involvement in the OP. The occupation managed to "regularize" its situation, earning the right to name its streets and to demand water and pavement, and residents are now owners of the small plots of land where their homes are. The association has a literacy program in partnership with City Hall, and there is talk of starting a day care center.

Neighborhood associations like Chácara da Fumaça and Parque das Orquídeas are the real centers of the world of the community, places where participants find important sources of friendship, cooperation, and collective problem solving. For someone visiting one of these neighborhoods for the first time, perhaps looking for a relative who lives in the area but who does not have a telephone or even a formal address, the first stop is "the association." These associations provide a wide array of services, from help with domestic disputes to basic information about public health services. Despite the importance of the OP and institutional councils, everyday community life still revolves around these associations, with their presidents often serving as important links to the outside world. Neighborhood activists today regard solidarity and militancy as the organizing values of the world of the community, and their central institutional base remains the association.

Porto Alegre has over 600 neighborhood associations spread out throughout the city, with heavy representation in its working-class and poor neighborhoods.[4] Over half of the associations that existed in 2002 had been founded or restarted after the establishment of the OP.[5] Most neighborhood associations solve collective problems or "defend the interests of the community." Whether founded before or after the OP, most neighborhood associations had been established to resolve demands involving urban services, as described in Chapters 2 and 3. In an effort to solve these collective problems, associations sometimes act like

TABLE 11

Activities of Neighborhood Associations in the Past Twelve Months,
Porto Alegre, 2002

Membership meetings	96%
Delegates in the Orçamento Participativo	94%
Social activities (incl. parties, activities for children, dances)	80%
Spaces of deliberation (debates, educational activities)	62%
Interfacing with the state (meetings with mayor, staff, other politicians)	78%
Contentious politics (protests, petitions, demands, media)	59%
Social services or day care	52%
Active committees	47%
Partnerships with the state	40%

SOURCE: Author's survey of associations, 2002.

"social movements," carrying out contentious activity in the defense of specific goals. These contentious activities continue today, although they were commoner in the past, as described in Chapter 2. Table 11 lists the main activities of neighborhood associations in Porto Alegre. Over half of the city's associations have in recent times circulated petitions, directly contacted the media, or made demands of politicians.

The vast majority of associations participated in the OP and actively sought funding for projects. While almost all associations carried out other tasks, OP projects were a priority activity for most associations' aggregate demands. This meant encouraging members to attend meetings, "fighting for" improvements in the OP, and actively fostering spaces for collective deliberation and discussion to address OP priorities and elect delegates. In Norte, for example, every March, each neighborhood association set up meetings with both OP budget councilors and City Hall employees. Associations also have talks on particular topics and occasionally bring in politicians to debate their campaign proposals at election time.

Inasmuch as most associations are involved in specific demands, most of which are met through the OP, the old distinctions between "combative" and "social" associations have become redundant. Associations continue to provide social services, whether formally or through informal networks of mutual assistance. In the past, they were directly involved in providing social services, but the current scarcity of such programs at the federal and state level means that they now provide services such as day care centers, adult literacy programs, and community health screenings in partnership with City Hall.

In practice, association leaders are informally expected to "solve problems" in the community:

> [T]he president of a *vila* is like a parent, you know? I see this now; after I got elected, when there is a problem with the neighbor, they come here. Look, last weekend this happened. "Vera, the neighbor in front had a lot of garbage in front of the house and scratched my car, can you talk to him?" So I have to leave home, go there speak with the neighbor, to solve the problem. Or the neighbor is drunk, screams all night long, nobody could sleep, so they come here. I thought we should call the police, but then I thought I would make an enemy, so I had to go talk to him. . . . If a light is broken in the street, they come here. When a pipe explodes, they come here. This is the president's job.[6]

Associations also frequently have social functions. Both Chácara and Parque elected delegates to the OP and hosted social events, including parties and dances. In terms of substantive concerns, both associations worked as partners in the organization of a day care center in Parque and a literacy program in Chácara. For Parque, the slum settlement, one of the main issues of concern was security and policing of the neighborhood. Responding to growing violence and inadequate police involvement in community affairs, the association organized a protest, and went to the media with its complaints. With substantial support from other neighborhood associations across the city, the Parque association held a meeting with the sergeant responsible for policing the area, as well as with the municipal Housing Department.

The structure of neighborhood associations in Porto Alegre fits the general pattern of neighborhood associations for the rest of the country.[7] That is, they usually have a board of directors headed by a president, a schedule of regular assemblies where important matters are voted upon, and a structure of councils that debate specific issues. The directorate is usually elected by the membership at an assembly (held yearly or biannually), and membership is for the most part open to residents, although a few associations charge dues as a prerequisite to voting. Associations may have links with organizations such as soccer clubs, mothers' groups, and groups working on projects. Most hold public assemblies where voting takes place on critical motions, with some variation on whether assemblies delegate the power to make decisions to the president or require ratification by the larger assembly. There is usually a board of directors, and the treasurer, secretary, and other officers of the association are elected. Most associations also have

TABLE 12

Proceduralism among 167 Active Neighborhood Associations in Porto Alegre

	Functioning since OP	Functioning prior to OP
Total	81	86
Direct elections or consensus	100%	100%
Elections open to all	72%	61%
Charges dues	25%	33%
Participates in Orçamento Participativo	98%	92%
Active committees	46%	48%

SOURCE: Author's survey of associations, 2002.

internal councils, such as a monitoring council and a deliberative council.

As shown in table 12, there is some evidence for greater democratic inclusiveness among newer associations.[8] More often than not, older associations tended to require that members pay dues in order to vote and were slightly less likely to hold open elections for the board of directors. A slightly higher proportion of newer associations participated in the OP. There were no significant differences in terms of engaging in contentious activity in relation to City Hall.

There are some notable distinctions between associations that reflect the economic standing of residents. Neighborhood associations in favelas perceived as "irregular" or formerly irregular areas were less likely to hold as many organized social gatherings and events. Few of these kinds of associations, for instance, have their own buildings. Associations in wealthier areas have more social events and recognizable sources of income, such as donations by members or renting out their rooms for parties. The distinction is evident if we compare Chácara, an established association with its own building in a working-class neighborhood, and Parque, a more precarious association without its own building in a squatter settlement. Chácara's association was able to fund the printing of a small newsletter, and local business donated uniforms for its soccer team. In Parque, in contrast, meetings are held in people's backyards, and the association has essentially functioned with no funding. Despite these material distinctions, resource-poor associations like Parque still manage to foster community discussion and deliberation in informal settings, even if those meetings take place in people's backyards.

Electoral Competition in Associations

One year after the founding of the Chácara da Fumaça association, a faction opposing the founding directors "staged a coup" and voted the board of directors out. The issue was fiscal impropriety, even though the association had little money at the time. The deposed board of directors sought legal action against the "usurpers," accusing their critics of "political motives." The woman who had led the charges of corruption and then became president of the association had been a "community advisor" to a prominent populist PDT politician. The previous board of directors had included one community activist who belonged to the PT. As I discuss below, association elections are one of the contexts in which "politics" manifests itself, although never explicitly. In almost all associations, neighborhood intrigue over party ties colors the election, and claims of election fraud, "politicking," and other sorts of impropriety are common. The normally affable proceedings of associations turn fiercely competitive, accusatory, and quasi-litigious as opponents debate the electoral minutiae of governing statutes and competing slates jockey for votes.

In this context, the OP provides proof of community leadership, rationalizing support for one candidate in neighborhood association elections rather than another. In 1998, a typical neighborhood association election flyer read: "VOTE SLATE 1 FOR THE DIRECTORATE OF THE ASSOCIATION: LEADERSHIP, PARTICIPATION, AND RESULTS. . . . The candidates of SLATE 1 have participated regularly in the OP since 1993 and have brought results."[9]

The OP is known as a place where neighborhood activists can make a name for themselves by bringing impressive numbers of participants, as well as by ensuring that their delegates are constructively informed about both the issues and the rules. The uncompromising posture of neighborhood leaders who are not intimidated by the college-educated talk of City Hall representatives is often seen as evidence of integrity. Carmen, who was elected to the board of directors of Parque, said she gained respect in the community because she does not "make a distinction between the government of different political parties; I am not like some of my *companheiros* who are afraid to criticize the PT. I am also not intimidated because some engineer has a university education."

Activists understood, in other words, that names and reputations were established, maintained, and challenged in the OP. Those who established themselves as community leaders were able to demonstrate not only competency but the skills that made them stand out at OP meetings. Some, who wished to be known for their tenacity and fighting spirit went out of their way to maintain an uncompromising posture in the meetings. The paradox, of course, is that by participating in the meetings, however militantly, they tacitly agreed to the rules of the process itself. However unruly participants became at meetings, they were still present and not outside publicly opposing City Hall. As I discuss below, this paradox left many organizations and activists with doubts about the purpose and meaning of militant politics in civil society.

Militant No More? The Role of Popular Councils

"I am afraid we have become tools of the administration," Nelson, a longtime PT activist on the Partenon Popular Council, told me.

The school where the Norte Popular Council meets every other week is a few kilometers from the Chácara da Fumaça Neighborhood Association. Meetings usually begin with announcements, followed by business items; these habitually include the admonition of particular municipal departments and complaints about ongoing intrigue within neighborhood associations, such as claims of corruption or voting impropriety. About once a month, municipal departments are invited to attend the Popular Council meetings to address activists, who hold them accountable for previous commitments. Thirty to forty participants attend any given meeting, and the proceedings often turn chaotic. Owing to a long history of grassroots mobilization, coupled with tensions between the populist PDT control of the Popular Council and OP activists, as described in Chapter 3, these meetings in Norte are more combative than "social."

Norte's Popular Council was created after intense confrontations over urban services, between neighborhood activists and municipal authorities in the mid 1980s. With the PT victory, some key Popular Council leaders left in order to join the new administration, thereby weakening the overall effectiveness of the organization and handing over political control to the populist PDT supporters. As a previously militant and politically heterogeneous organization whose primary objective had been democratic access to urban services, the Popular Council in Norte faced a dilemma over its organizational role within the new PT regime.

Popular councils in Brazil are autonomous institutions that hold regular district-level meetings on a weekly or bimonthly basis for representatives of neighborhood associations and citizens who wish to discuss the district's problems.[10] While popular councils do not have any formal power over neighborhood associations or over the OP, they serve as intermediaries between local associations and the municipal government, coordinating activities between neighborhood associations, for instance, to make sure a fund-raiser does not overlap with a cultural event in a nearby neighborhood, settling disputes among and within associations, and deploying collective resources to solve district-level problems.

The Norte Popular Council was not involved in the OP, and its directors made it a point not to participate. In the past, the Popular Council had, in fact, organized opposition to the establishment of the OP, which for some years had caused participation to "dry up" according to one participant. At the time of my fieldwork, the Popular Council oriented its activities toward the municipal government, serving as an "autonomous" intermediary body, often taking up the causes of associations that felt wronged in the OP and sometimes acting as an "independent overseer" to the process.

Norte's Popular Council had historically counted on participation from the twenty neighborhood associations in the district, but by 2000, only eight associations were participating in its meetings. The leaders of the Popular Council would at times solicit participation from favela residents precisely because their demands within the OP were among the most difficult to solve. PT activists saw this as strategic, since the PDT loyalists were the same neighborhood leaders who had earlier shunned favela residents, labeling them as outside of the "good community." The Popular Council now actively took up their cause and used its stature in the community to demand to speak first at OP meetings in order to criticize the administration for, among other things, failing to meet the needs of favela residents. Lauro, a longtime resident of the district and once the head of the Popular Council, explained that "community activism has died. No one around here questions the administration any more, so that's what we do." The difficulty for the Popular Council, however, was that as its leaders pursued a strategy of opposition, they began to be seen as disruptive by other participants. As a new delegate in the district's OP forum told me, "I don't know about people like Lauro who just come to make noise to oppose the process. I don't think it's honest." The Norte Popular Council faced the dilemma of being a "militant" organization in an environment where many of its demands were met through other means. Its unremitting opposition to the OP had costs in terms of long-term legitimacy and new participants. In fact, the council had steadily lost participants over the 1990s, and one of the directors confided that he was unsure "whether the Popular Council would survive much longer."

The Partenon Popular Council (CPP) took a different route, since many of its activities revolved around proposing policies to the municipal government. Originally an autonomous umbrella organization dedicated to fostering discussion on common problems in the district, it drew participants from various neighborhoods. Community activists involved in the CPP noted that "before the Budget Forum meetings, it was almost impossible to count on people showing up to a meeting."

By 2000, the CPP had become an important district-level forum for conversations about community affairs, although it was also closely linked to OP meetings, to which its yearly schedule was always tied. The principal community activists in the CPP were the same as those in the OP meetings, and they coordinated activities between the two. Moreover, a significant portion of CPP meetings was dedicated to the issues raised in OP meetings, and the same City Hall facilitator attended both sets of meetings. On a few occasions during my fieldwork, entire meetings were dedicated to solving community disputes, such as the one between Claudio and Marcos discussed in Chapter 5, which initially erupted in an OP meeting. In other words, the CPP complemented the OP.

Nonetheless, even in Partenon, recurring tensions arose about the appropriate role of the Popular Council in relation to the OP, and a handful of activists clearly want greater autonomy. At every other CPP meeting, activists spent some time arguing about whether one another's "interventions" in the OP had been too uncritical of the PT. They also argued about whether delegates were "personalist" or self-serving in their deliberation—as when one of the community activists in a plenary OP meeting announced publicly that a particular "road would not have happened without me." In this way, activists in Partenon used CPP meetings as an additional site to collectively think through their practice in the OP.

Political Parties and Soccer Teams: Connecting to the World of Politics

"I have my political party, and I have my soccer team," Arno, a PDT activist, told me. "Those are separate things from the OP and the community movement."

In interviews, most activists described associational activity of any kind as unconnected with political activity in the sense of party and electoral politics. In Porto Alegre, for activists, there is an important division between "the world of parties" and "the world of the community." While it is understood that community activists are entitled to participate in party activities, there is a tacit rule that those activities are not to take place within the OP or within community organizations. Survey data revealed that the majority of OP delegates did not participate in PT activities. Although there are more people registered with political parties today than in 1988, and the PT has gained substantial support through registered members and elections, party activity is considered separate from community activism, and OP participants and community activists monitor this distinction, often accusing one another of having "partisan" motivations. Even though community activists understood "politics" as a separate realm, many community leaders campaigned for politicians during elections, and at times "party politics" provided a tacit subtext for OP or community discussions. Community activists repeatedly described the divisions between community and politics, as Arno continued:

> In the association, no one has a party. It is like religion: you have yours, I have mine, and we do not discuss it. In the association, our party is the community.
> Q: But what about elections?
> A: During election time, we all work for our candidates. You have yours, I have mine, and we work for them as individuals, but not the association. The association has no party.
> Q: But don't candidates come to the association?
> A: At the association, anybody can come to talk during election time. It is good for the community. It can even be someone I am working for or you are working for. If someone wants to come to the association, he can come and talk. But the association is neutral.

Approximately one-tenth of the neighborhood activists I interviewed admitted they had some kind of "patronage" relationship with a politician. Newer leaders were less likely to admit to such relationships.[11] Many more claimed that while this had previously been true, it was no longer the case today. During the years of the dictatorship, the military-appointed municipal government sought to establish sympathetic neighborhood associations throughout Porto Alegre. The municipal government often wrote the associations' bylaws and ensured very close ties to neighborhood leaders.[12] But the routinization of the OP made this version of clientalism essentially counterproductive at the municipal level, since the outcome of the budget was decided through the OP. Community activists who admitted accepting benefits from politicians, described it as a pragmatic choice, resulting in a "small gift." As Maria, a neighborhood activist in Nordeste, confided, "Yes, I work for a politician at campaign time, and then he helps us out during the year. But look, there is not much more they can do as far as helping, maybe something with the [association] building, but everything is through the OP now." Her father, Seu Sílvio, who had been an association president in the past, said his rule was, "I let them [politicians] pay for a party for the kids at election [time], but we are not working for them. If politicians from other parties want to pay for things, we'll take that too."

Activists in neighborhood associations actively monitored the boundaries between "community" and "parties." According to Seu Sílvio, the "correct way" to use politics is in the interests of furthering the community's goals. This seasoned activist understood the way "some people try to turn the association into something political" as a sign of inexperience. "They don't know how to use politics without bringing in their community work, when it should be the opposite," he said.

Party Locals and Coded Political Contests

In two of the three districts I studied, there were PT "party locals," but these are neither as hierarchically organized nor as disciplined (or secretive) as the Portuguese term *núcleo partidário* might suggest. Rather, in keeping with PT practice, they are relatively autonomous sites of activity and discussion, which function to coordinate many of the party activities in their areas. While party locals do not dictate the activities of neighborhood associations and do not receive instruction from the party as far as a political line goes, they do coordinate protests and election campaigns. In principle, the centrist PMDB, the populist PDT, and the right-wing PTB had party locals in all three districts. In practice, however, only the PT had active party locals that functioned outside of election periods in both Nordeste and Partenon.

These party locals were important for the party but did not have any impact on the community at large. Instead, political contestation took place, however implicitly, in the OP itself. For example, the 1998 state elections were charged for the community movement. Both the PT's first mayor, Olívio Dutra, and Alceu Collares, the populist PDT mayor from 1986 to 1988, were candidates for state governor. OP meetings in some districts emptied as the election approached. This also occurred in associations and the popular councils, because neighborhood activists campaigned for one side or the other.

OP meetings became more charged during the run-up to elections, because participants campaigning for parties such as the centrist PMDB and the populist PDT articulated their opposition to the PT. Some of these community activists continued to participate in the OP, but they vocally criticized the administration as a means of attacking the PT. As one City Hall employee put it, "[O]ne of the things we have to do here is always to allow the opposition [the PDT] plenty of time at the microphone," even if they "always go first at the plenary meetings with the mayor, and always attack him." He said if PDT activists were not allowed the chance to publicly castigate the PT, the administration "would be accused of being undemocratic."[13]

At several meetings in this period, disagreements became a way for activists to distance themselves from the administration or overtly criticize the PT. In Nordeste, one participant became angry with what he perceived as the acquiescence of another participant and accused him of partisan PT motives:

> João: Unlike Maurício, I don't have ties to the PT, and I don't have to apologize for an administration that never does anything for us here in the Nordeste district. I don't feel we should waste our time making demands in the OP, because we never get anything anyway.
>
> Beto: I have to say that I am pretty disappointed with what happened last year with the projects we wanted, and that I hope the PT follows up on its promises this year, which is an election year! [He went on to discuss what they had asked for at an identical meeting the year before.]

Community activists like João and Beto used the discussion of projects as a way to criticize the PT, implicitly accusing the party of populist tactics, such as proposing building projects in an election year, and accusing OP delegates of partisan motives. Other delegates tried to keep the terms of debate to issues of community participation and relevant projects. Keeping political party machinations separate from the OP was important to the majority of delegates.

Community Leaders, New and Old

Competing styles of civic practice have also given rise to recurring conflict in civil society. Neighborhood association presidents were for decades the most important mediators between municipal authorities and local communities in Brazil. In Porto Alegre, neighborhood association presidents and well-known activists from the 1970s and 1980s were respected public figures, whether or not they had any official power. In contrast to this earlier generation, new generations of neighborhood leaders have started out in the OP, as opposed to local associations or even social movements. New leaders have been schooled in participatory governance rather than the conflictual tactics of social movements or the deal making of neighborhood politics. But the rise of new-style activists to perform this role has not been met without some resentment from old-style activists, particularly those with origins in the community movement.

In each of the city's districts, there are eminent older activists with origins in civil society, primarily the community movement, although in some cases, they have ties to church activism or other social movements. Many of these activists have party preferences, but their ties to political parties are seen as secondary to their work as community activists. Here I have chosen to portray three older community leaders still active today: Dona Maria, an ex-nun and activist with a liberation theology background, representative of the progressive clergy in Nordeste; Seu Sílvio, an association president since the 1970s, also from Nordeste; and Marcos, who was an activist in the social movements of the 1980s in the Partenon district.

As one of two elected councilors from the Nordeste district for two years in the early 1990s, Maria developed a reputation as a skilled negotiator by playing a key role in securing approval for the district's school project, which required that virtually all delegates forgo asking for pavement for one year. Maria, who is in her sixties, has been a member of the PT since its founding in Porto Alegre. Since the beginning of the OP, she has been central to many of the civic activities in her neighborhood, the favela of Parque das Orquideas. Maria was one of the organizers of the protest of the women of Parque against police apathy described in Chapter 5, which caused the PT much embarrassment. Although Maria is critical and sometimes even combative in relation to the PT, she is a committed participant of the OP.

Maria describes her own job as that of a teacher, "bringing the people along." Coming from a religious order committed to social justice issues, she voluntarily moved to her poor neighborhood from a middle-class home in a small town twenty years ago. Active in her neighborhood association, the OP, and health and human rights forums, Maria knows the district as well as anyone else. She has contacts in most neighborhood associations, and is often invited to help associations run elections and deal with problems in the neighborhood. For instance, Maria was often asked to be the spokesperson to explain neighborhood concerns—ranging from uncollected trash to lack of child care—to the local media. At OP meetings, she often facilitated discussions and rarely hesitated to take strident positions on all issues, even though she was not always successful in convincing her peers.

The leadership style of the well-respected, longtime neighborhood association president Seu Sílvio was a very different from Maria's. For him, *comunitários*, or community activists, should above all strive to be honest rather than to benefit personally from getting things done. Seu Sílvio lived in a building designated as a day care center, "donated" by a politician who wanted to assure the allegiance of the neighborhood in a crucial election in the 1980s. He does not hide the fact that he has been associated with a variety of politicians from various right-of-center parties, and he is known in the neighborhood as someone who brings food to the neighborhood during election time, although, as he acknowledges, it is not possible to bring things "like in the old days," when a skilled president could bring construction materials at election time. Seu Sílvio also actively participates in charity networks, seeking out philanthropic assistance from a wide range of private donors. In addition, he considers himself the de facto lifetime president of his association and used his status to gain a seat as one of Nordeste's two councilors in the citywide Budget Council in the early 1990s. Although Seu Sílvio was an active participant in the OP, his leadership practices were pointedly out of sync with those of most new community activists. At OP meetings, he often assailed City Hall employees with threats of negative election outcomes resulting from popular dissatisfaction with the budgeting process.

Marcos, who worked for a PT councilperson as a community liaison, but essentially used the city-funded position to work as an autonomous activist, is another example of this earlier generation. He was active in the fledging citywide Movimento Negro (Black Movement) and served as a board member at several samba schools and as a soccer coach for underprivileged youth. He was also active in human rights organizations as a representative of Afro-Brazilian interests. Marcos was a founding member of Partenon's Popular Council, as well as of his neighborhood association. He would sometimes facilitate meetings of the Popular Council, resolving disputes or explaining laws and procedures. He often helped other activists state their points more concisely, even if he did not agree with their positions. Marcos commanded a great deal of respect in all these settings and was rarely challenged.

Sílvio, Maria, and Marcos all played crucial mediating roles in their neighborhoods, and despite the differences between them, all three had backgrounds in civil society prior to participating in the OP. Today, all three have had to adapt to the new state–civil society regime centered around the OP, although they had different routes of access to the world of government in the past. Maria and Marcos may have had an easier time of it because of their political dispositions—Maria had run for the Porto Alegre City Council under the PT, and Marcos was closely connected to the CPP, which had played such an important role in facilitating the introduction of the OP in Partenon. The politicians who did Sílvio favors in the past have steadily lost influence, thus forcing him to adapt to "get things done" through the OP. Despite the variation of styles among these three activists, they all occasionally clashed with the new style of community leader who got involved in civil society organizations only after acquiring both experience and a reputation in the OP. Typical of this new kind of leader was Jonas, a councilor in Nordeste.

The Councilor as Community Figure

Jonas was elected one of two budget councilors for Nordeste for the first time in 1998, a few months before he was asked to resolve a dispute about an election in a nearby neighborhood association. During his term in office, this kind of request became increasingly frequent. He was asked to step in and resolve disputes in the community or to intercede with the administration on behalf of residents. Despite his few years of formal education and his relative lack of community experience before participating in the OP, he became well known in the area as a community leader and a trusted and honest individual with access to the administration. After being persuaded by some members of the PT local, Jonas joined the party before the 1998 election, and rumors spread that he wanted to eventually run for city council. Jonas never participated in the party local's activities, and although he was by then a PT party member, he presented himself as a community leader and not as a party activist. His work as a self-employed general contractor fitted in well with his community involvement. His time was his own, and as he moved about the district, sometimes between jobs, he would stop in to visit one neighborhood or another.

At the end of his first term as an OP councilor, Jonas became involved in a public political dispute that made its way to the local press, including the city's newspapers and television channels. A woman in his district claimed to have been neglected at a public health clinic, and argued, furthermore, that OP councilors had tried to cover up the "poor services" provided by municipal public agencies and had failed to respond to her complaints. A city councilor from an opposing political party took the opportunity to attack the administration and the OP publicly in the media. The opposition politician released several provocative public statements about the "poor services" of the administration and the "farce" of the OP.

Jonas decided, on his own initiative, to respond to the city councilor publicly, making use of a weekly "community hour" in which city councilors listened and responded to community problems. Together with a few other delegates from Nordeste, he made his way to City Council that Friday wearing a borrowed coat and tie, and read a brief prepared statement about participation, transparency, and the hard work by public clinicians. In the tense minutes following, the city councilor who had criticized the clinics viciously attacked Jonas as an "uneducated" "parrot" (*papagaio*) of the administration and "tool" (*boneco*, literally, "doll") of the PT. Jonas stood stoically at the podium, while the PT legislators remained silent in response to the accusations.

I later asked Jonas why he had chosen to go to the city council:

> Jonas: I came down because he attacked us and our work in the district, and people work hard in that clinic, and he is trying to "make gains" [*faturar*, literally, "invoice," or "submit a bill"] at election time.
>
> Q: But don't you think the PT city councilors could have defended you after those insults?
>
> Jonas: I did not come down because of the PT. I came down because he is a liar and he is attacking our work in the district, and so I had to come tell the truth.

The incident involving Jonas was particularly striking because the public health clinic in question did not, in principle, have any direct ties to the OP. But the woman with the original complaint, the city councilor, and Jonas all understood it as a reflection of the OP and of the work of OP delegates. Moreover, both sides implicitly understood the role of the OP councilor as one that implies standing up for all of the work in the community.

Budget councilors perform functions in associative life at large in all districts that are much broader than facilitating budget meetings and participating in the OP. Jonas understood his role as defending the overall objectives and everyday functioning of community projects. His role included mediating between the community and the government, but also speaking out as a public voice on larger matters. Invariably, in interviews, respondents revealed that the "role of the budget councilor" was broadly understood in this way. Their responses also indicated that for city councilors, the OP was a project of the PT, but for Jonas, it represented something beyond the party's interests. OP leaders like Jonas see themselves as leaders of the community, as opposed to individuals responsible only for the functioning of the budget process. At the same time, the world of politics remains distinct, as evident in the absence of direct intervention on Jonas's behalf by PT councilors.

Contestation Between Old and New

Whenever a dispute arose between the earlier and newer generations of activists, it was usually the latter—those who had started their associational lives prior to the OP—who picked the quarrel. Often, but not always, such disputes were contests with activists who had ties to older political parties, like the populist PDT. In the elections for budget councilor in the Norte district in 1998, this dispute became explicit. Two groups contested the election. Longtime community activists and neighborhood association presidents, some with ties to the PDT, made up one group. The other group consisted of activists who had less experience in community politics but maintained closer ties to the OP; activists in this group had begun their involvement through the OP and not the other way around. The self-representation of each group was telling, as each claimed a very distinct trajectory. Joelci, of the group with OP experience, spoke at a meeting to elect budget councilors:

> I have been involved with the OP since its early days. I was a councilor in 1993, a difficult year for us all, a year in which we were trying to improve ourselves, to understand what the OP is. But it was a year in which we brought many different projects to the district, including the river project that even brought us problems. But we fought for it, and along with Walter,

who was also a candidate, we were able to get the support of the other districts to show them that our projects were important. That year I criticized the land reform formula in the OP, and I fought with the Housing Department so that the process became more prompt. . . . I have participated in the OP since year one, [and] I have always taken the process seriously, because if it weren't serious, the authorities would not be here today.

In reply, one of the candidates from the competing group asserted that he was a "communitarian," a person from the community movement. Like him, his entire group had several years of experience in neighborhood associations, and believed in community values:

All the groups running today are qualified, and you will have to vote to decide democratically, but I want to tell you why I would vote for our group. Everyone [in the group] has a history of work in the community and has respect. Claudia is a longtime neighborhood association president and has fought for the people for a long time. She does not defend A or B or political party A or B. Then there is Laura, who organized the Parque association, which brought together 1,700 families. Then there is Vanda, our great *companheira*, who has fought for day care centers and organized them so well. We have people from all kinds of associations and groups in our Slate 2.

After the vote was counted, the OP activists won with 65 percent of the votes and had to select the two budget councilors for the district, along with a substitute. The community activist group was supposed to provide one of its members as a second substitute. The substitute from the community activist group eventually dropped out of the process, and the district continued with two councilors and one substitute for the rest of the year.

Many older neighborhood associations had ties to the populist PDT, but this changed with the OP's increasing popularity among civil society activists. One of the changes activists described was a change in the "ways of doing politics." As in the example above, we find activists claiming different sources of competence. The first group claimed previous successes in the OP and competence in its tasks, while the second group emphasized its history of struggle and work "in the community." The second group of candidates stressed that they were neighborhood association presidents, while the first group of candidates stressed their experience in the OP. The losing group would later grumble that the first group of activists "are a new kind of generation who know nothing about real community work, all they know is the OP and they know how to talk nicely [*sabem falar bonito*, literally, "know how to talk pretty"] in front of the meeting."

In a sense, clashes like these are no surprise. The routinization of the OP meant that new kinds of civic practices would become more valued and effective. For community leaders to maintain respect and standing, it was necessary for them to continue to respond to the needs of their communities, which now meant having to go through the OP process. Although clashes between these two types of groups were sometimes abated thanks to the work of experienced and respected activists, they did nevertheless occur on a relatively regular basis.

New Civic Practices, Old Dilemmas?

In an interview, Seu Sílvio became upset when asked if the low level of education on the city's periphery was ever a problem for the OP:

> Seu Sílvio: I totally disagree. We don't even have to discuss it.
> Q: But do you think it is a challenge for the OP?
> Seu Sílvio: No. I think it helps the OP, because it begins from below. It is not the suits [*colarinhos-brancos*, literally, the "white-collars"] who come here and tell us what to do. It is us. I am a humble person. I have participated since the beginning. And like me, there are many more poor people who are there with me, debating or helping in whatever way possible. And so I think the OP is enriching in this way, because it makes people talk, even the poorest ones. It has not let the suits take over.

Later in the interview, Sílvio described what he considered the "real" bases of authority:

> Someone who gets respect in the community or the OP is someone who is honest, works hard, and does the job the community has given him. He has to have all three: work, honesty, and respect for the community. A good [neighborhood association] president, for instance, has to have work in the community and always to be available. If people need him, and he is not home to help, then he becomes known as a bad president.

Dona Carmen, another longtime community activist in the district, who works as a domestic during the week, expressed similar feelings:

> There needs to be a community spirit, a spirit of participation. If not, it doesn't matter if the person goes to meetings, she won't understand anything. . . . You don't have to be a doctor or anything. . . . there is a lawyer who is participating these days who is making everything more personal. That won't do.

Implicit in both Sílvio's and Carmen's comments is the common sentiment among neighborhood association activists that there is a popular logic of authority in the world of the community that is completely different from that of "society at large." In the world of the community, "work for the community," respect, and solidarity are what count. Rules and behavior are such that in OP meetings, where community rules are in effect and where the "community spirit" is the accepted norm, values like honesty and dedication to community count for more than money or formal education. In the speech of activists, like much of the academic discourse on civil society, the world of voluntary association is one of cooperation, trust, and solidarity, where citizens take care of one another. Scholars writing on Porto Alegre have emphasized the importance of the renewed "civic ethos" in the city.[14]

Community activists also point out another side of the world of the community, one that some feel has declined. The earlier generation of activists from various political orientations on occasion lament the decline of the "movement" side of the community movement in Porto Alegre. Even those who said they were convinced of the OP's merits spoke of the diminished "militancy" of social movements and associations. They blamed the OP and the administration for making "the movement" less militant and combative and abolishing some of its principal functions. Arno, a community leader who had ties with numerous different political parties, although not the PT, admits: "Some things have really changed. Today it doesn't matter if you collect signatures and take them to City Hall, or if you get along with the city councilor. Everything is more correct now. Really, everything is through the OP. But the OP has almost ended with the community movement. Everything is through the OP."

As the OP has become routinized and brought in more participants, its impact has grown and transformed the rules of civic life. Although political party activity was considered a separate realm from community activism, the OP democratized access to governmental decision making. This has affected the functioning of associations in civil society, as the OP itself has become a central locus where activists both resolve issues and display political competence. Budget councilors become important figures in the community, and the OP itself becomes a setting where activists debate politics in a coded way. It is broadly understood that while explicit party activism is off-limits, critiques of the OP are directed at the PT. Only a minority of any given district's residents engaged explicitly in political party activism.

Many older activists with backgrounds in social movements argued

TABLE 13

Active Neighborhood Associations in Porto Alegre, 2002

Active associations (est.)	600
"Legally" registered associations[a]	94%
Percentage of associations once paralyzed	25%
Percentage associations that have	
. . . day care	20%
. . . bulletin/newspaper	20%
. . . own building	58%
. . . formal statutes	66%
Percentage associations that held[b]	
. . . party or barbecue	58%
. . . raffle	27%
. . . activities for children	66%
. . . petition	31%
. . . protests	37%
. . . debates	42%
. . . meeting with mayor or vice-mayor	20%
. . . meeting with a municipal department	69%
. . . more than four open assemblies	68%
Sources of income of associations	
. . . membership dues	29%
. . . sale of products	5%
. . . parties and raffles	46%
. . . renting out rooms	22%
. . . donations	22%
. . . partnerships	29%

SOURCE: Author's survey of associations, 2002.
[a] Registered with a notary public (*cartório*).
[b] In the past twelve months.

that it had been difficult to establish an autonomous forum like a popular council in districts like Nordeste, where despite a renewal of civil society, community activism had become so centered around the OP. Autonomous popular councils are important as a counterweight to the OP. But even when such institutions existed in particular districts, the dilemma of retaining the popular council's original function as a "militant organization" was complicated for numerous activists. Relating to the state after it has been "taken over" by sympathetic forces obliges activists in formerly oppositional organizations constantly to reimagine and reinvent the roles of their organizations.

CHAPTER SEVEN

The Civic Is the Political

The Many Crises of Democracy

In 2004, after the research for this book had concluded, Brazil's democracy made international news again. Whereas in 2002 it appeared that Brazilian voters were ready to take their chances with a political outsider with little formal education or government experience—perhaps a hopeful sign of the system's openness—in 2004, Brazilians' responses to surveys indicated dangerously low levels of support for democracy, registering some of the world's lowest levels of trust and belief in their democratic institutions.[1] And it is not only in Brazil that democracy is in crisis; the late 1990s and early 2000s, academic discussions were dominated by whether U.S. democracy was in decline, a theme also echoed in discussions about many other industrial and developing countries.[2]

As John Markoff has noted, although democratic transitions were greeted with post–Cold War triumphalism only a few years ago, the current mood is one of alarm about the state of democracy, especially in the face of globalization.[3] Jürgen Habermas and Max Pensky, for example, describe the dangers of the consequences of the national state's inability to provide the basis for national solidarity as global pressures that erode the power and capacity of states weaken its ability to assure even basic rights that are prerequisites to democracy.[4] Yet, if instead of reading the literature on national trends, a reader focused on local-level experiments in direct democracy, the impression would be very different—for every country facing democratic woes, from Brazil to South Africa, Mexico, and the United States, there are dozens of experiments

in local democracy, from shared management of environmental resources to novel forms of community policing and all manner of participatory governance, including a very widespread diffusion of participatory budgeting experiments. These two images appear at odds—on
one hand, mistrustful, apathetic, and isolated "lone bowlers," and on
the other, trusting and engaged citizens involved in local problem-solv-
ing, much as the descriptions in this book contradict the images of
Brazilian citizens evoked by surveys.

Both images have some merit, and the disjuncture between them is
more than a matter of methodology or choice of sites. It is not, in other
words, simply that although Brazilian democracy is a shambles, Porto
Alegre is an island of civic consciousness in a sea of apathy (or that Eu-
gene, Oregon, is such an island for that matter). One of the lessons of
the Porto Alegre case is that purely examining society-side factors (such
as citizens' levels of trust) in the absence of what I have called a relational context will not yield much about the actual potential for democracy or civic engagement. As national states have decentralized since
the 1980s, these relational contexts have become more and more local,
as societal demands and experimentation have increasingly shifted to
local administrations, which are often distinct from other local administrations within the same national context. Although national contexts
obviously matter, because local regimes are located within them, surveys that do not consider local relational contexts are of doubtful use.
This book discusses the way in which one empowered participatory
regime transformed a local associational landscape in a break with previous regimes defined by tutelage.

Porto Alegre's Empowered Participatory Regime

In Brazil, the decentralization of the state in the late 1980s allowed a
great deal of new discretion with regards to municipal finances and
planning, and the central innovation undertaken was the establishment
of the OP in Porto Alegre, beginning in 1990. As a society-side innovation that emerged from urban social movements frustrated with previous attempts at participatory governance, the OP took its present shape
partially as a result of the political weakness of the Workers' Party,
which turned to getting unorganized sectors to participate. The city of
Porto Alegre proved to be fertile ground for this innovation.

Chapter 2 compared tutelage regimes from the 1940s to 1988 with the later empowered participatory regime. Tutelage fostered cycles of protest and acquiescence, sometimes encouraging the creation of neighborhood associations, but the administration selectively recognized associations on the basis of political allegiance, which had a demobilizing effect over time. The state–civil society regime established since the PT administration, however, was based on the broad recognition of societal demands from various sectors of civil society without regard to political allegiance, which I have called the *empowered participatory regime*. In time, it brought several thousand participants into the OP to demand accountability and to make real decisions, which deeply transformed civic life in Porto Alegre. In the city's different districts, new players began to participate in civic life and formed new organizations. There was also a transformation in the *civic practices* of associations, which tended over time to engage less often in contentious activity. Chapter 1 asked what the impact of participatory governance on civil society is, and Chapter 2 concluded that the Porto Alegre experiment offers us one answer: participatory governance of this sort can make civic engagement more likely, addressing the paradox that "neighborhoods with the most serious need for community organization are the ones with the least capacity to create and sustain them."[5]

The routinization of the OP was not conflict-free, however, and embedding participatory governance in three of the city's districts forced the realignment of civic networks, as discussed in Chapter 3. The configuration of these networks around the OP was seen to be crucial in determining its future routinization, and three possible scenarios were considered: government-induced activism, scaled-up networks, and a system of competing allegiances. Ironically, preexisting civic networks were not found necessary to assure the routinization of the process, and in fact, very strong associations proved a stumbling block. The district with some of the most combative associations in the city, Norte, was one in which neighborhood associations actively boycotted the OP process for many years, and then controlled it to forbid the entrance of new participants. Only when the rules were changed to a more open format (surreptitiously, according to some), did a broader spectrum of participants start to attend. The distancing of civil society from the process would cause difficulties in later years.

The next three chapters explored the day-to-day activities of participants in the OP and activists in civil society. Chapter 4 looked at decision making within the OP—which contained a significant deliberative element, although the process is not without its difficulties—and a number of the dilemmas that participants face when they consider leaving or undermine the deliberative process. Deliberation, as an ideal of democratic theorists, did occur, but it was not a smooth process, and the crucial presence of "respected activists" who created compromises that permitted it to continue helped make it happen. Chapter 5 went on to argue that public-sphere type discussions appeared in each of the three district-level fora that served broad, open-ended types of purposes.

Chapter 6 examined the political culture of civil society in Porto Alegre, specifically, the way in which the city's civic activists organize and the "three worlds" that structure their worldview: the world of the government, the world of political parties, and the world of the community. I contend that the political culture of civil society in Porto Alegre goes beyond the dichotomy of citizen/militant, because the meanings of those two poles have become blurred: what one does in a social movement is largely what one does as a citizen when participatory governance plays such a central role in civil society. By merging the two roles, this political culture has both institutionalized social movement militancy and expanded what it means to be a citizen. This meant that certain previously militant organizations now had a difficult time assessing their mission. And while the PT has made electoral gains with the OP, careful attention to the activities and speech of activists shows that the PT did not control associations, and that activists generally maintained a pragmatic attitude toward political parties in general. The OP itself, however, was what much of community life revolved around. For example, community leaders established themselves by their participation in it. Chapter 6 speculated whether the OP has perhaps become too central to community life in Porto Alegre.

The Importance of Configurations

The routinization and experience of the OP in each of the districts was different. Comparative historical, aggregate, and ethnographic evidence shows that civic configurations set the context for the establishment of the OP and conditioned the types of engagements within it. Table 14 summarizes the argument about the three districts.

While each of the districts hosted the establishment of the OP, and deliberation and open-ended discussions within it, the civic configurations in each were strikingly different. Nordeste had the lowest level of

TABLE 14

Civic Configurations and the Orçamento Participativo

	Nordeste	Partenon	Norte
CIVIC CONFIGURATIONS			
Level of organization	Low	High	High
Organized opposition to OP	No	No	Yes
Cohesive civic networks	Yes	Yes	No
OUTCOMES			
Routinized OP	Yes (High)	Yes	Yes
Trust in OP	High	High	Lower
Deliberative breakdowns	Sometimes	Sometimes	More often
Public sphere	Yes	Yes	Less often
Public sphere breakdowns	Yes	Seldom	Seldom

autonomous organization, but civic networks were cohesively organized around the OP and there was no organized resistance. Numerically, participation was highest there, and the levels of trust in the
process were also high. Nordeste's OP deliberations occasionally broke
down (although City Hall facilitators were sometimes able to forestall
this), but the local Budget Forum was also a place for public sphere discussions for the district. The ethnographic evidence presented here also
highlights some of the contradictions of "government-induced" participation in Nordeste, where there were so few preexisting civic networks. It was here that strategic interruptions by participants to manage their reputations took place, because it was the only place in the
community where this could be done. As Chapters 4 and 5 illustrate,
the lack of "recognized activists" to maintain order, create collective
platforms, and assure the quality of discussion meant that the quality of
discussion was not the same as in Partenon.

Partenon was where the Budget Forum functioned most smoothly,
owing to the experience of activists, but also to the fact that there was
an active popular council parallel to the OP that effectively mediated
demands, protecting smaller neighborhoods and creating compromises. Participation in Partenon was also not as high in terms of numbers as in Nordeste, and popular council activists often expressed un-
ease at the closeness to the administration their role created. Finally,
Norte was where the establishment of the OP was most difficult. The
district's developed civic networks were not integrated with the OP, because its popular council activists boycotted the OP. The conspicuous
absence of popular council activists led to more frequent deliberative

breakdowns at the Budget Forum, and also did not lend it the quality of public-sphere-type discussions, because it was not a place for the "whole community to meet," as was the case in the two other districts.

The comparison shows, first of all, that civic configurations matter, although not simply in terms of sheer "stocks of social capital." The presence *and* alignment of civic networks are both crucial. Having an organized civil society that is integrated with participatory governance made for the most successful outcomes, but a civil society that is split and oppositional made for the worst. Having virtually no civil society at all did not prevent the routinization of the OP, although the lack of an organized associational counterweight to the OP was detrimental to the meetings in Nordeste in comparison. There is no reason to assume that Nordeste will not, in time, develop such networks, but they will be composed of community activists practically all exclusively schooled in the OP rather than in autonomous civil society. Whether that will be detrimental is an open question. But it should be noted that bodies like the CPP that provide a counterweight to the OP were originally conceived of as militant organizations, and to many community activists, their purpose today is unclear. In Nordeste, many activists thus probably do not see the point of creating a popular council. The paradox is the existence of organizations like the CPP that enliven the quality of participatory governance.

Despite these uneven results, is Porto Alegre's OP still a "grassroots answer" to the problems facing modern democracies? What, finally, are the limits and potentialities of participatory budgeting? As a conclusion to the book, I address the implications of this case study for those interested in the "limits of democracy within late capitalism."[6]

Relational Insights: Toward an Alternative Account of Civil Society

The Porto Alegre experiment, remarkable as it is, could be studied from a number of other perspectives than the civil society approach I have posited here, such as its impact on municipal governance and finances or the dilemmas of political parties in power.[7] The reason for this emphasis on the associational realm is, beyond analytical clarity, normative. Normatively attractive concepts in democratic theory like "radical democracy" and "public sphere" are often elusive in their "real-world applications," and this book has sought to contribute to the already extensive discussion of democratic theory through an actual examination of instances of popular participation in governmental decision making. As important as it is to understand whether, how, and when participatory budgeting will take hold and improve governance, the limit of such an approach is that it does not tell us about the *quality* of democratic participation, often the province of normative theorizing rather than empirical research.

Another of the book's contributions is to develop an approach that grasps the potential impacts of participatory reforms on actual practices in civic life. The framework I develop focuses on the relationships between civic practice and state–civil society regimes. In order to understand these changes, I have borrowed from relational sociology and developed the analytic lens of the concepts of *state–civil society regimes*, *civic configurations*, and *civic practices* and used them to examine the establishment of participatory institutions and their impact. Instead of a society-centered approach or a social movements approach, I have relied on a relational approach that highlights the logic of civic engagement within specific regimes and the way states manage their openness to societal demands. This approach necessarily treats politics and conflict as central to discussions of civil society, challenging the notion of its "separateness," implicit in much theorizing. Civic activism is embedded in fields of social relationships, and to shed light on it, we need to investigate the relationships between government and civic organizations and how these structure the context of civic engagement.

By relying on relational sociology, I have sought to avoid romantic notions about "participation" and public-minded action when borrowing from normative theories of the public sphere and of deliberation. The relational approach and case study here touch on at least three important debates with respect to the state and the public sphere, social capital, and deliberative democracy.

The State and the Public Sphere

Although participatory institutions in Porto Alegre have involved tens of thousands of participants, the quality of democratic practice in their meetings is not evident from the City Hall brochures that describe them. The fact that they encourage participants to engage freely in discussions, and thus to contribute to the construction of a "collective will," means that these institutions have a greater impact than they would if they sought merely to improve the quality and legitimacy of governmental decision making.

One of the principal analytic threads running through this book is not dissimilar to what de Tocqueville observed in America's townships: sharing in governance led people to become involved in civic life at large and to develop a "public orientation."[8] The role of the state in much of the theoretical discussion on the public sphere is ambiguous, however, and this case allows an investigation of its potential role. On the one hand, according to Habermas, the state plays a crucial role in assuring the rule of law and buffering the most egregious social inequalities to permit the public sphere to exist. But on the other hand, civil society forms its will beyond the reach of the state or the market in the networks of the life world that regularly places checks on the state.[9] While democratic theorists agree that neither the market nor the state can "carry or house publics," this formulation creates an ambiguous status for instances where participation is directly linked to the "exercise of public power."[10]

In the case of Porto Alegre, a set of institutions emerged from the encounter between demanding community activists and a politically weak political party that has fostered activities that bear a family resemblance to the practices of a "virtuous citizenry" advocated by liberal theorists.[11] This begins to address a crucial unanswered question about whether state-side reforms can "conduce to democracy in the absence of a self-organized citizenry, or an autonomous associational realm," also correcting the notion that the only place for open-ended community discussion is within the networks of civil society, or in its "free spaces."[12]

This insight, however, runs afoul of much of our commonsense understanding of these concepts. First, adding to the burgeoning sociology of democracy, the evidence here makes a case for a significant broadening of the potential cast of actors for civic activities. Habermas's version of the public sphere has been criticized for too narrowly conceptualizing the types of activities and actors thought to be its participants.[13] This book has sought to contribute to the critique, although from a slightly different perspective from those who have attempted to theorize the public sphere from the perspective of those excluded from it, as in the concepts of "subaltern publics" or "plebeian public spheres."[14] Rather, I have tried to show that even holding the definition of the public sphere constant, it is present in a context considered unlikely according to dominant approaches, given the material difficulties, lack of education, and lack of a liberal political culture. Well-proven models for predicting civic engagement and participation have consistently shown that education and economic resources are important predictors of civic engagement, and recent applications of these models to Brazil have replicated these findings.[15] In addition, the political cultural bases for an active citizenry may be absent. Habermas, for instance, intimates that the public sphere "can only emerge in the context of a liberal political culture and corresponding patterns of socialization."

The appearance of the public sphere calls attention to the role of state-sponsored institutions as enabling their appearance in otherwise difficult settings. While participatory institutions may be more relevant in those societies where the state historically played a larger role in nation building than in North Atlantic societies, instances of participation in government are increasingly common in many countries. In the United States, for example, participatory instances around policing are now commonplace and have been shown to attract many participants who otherwise have had little community involvement.[16] Nancy Fraser has criticized the conception of the public sphere precisely for neglecting the possible connections with empowered state settings, and I have argued that empowered state settings such as the OP are important objects of investigation, because they have the potential to foster the participation of unlikely candidates in these public spheres.[17]

Regimes: An Alternative to Social Capital

The approach developed here can also be juxtaposed to the argument, put forward in *Making Democracy Work*, by Robert Putnam, Robert Leonardi, and Raffaella Nanetti, that the dynamics of an active civil society take centuries to evolve and that there is little potential for such a society anywhere outside of the North Atlantic region.[18] Not only does *Militants and Citizens* call into question the long-term assumptions of these authors, it challenges their view on the way that legacies influence state institutions. Putnam does mention the role of the state at certain points in U.S. history in facilitating civic engagement in his more recent book *Bowling Alone: The Collapse and Revival of American Community*, but the observation is not central to his argument about the dynamics of civil society.[19]

The Porto Alegre story suggests, echoing Tarrow, that perhaps the "culprit" in declining civic engagement in the United States is to be found, not in a factor endogenous to civil society itself, but perhaps in changing sets of local conditions, where the changing levels of openness of the state to societal demands have interacted with civic configurations.[20] This argument follows the insights of several other scholars who point to the ways in which the state side of the state–civil society relationship structures the context in which civil society functions. Notably, based on the experiences of the United States, scholars such as Theda Skocpol and Morris Fiorina have examined the ways "in which the institutions and activities of the US government have influenced the identities, organizational forms, and strategies of voluntary organizations."[21] Similarly, studying Mexico, Jonathan Fox has argued for a "political construction" approach that shows how social capital has, in some instances, been politically constructed.[22] Fox thus argues for an analysis of the interdependent democratization of civil society and the state. Drawing from Central American examples, John Booth and Patricia Richard argue that governments create incentives and disincentives for participation in civil society by making community arenas more accessible.[23]

From a relational perspective, some of the causes of declining civic engagement in the United States might be found in the closing of avenues for societal demand making, which raises some suggestive hypotheses. For example, it could be productive to examine the changes in state–civil society regimes during the period of civic decline. As rightly critical as scholars have been of the paternalist and inefficient "great society programs" of the 1960s, those programs provided avenues for societal demand making. Since the 1970s, the welfare state has retrenched, and social spending to meet precisely the types of local demands I describe in this book has steeply declined, "breaking the social contract," in the words of Frances Fox Piven and Richard Cloward. The avenues for civil society demand making have been largely mediated through representative institutions, but access to those has diminished. Since the 1970s, electoral campaigns have become increasingly dominated by large donors and expensive political apparatuses that have sidelined civil society activists in favor of corporate actors. William Domhoff, argues, for example, that since 1975 not one piece of legislation favored by environmental movements has passed against corporate interests.[24]

Deliberative Democracy and Political Institutions

Theorists of participatory governance and deliberative democracy have similarly attempted to shift the current debate on the normative foundations of democratic renewal toward a discussion of "the exercise of public reason" and the nature of state institutions, away from an almost exclusive focus on communicative action in the public sphere, or in civil society's "free spaces."[25] Theorizing forms of coordination across non-state-related and state-empowered publics, they have developed proposals for associative governance and for direct citizen control of government functions.[26]

The Empowered Participatory Governance (EPG) approach proposed by Archon Fung and Erik O. Wright, which is partly based on the Porto Alegre experiment, is principally attentive to the ways in which the institutional design of participatory institutions may lend itself to good governance outcomes, effective participation and voice by broad segments of the citizenry, and resistance to bureaucratic rigidity. In the case of Porto Alegre, for example, the OP's decentralized and transparent system of decision making on pragmatic issues, which is open to all citizens, accounts for its success in attracting participants and assures its continued existence.[27] In pointing to institutional design as causal, Fung and Wright remind us to avoid becoming mired in local contingencies and not to lose sight of the potential role of the reform of state institutions. In contrast to what might be construed as the political pessimism of society-centered approaches, the EPG approach does not concern itself with long historical legacies. In the case of Porto Alegre, while not denying the social movement origins of the experiment, Fung and Wright point to the importance of participatory institutions in themselves, and their institutional design, as schools of democracy.

By extending the insights of EPG forward (to its potential outcomes in civil society) and disaggregating civil society to its component parts, a relational approach also extends its insights backward away from the moment of participatory institutional design to the recursive and structured "rounds" of state–civil society prior to the reforms, in which, at each turn, the balance of power and the institutional legacies of the previous turn limited some possibilities but also opened up others.[28]

In terms of implications, this book points to "civic outcomes" once EPG institutions emerge. Assessing the implications calls for research into both institutional designs and the interactions of institutional designs with civic configurations. In terms of EPG research, one further issue to be explored is the impact on civil society of specific institutional design features themselves within otherwise comparable settings or comparable state–civil society regimes.[29] In this book I have treated OP rules as a specific feature of a broader empowered participatory regime that was highly open to societal demands. But it is possible to imagine equally empowered participatory regimes based on different sorts of rules, such as one that emphasizes sectoral interests over geographical ones.

Another important factor is the surrounding social context of institutions and the way they interact.[30] Attention to these interactions may significantly qualify both criticisms of and praise for instances of "participation in government," because it may shed additional light on the desirability of such arrangements in a variety of contexts. One insight from this book is that whether participatory sites involve certain downsides or patterns of communication may have as much to do with the surrounding civil society as with the institutional participatory rules. Thus, for example, in the case of Porto Alegre, although meetings were not dominated by the articulate few, as might be expected by some critics of participatory democracy, they did manifest the problems of unruly meetings in settings without existing civic networks.

Yes, But Can the Orçamento Participativo Fix Brazil's (or Any Other "Bad") Democracy?

The OP has captured the imagination of local administrators and electors throughout Brazil. In the 1997–2000 period, at least 100 administrations experimented with it, and in the 2001–4 period at least twice that many have been attempting it, with very many cases of municipalities run by other political parties doing so. Many draw inspiration from Porto Alegre, which raises several issues for further comparative work. Can Porto Alegre's lessons be extended throughout Brazil, or is it an exception? Would OP reforms have the same outcomes in places with much less developed civil societies, for example?

Civil society was demobilized in 1988 in Porto Alegre as a result of the tutelage regime, but it was already quite developed there as compared to other cities in Brazil, particularly those in areas of the country where associationalism has traditionally been weaker, such as the north.[31] Porto Alegre's large number of European immigrants, *gaúcho* culture, and past as an "oppositional" city have also been cited as making it an exception.[32] Perhaps more important, the city's union of neighborhood associations, UAMPA, originally called for the OP as early as 1986, and the presence of organized neighborhood activism were crucial in fine-tuning and improving the participatory process. In sum, it can be argued that the rapid and significant changes in civil society in Porto Alegre would not have been possible in some settings without these factors, if, indeed, participation could have been instituted at all.

However, there are also reasons to qualify the case for the "Porto Alegre exception." Some districts of the city without significant associational life in fact experienced the most significant changes over time. The Nordeste district, for example, is an example of how the process can take hold in an inauspicious setting. It is one of the poorest and most remote districts of the city; and most of the "popular settlements" there are resettlements from other parts of the city. Despite only four functioning neighborhood associations in 1989, the district has had some of the highest numbers of participants in the OP in the whole city. Working around the OP has also been an important impetus for fostering other associations. In the second year of the OP here, participants rented a bus that drove around from settlement to settlement to decide on priorities and needs, because "it would be impossible to know what was going on in another settlement without seeing it." By 2001, twenty-eight different associations had elected delegates in the proceedings.

Studies from other settings in Brazil, both in the north and northeast, thought to be less civic than the south, or from smaller municipalities, call into question the conclusion that there is some rigid necessary precondition for the establishment of OP. Successful examples exist in discouraging settings, such as in the municipality of Icapuí in Ceará and in Belém, the capital city of the state of Pará, where lack of autonomous organizing and the strength of clientelistic traditions might have been thought to make participatory democracy "impossible." A number of contextual factors and local interactions in fact account for whether democratic experiments like Porto Alegre's are possible.[33]

The most important precondition is the lack of organized opposition in civil society. Insofar as municipalities have few or no associational networks, there will also most likely not be much organized opposition. Those who have relied on regional stereotypes about the south of Brazil as an explanation for Porto Alegre's success forget that one key problem with many of the early PT administrations was the inability to find a way to give voice to organized social movements within the administration without succumbing to the charge of privileging "special interests" and without becoming embroiled in factional disputes between social movements within the party. Highly organized civil societies have thus just as often had trouble with participation. The presence of participants who do not belong to organized sectors has helped the PT administration in Porto Alegre shield itself from such charges, as well as helping prevent the demands of organized sectors from overwhelming the administration.

On the other hand, the same reviews have pointed to the importance of an adequate municipal resource base. In some municipalities in the metropolitan region of Porto Alegre, for example, OP-type reforms have not been very successful in activating civic engagement, partially because of the lack of resources for the OP.[34] But what the Porto Alegre case shows very clearly is that one lesson is that those outside of social movements and neighborhood associations have provided as much of the dynamism and legitimacy of participatory governance as those inside them, and that the central issue in capturing the dynamics of participation in the OP lies in the relationships between local configurations of civil society and a state–civil society regime.

Militants in Power: Reimagining Party-Movement Dynamics

Another important lesson of this study is the urgent need to reimagine the role of political parties and their relationship to civil society. The traditional political process model has treated political parties as institutional players in the polity that can occasionally be an ally to social movements, but owing to institutional imperatives, political parties can often cause social movements to demobilize. Social movement researchers and civil society theorists have often been skeptical of political parties, pointing to the inherently conservative logic of institutional structures, as opposed to the democratic logic of social movements.[35] A sophisticated rendering of the potential relationships between parties and movements is offered by Roberts, who argues that leftist Latin American political parties have faced considerable challenges in creating popular constituencies that span different social movements.[36] The PT has often been treated as an exception to this rule, as a political party that organically reflects social movements and has maintained a kind of internal democracy that preserves the autonomy of social movements within it.[37] In fact, the PT's dilemma early on was to decide whether it was a social movement or a party.[38]

The Porto Alegre story in the late 1990s suggests a rather different analysis. It is clear that the PT in the administration of Porto Alegre is not a social movement, and administrators no longer harbor such illusions. Its relationship to civil society is largely mediated through participatory forums like the OP. The party's relationship to civil society is not an instrumental one, however, as its reproduction in power does not depend on its direct influence on civil society. Its ability to remain in power depends on supporting forums where civil society is autonomous and empowered to make claims. This is a novel way for a political party to operate.

This kind of party practice—relating to organized and unorganized sectors via the sponsorship of autonomous participatory spaces—reflects a decade of experience with participatory democracy that has radicalized the party's attitude to civil society. This represents a shift away from traditional leftist visions of party hegemony over civil society, in which a leftist political party dominates associational life, as described by David Kertzer in the case of "Red Bologna."[39]

The stance of the PT today, honed through its turns in government, is one that neither seeks to bring social movements under the tutelage of the party (as its appendages) nor is predicated on imposing the party's ideology on government. Rather, this participatory stance is one that turns the instruments of government into tools to facilitate and foster discussion among organized and unorganized sectors in local settings so as to negotiate their relationship to government (and thus to the party) and to one another. This form of radical democracy turns social movements and unorganized citizens alike into participants, and its quality depends precisely on the autonomy of these participatory spaces from party control. At OP meetings, for instance, PT members do not participate as "party members" but rather as independent citizens or members of autonomous civil society organizations. In fact, from the purely instrumental point of view of the party's electoral reproduction there could be a danger that these spaces could be used against the party itself.

There was little attempt to control the content of discussions in participatory budgeting in Porto Alegre, and OP meetings there were far from being party-controlled spaces. It is possible to imagine, of course, that with less disciplined local parties and less vigilant community activists, such meetings might deteriorate into settings serving only to bolster the party administering them, thus subtly reintroducing tutelage. This has not, however, been the case in Porto Alegre, where participants are vigilant about what they see as political party activity and the instrumentalization of the OP. A 2001 survey of participants in the OP showed that while expressed "political sympathy" for the PT ran high among them (54 percent), this was no higher than the citywide preference for the PT (64 percent). Participation in a PT local was low among participants (less than 5 percent), and did not translate into any greater likelihood of being elected a delegate or councilor.[40]

There is also little evidence of the instrumentalization of civil society. Although the PT has continued to be elected to municipal office, voters continue to vote for other parties in the municipal legislature, who still control two-thirds of it. In fact, the distance that most civic leaders took from party affairs and their professed autonomy from party politics might mean that Porto Alegre's civic organizations would not shy away from mobilizing against the PT. When Tarso Genro quit his position as mayor in 2002 to run for governor, he won in Porto Alegre by only a few hundred votes, suggesting that this is an active civil society whose support cannot be taken for granted. Some anecdotal interviews suggest this was a targeted vote to register dissatisfaction with the ex-mayor.[41]

Nonetheless, insightful case studies raise questions about whether there has been a reintroduction of tutelage in the guise of participatory budgeting in some other PT-controlled cities.[42] And the quality of democracy has been questioned in the very large assemblies of the state-level OP in Rio Grande do Sul.[43] Certainly, an important issue for future comparative work on participatory democracy will be understanding if there are specificities that account for instances when empowered participatory reforms deteriorate into tutelage. A challenge for party and community activists who introduce empowered participation will be to protect the autonomy of participatory spaces.

The Porto Alegre case is one in which a political party remains in power by requiring the allegiance of civil society, not to a political ideology, but to a set of rules of engagement that leave civil society both its autonomy and the power to make meaningful decisions about governance. This kind of relationship is much beyond the purview of current political process theories, as well as still outside of the political imagination of activists who draw sharp distinctions between the logic and goals of political parties and civil society and who wish to preserve the purity and autonomy of civil society. Reimagining the party–civil society relationship with examples like Porto Alegre in mind is an important task for activists as well as scholars, and this book was written to help that process along.

Politicizing the Civic and Not Civilizing the
Political: Implications and Limits

Ultimately, the greatest innovation of the empowered participatory regime in Porto Alegre has been to create institutional channels to connect civic participation to what the political philosopher Chantal Mouffe, pace Carl Schmitt, calls the "the political," the inescapable realm of human conflict, which in urban peripheries in Brazil is so often about material resources and access to urban services. This empowered participatory regime has translated the innovation of social movements of the 1980s in Brazil, movements that sought to "politicize" and expand citizenship, into citywide practices of demand making that radically democratized access to resources and services. Civic participation in Porto Alegre today is not neutral, in the sense that it is not disinterested. On the contrary, civic life for most community activists in Porto Alegre today is very much about achieving collective goals, contesting resources, and engaging other collective actors who seek the same. But civic participation has clear explicit and implicit rules—in the OP, there are only antagonists, those whom we respect as fellow participants and with whom we can reconcile, and not what Mouffe would call enemies. Coordinating different interests in the OP is about finding compromises that are conditional on all parties accepting the rules of the game.

Literally thousands of Porto Alegre's poorer citizens have participated and made claims as empowered citizens in this way. But requiring participants to accept the rules may ultimately imply limits, and the continued democratic dynamism of the OP and of participatory arrangements like it depends on realizing immediate needs but deferring action on questions that cannot be resolved locally, because they require broader social changes.

It is important to continue to expand the participatory logic outward to other settings and issues. Much has happened in Porto Alegre in this direction, especially since the mid 1990s, with new avenues opening up for decision making on social services, health, and longer-term urban planning, for example. But continuing to extend it to other areas and levels of government, although complicated, will be important. One recurrent issue for community activists in the districts I studied, for instance, was the problem of violence and policing. Eventually, opening up areas such as policing to democratic control is likely to be an important extension. Another important issue that institutions like the OP will also have to face is the discussion on racism and reparations in Brazil. While some Afro-Brazilian interests are represented in the Thematic Culture Budget Meetings in Porto Alegre, the challenge will be to meet black claims for redistribution. Policing and racism are currently important issues, but addressing them largely falls outside of the jurisdiction of the municipal government.

Another limit may be that the process has become *too* successful in attracting participants and channeling the energies of civil society. Porto Alegre's citizens may become overly involved in local questions, at the expense of broader issues. Many older activists decry the "excessive pragmatism" of a younger generation more concerned with urban services than ideological discussions, in the words of Marcos, the social movement activist described in Chapter 6. And many activists mentioned the decline in contention as a worrisome issue. The question that remains is whether civil society's focus almost exclusively on local issues, as a result of the success of the participatory process in delivering results, is to its detriment. One recurring critique leveled at the process, already in its early years, even from within the PT, was that it denied access to "more comprehensive" and longer-term questions. João Couto, head of the Social Movements Department of the PT for Rio Grande do Sul, charged in 1992 that social movements had become very "localized . . . from dealing with local, current problems," and that this had made it difficult to "organize around broader questions."[44] While the municipal government has attempted to address these criticisms by expanding the participatory process to include broader areas of municipal governance, activists today express disappointment at the inability to mobilize around concerns aimed at the federal government.

A related limit involves the future of the experiment. Predicting electoral results is risky, but the PT will doubtless eventually be voted out of power in Porto Alegre, whether in the next election or twenty years down the road. It is impossible to know how the civic transformation in Porto Alegre is ultimately likely to affect the city's electorate as a whole, especially given the deeply personalist nature of Brazilian political culture and the fact that organized civil society and participation in the OP still only span a fraction of Porto Alegre's adult population. When the PT is voted out, it may be the result of popular dissatisfaction with the OP, but it is also just as likely to be due to other factors, such as dissatisfaction with the national PT administration.

In any case, it is not clear what would happen in Porto Alegre if the

PT were to lose power. Since the 1996 election, opposition candidates have proposed they would maintain the OP. Whether that would mean an unchanged OP is another question, but there is reason to believe it would likely remain in some form. But even if dismantled, from the perspective adopted here, the vibrant civil society organizations and networks may be able to sustain activism for a time, even if the state–civil society regime becomes less open and civil society actions shift to more combative claims-making. These networks may be so well organized that they may be able to pressure a new administration into reestablishing a participatory system, as happened in Recife in the late 1980s.[45] Community activists and administration alike today resist making the OP an official municipal institution, regulated by municipal law, arguing that this would, for example, undermine the process that allows budget councilors to radically alter the rules from year to year. But this makes the OP vulnerable to such electoral vagaries.

Porto Alegre's significance may lie in its impact on other places. The idea of participatory budgeting has spread widely in recent years, partially as a result of the impact of the World Social Forum. There are several reported experiences on various continents. In Latin America, there are *presupuestos participativos* in Rosário, La Plata, and Buenos Aires in Argentina, Montevideo in Uruguay, Bogotá in Colombia, Quito in Equador, and San Salvador in El Salvador. In Europe, there are the cases of Saint-Dennis in France, several municipalities in Spain (Sevilla, Córdoba, and Puente Genil), and Mons in Belgium, among others. In Asia and in Africa, there are versions of "participatory budgeting" in several municipalities in the Philippines, including Naga City; in Mumbai in India; and in Durban in South Africa. The actual number of municipalities with such experiments, whether in name or in spirit, is probably in the hundreds worldwide.

There are today a number of international initiatives to track and disseminate participatory budgeting, among them the International Budget Network,[46] the UNDP-funded International Observatory of Participatory Democracy,[47] the European-based Budget Participatif network,[48] and the International Forum of Local Authorities,[49] which convenes with the WSF. This list does not include international efforts funded by agencies like the World Bank to promote "good governance." In most cases, Porto Alegre is cited. Since the establishment of the OP in Porto Alegre in the 1990s, the city has apparently become an important international symbol of democratic innovation. The charter of the "Radically

Democratize Democracy Network," a group based in Europe with members in over twenty countries, reads, for instance,

> We have gathered because we all agree upon the fundamental innovation launched by Porto Alegre's Participatory Budget policy: the whole town's budget is discussed, decided and controlled by the citizens, in close contact with the mayor. The working rules of the process are co-elaborated and discussed again yearly by the municipal authorities and the people citizens [*sic*]. On a day-to-day basis, a new relationship is established between the legally elected municipal authorities and the civil society.[50]

The network was founded in 1999 in order to study, defend, and disseminate the experience of Porto Alegre's OP as a means of fostering similar innovations in the home countries of participants. The political vision of different networks around the idea of participatory budgeting varies, from those who emphasize "good governance and transparency" to those who see participatory budgeting as a step to socialism. Nonetheless, Porto Alegre's OP clearly occupies a central place in the democratic imagination in these networks that disseminate its principles and find inspiration in it for similar developments.

Much like Bolognese city management under the Communist Party in the 1970s, or the Mondragón cooperatives in Spain in the 1980s, or the Zapatistas in Mexico in the 1990s, Porto Alegre has achieved mythical status among activists. But its contribution to democracy should not be based on myths, but on the lessons to be learned from a dispassionate look at just what is possible in one place. Its contribution may ultimately lie in what it has to teach activists in far-flung places, more than in any particular benefit to the citizens of the city of Porto Alegre itself.

November 2004—The End of an Era?

Participatory Budgeting belongs to the city of Porto Alegre;
it is a conquest of its civil society and reflects the associative
capacity
—Porto Alegre's Mayor-elect José Fogaça (PPS)

The early polling results on October 31, 2004, were met with nervous silence and then collective reassurances at PT headquarters. Polls had closed at 5 P.M., and now, at 6, the first results were coming in. The first polling districts to announce results were upper-middle-class neighborhoods where the PT had not done particularly well in previous weeks. By the time the PT's candidate, Raul Pont, arrived at headquarters, at 7, a third of the votes had come in and the gap between him and José Fogaça, the opposing candidate at the head of the twelve-party anti-PT coalition, had decreased but remained high at 12 percent. By 8 o'clock tearful hugs among activists made it clear that most accepted defeat. With some 20 percent of the votes to be counted and a lingering 5 percent difference, a victory was still a mathematical possibility but was extremely unlikely. At 8:30 Raul Pont conceded defeat in a polarized run-off election that had pitted him, the mayor from 1997 to 2000, against a challenger from the politically insignificant PPS, or Popular Socialist Party, who had managed to create a coalition of virtually all the other political parties in Porto Alegre from the far right to the populist left. Given the electoral defeat of the PT state government in 2002, and dissatisfaction with Lula's policies at the national level, local newspapers gleefully described the new defeat as the end of the sixteen-year PT hegemony in Porto Alegre and the precursor of a national movement against Lula in 2006. The concurrent defeats in Porto Alegre and São Paulo indeed shook the party nationally, despite gains in other regions. The Mecca of the Left was no longer under PT control. Porto Alegre, according to one analyst, had declared on October 31, 2004, that it "does not belong to one party."[1]

The reasons for the electoral defeat were not straightforward. The opposition candidate ran a well-planned campaign that capitalized on anti-incumbent sentiments, calling on Porto Alegrenses to vote for "democratic alternation" (referring to the tradition of parties alternating in power) and an end to "one-party rule." Fogaça also capitalized on the lingering negative sentiments that the one term of state-level PT rule had left, not to mention the dissatisfaction with Lula's national administration. The ill-resolved national strike by the bank-tellers' union earlier in the year cooled the enthusiasm of the unions, among the party's traditional supporters in Porto Alegre. And a doctors' municipal strike close to the election also hurt the party, which was perceived as having accommodated activists on the eve of what was assumed would be an automatic electoral victory. Moreover, street campaigning did not get under way on a large scale until the run-off election, when the specter of electoral defeat was imminent. Some votes were probably also lost due to the mid-term resignation of Mayor Tarso Genro following a failed bid for state government.

But the decisive factor in the electoral upset was the middle-class vote. In this election, unlike earlier ones, the middle class voted heavily against the PT, wooed away from it by myriad forces that been galvanized under the anti-PT umbrella around Fogaça. His campaign strategy of "keeping what is good, improving the rest" proved particularly effective with middle-class voters who were ideologically opposed to the PT but recognized its effective style of governance. Fogaça's campaign promises included improving service delivery in areas such as health and social services, removing all street children from the streets, and de-bureaucratizing the municipal licensing of business, but at the same time not changing what his campaign recognized as improvements made by the PT administration. His campaign materials described him as "change in a safe way, the way we want. He knows that some changes are necessary, but without destroying the good things the city has achieved in the last few years. Fogaça will maintain the OP, the World Social Forum, and ongoing projects."[2]

With respect to the OP in particular, Fogaça cited administration materials about currently delayed projects and promised an improved and more responsive OP; unable to claim that a vote for the opposition was a vote against the OP, the PT lost one of its trump cards in its bid for a fifth municipal term. Alluding to academic discussion in Brazil (and the United States) about the origins of the OP, Fogaça often claimed in his campaign speeches that the PT did not invent or therefore "own" the OP; rather, he said, the OP was a "triumph of civil society" and reflected "the city's associative capacity." Fogaça spent the first day of his electoral campaign, in July 2004, with councilors of the OP visiting neighborhoods, and one of his first campaign promises was to "preserve and improve the OP"—by devolving more funds to it, and by creating a council for emergency expenditures without waiting for OP deliberations.[3] In a debate with Pont, Fogaça contended that he'd never deny that the OP was introduced by the PT, but that it belonged to the city, not to the party. "We understand that the OP belongs much more to the city than to the government, much more to civil society than to the state. It belongs much more to the citizens than to the municipalities. It is not a PT instrument."[4]

As to the implications of the arguments presented in the preceding chapters, little is changed. In one way, the election results confirm the importance and acceptance of the OP as a facet of civic life in Porto Alegre and as one that will outlast the PT. They also confirm what the data have shown about participants and what I have emphasized throughout, that the OP largely drew in Porto Alegre's poorer citizens and had relatively little impact on its middle class. And they confirm what the ethnography has shown: that the OP was not a partisan space—indeed, facilitators and participants made sure it did not become a staging ground for PT organizing—and that most participants saw the OP as something separate from political parties. That an opposition candidate might visit the OP and would go on neighborhood visits with councilors was regarded as quite natural; according to interviews, some councilors actively campaigned for Fogaça confident that another administration would preserve the OP.

The argument and evidence I have presented also allow us to speculate about the future of the OP under a different administration. As I have argued, the OP constituted a central axis in a state–civil society regime of openness to societal demands. This highly open regime established a logic for civic engagement that de-emphasized conflictive engagement and instead fostered engagement based on proposing policies and on participating in governance. This distinctive political culture straddled militancy and citizenship. The OP was off-limits to political party activity, but coded conflict around political positions did take place.

What happens now to the OP and to civil society depends in large part on the new administration and the overall pattern of openness to societal demands. It is possible, of course, that the new administration will indeed preserve the institution as promised and remain open to civil society demands. One would expect in this situation a continuing high level of civic engagement, and of participation in the OP. Civil society is highly organized in Porto Alegre, and highly educated in matters of governance, and it may provide an important monitoring role. Since the new administration will be greeted with skepticism by organized sectors—particularly since areas with organized workers and poor people voted for the PT, one would expect this monitoring role to be a priority at first. According to this scenario, the institution is unchanged, the logic of civic engagement remains, and political parties alternate in power.

There is alternative scenario, however, according to which the OP is not codified in law and there is no necessary presumption that, under a new administration receptive to societal demands, something called the OP will still be needed as an empowered participatory forum. It is possible, in other words, that institutions called the OP, with a similar formal structure and set of meetings that appropriates the language and symbolism of participation, will become something altogether different. The PPS is not a party with connections to social movements, and the coalition of parties in its government is composed both of politicians (especially right-wing politicians) who have been against empowered participation by the OP and of politicians (such as the populist politicians) in favor of tutelage instead of participation. The likely head of the municipal department of urban works, for example, was an appointed mayor of the city during the dictatorship and a critic of the OP. Unless political society in Porto Alegre has been won over by the logic of empowered participation and all these politicians have changed their perspectives in forming the pro-OP and anti-PT coalition for mayor, the ideological spectrum will likely include a range of positions both for and against truly empowered participation and openness to societal demands. In this case, the OP will be at first an ambiguous institution; the formal rules may remain, but there may well be attempts to reduce the actual decision-making power of the COP or to informally favor politically sympathetic organizations within the OP.

If this is the case, there is also good reason to count on organized civil society to monitor the institution and press for continued openness. If the PT does not leave behind an OP that is set in law, it leaves behind literally thousands of ex-OP participants in dozens of new neighborhood organizations who are connected to their communities and are intimately aware of the ins and outs of government functioning and budgetary affairs. This organized civil society has an immense capacity for monitoring the government and putting pressure on it. It will be practically impossible to run an institution of participatory budgeting that does not conform to high standards or that tries to manipulate participants. Since the latter scenario is the more likely, we can expect that organizations will return to combative practices, to the separation between government and movement, and to "that old militancy of going door to door" that so many activists told me they missed. Parallel cases where a government that promoted a successful participatory scheme suffered electoral defeat and the scheme was dismantled, as in Recife in the late 1980s, have ended in the eventual re-adoption of the scheme if not the re-election of the party that promoted it precisely because of this pressure. The irony here is that it can take an electoral defeat for such a highly organized civil society to become combative again.

Another irony is that had the PT adopted a different strategy in implementing the OP, one founded on a traditional vision of party hegemony over civil society, the OP and PT might have been more closely identified in Porto Alegre, making it impossible to run an opposition campaign for the OP but against the PT as Fogaça did. Of course, had that been the case, the OP would have never been a vibrant institution that so contributed to Porto Alegre's democracy and more generally to our understanding of the potential of participatory democracy around the world as I have described in these pages.

Ethnography by Numbers

Extending the Case

By the time I showed up at Dona Maria's house, six months into the fieldwork for this book, I had spent many afternoons in people's homes looking through old photographs or social movement pamphlets in the complicated process of reconstructing the history of this or that neighborhood association. A few weeks into the fieldwork, I had learned already that asking direct questions such as "Are you involved in a clientelistic relationship?" or "Do you believe in democracy?" was essentially useless.[1] People, as a rule, did not respond well to accusations, or simply knew what to tell foreigners doing research ("Me? Never." Or "Me? Always."). It had also become clear that interviews with anyone very institutionally central to the process, such as facilitators, directors of municipal departments, and so on, were not very useful in themselves. While they had tremendous knowledge and were invariably generous with their time and their contacts, these were often the situated perspectives from the institution itself, not to mention the fact that many of them were sociologists themselves with ready-made opinions on Putnam, Bourdieu, Habermas, and others.[2] In order to pursue my research questions, I thus decided instead to interview community activists, usually in their homes or walking around the neighborhood.

But I was not prepared for what Dona Maria did. She resolutely told me that I could not come into her house because she was a lifelong Catholic and she'd figured out that since I hadn't told her when we met what "university abroad" I was at, I must be doing research for the Cuban government, and she would have nothing to do with a communist. After I explained that I was studying for a Ph.D. at a U.S. university, she seemed more at ease, but she didn't want me "stealing" ideas from Porto Alegre and taking them back to the United States. I found it ironic that Dona Maria, a professed follower of Leonel Brizola, a populist labor leader exiled for almost two decades, who was once described as the "greatest threat" to Brazilian democracy, would have such strong aversion to possible Cuban agents, but felt better with a U.S. researcher.

Dona Maria had nonetheless caught me in an unconscious omission when I had introduced myself at a meeting some days before: as a Brazilian with a *gaúcho* accent (which I must have inherited from my parents, since I had never lived in this part of Brazil), I found myself comfortably letting people assume what wasn't true: that I was also a local. And although I would have gotten around to telling them what university I was at, because I (unfailingly) carried out the human subjects protocol before interviewing someone, it seemed better to talk about where I was from then, using the inevitable questions about how I wound up in the United States as a way to get started. This was partly a matter of building rapport, because I early on had the mistaken idea that an environment full of leftists must be imbued with anti-Americanism. But probably more to the point, this was a reflection of my "sense of the field"—I hated the treatment foreigners sometimes received, so full of pomp and deference, especially in the city's working-class and poorer neighborhoods. I had witnessed this many times and probably hoped to avoid it.[3]

The visit with Dona Maria was a turning point for the project, as at that point I realized that I not only had to be more self-conscious about my presentation, but also that the whole enterprise of getting to questions I was interested in (at that time, a diffuse set of concerns about the political cultural impact of participatory democracy) required a more careful and nuanced understanding of the meanings actors attached to political practices, as well as attention to the way this understanding varied across social space. This would be the only way to deal with conflicting accounts, for instance, and the set of investments actors like Dona Maria had in a certain way of telling the story. It was not simply that Dona Maria's understanding of me stood in the way of the truth, but that her understandings of politics (a connection to populist politicians, a rejection of overt leftist politics) were connected to her practices and her place in the social world of community activists. As a community activist, she was guided by a certain set of understandings and had a reputation to protect; as I learned, part of this reputation depended on avoiding the kinds of relationships one might impute to someone who would collaborate with a Communist Party activist. In short, I realized that to address the questions I was pursuing to my satisfaction would require more than counting the numbers of neighborhood associations and asking actors about them; it would require ethnography: paying attention to meanings, practices, and relationships across social space. But I was also keenly aware of the need for other types of research: U.S.-based ethnographers can often make assumptions about background contexts that I would not be able to make, at least for a U.S. audience. And particularly in this case, the historical specificity of the social changes here (possibly unique ones) frankly required me, the researcher, to document in some detail these changes in order for the case to be believable to those reading the account.

Luckily, the theoretical body of writing from which I drew inspiration, what I've referred to as "relational sociology"—lent itself easily to the research strategy I came to define, one that drew on ethnographic, historical, and aggregate types of evidence. Bourdieu, for instance, calls for "a multivariate ethnomethodology" and a rejection of a priori methodological stances.[4] Less fortunately, current trends in North American sociology dictate against this kind of eclecticism, and despite inspiring examples of theoretical ethnographies, there are few models for the mixing and matching of approaches. This appendix offers an account, by way of justification, of the methodological strategy I pursued in this study, first discussing the case study itself, then the ethnographic choices I made, followed by a brief discussion of nonethnographic methods and how they were related back to the research.

The (Exceptional) City as Case Study

Although my research contains comparisons within the city as well as comparisons over time, I have framed my research as a theoretically driven case study. Many of the most famous studies of city politics were case studies, such as Robert Dahl's study of New Haven (1961), Robert and Helen Lynd's study of Muncie (1929), or Floyd Hunter's study of Atlanta (1953), because the case study allows a certain "situated groundedness" (Walton 1992). The logic of inquiry with this project is slightly different, however, and is related to the insight that although case studies do not permit certain types of generalizations that comparisons or "larger-*n*" studies permit, the case study of a relevant or unique case can allow for theoretical innovation because of its attention to process and anomaly. The apparent success of the project in Porto Alegre is unusual in terms of our expectations and of the bodies of theory in question. As an instance of state-civil society relations, it forces us to *rethink theory*.

This is akin to the "extended case method" (Burawoy 1992: 2000), in which there is a constant dialogue between field notes and theory. This method focuses on theory building by contradiction and difference, rather than attempting to use cases to illustrate general principles or creating generalizable theories by pure induction. Theoretical gaps and contradictions or empirical anomalies force our attention to the case at hand with a view to reconstructing theory. Michael Burawoy suggests that the extended case method is thus immune to the criticism of significance. If case studies are prone to being criticized for being "insignificant" in the potential universe of cases, this is because they seek abstract explanations and theories founded on "covering-law models." Explanations founded on historically specific cases that are anomalous are significant for the theory by virtue of their uniqueness (Burawoy 1992: 280).

The extended case method also deals with the question of theoretical relevance of ethnographic work dealing with small-scale action, a problem distinct from that of the relevance of the single case. In principle, the logic of my project is that while the *case* of Porto Alegre merits interest and points to gaps in theory, close analysis of specific situations, such as meetings or the functioning of one neighborhood association will shed light on the case of Porto Alegre. It was a study that required attention to micro-interactions (ethnographic detail, life-history interviews) in the context of the city as a whole. This meant ethnography with an eye to relational setting, as well as "sampling and variance" in the field, as Becker (1998) suggests, complemented by an array of nonethnographic evidence.

Why Ethnography?

The principal component of the research was ethnographic. Recent work on civic networks and political practices has begun to rely on participant observation and ethnographic methods for its specific insights (Eastis 1998; Eliasoph 1998; Lichterman 1996, 1999; Patillo-McCoy 1998), echoing calls for ethnographic interventions in social movement theory and for analyses of culture to engage studies of politics (Berezin 1997; Johnston and Klandermans 1995). Despite drawbacks, ethnography allows us to answer a number of questions simply not accessible by other means: questions of meaning, intention and purpose, implicit rules, among others, which cannot be answered by interviews alone (Lichterman 1998).

Research on the themes of civil society and citizenship has recently developed a robust English-language tradition (Eliasoph 2002; Lichterman 2000; Wood 2002; Becker 2002; Brown 1997), compounding a resurgence in interest in ethnographies of politics and social movements among the Latin American urban poor (Auyero 2002; Rubin 1999; Hanchard 1998; Gay 1994; Lancaster 1992). As all of these ethnographies attest, projects about "ways of doing politics," practices, and performances require a certain amount of observation of these *as they happen, and where they happen.* In this case, this meant OP, popular council, and neighborhood association meetings. To simply ask people about "politics" and "citizenship" would be to miss an important facet of the phenomenon (cf. Lichterman 1996).[5] Studies of language and culture have to pay attention to the internal coherence of cultural codes but also to the unspoken, performative, and structuring elements of these codes, the "extralinguistic" factors, as the implicit rules of who can and cannot speak, who determines the rules of "proper" speech, and access to proper ways of speaking (Bourdieu 1977, 1984, 1989). Deployment of political identities involves strategies of presentation of the (political) self (Eliasoph 1995).

The concepts I explore in this research project—among them, "tradition," "civic practice," and "public-minded communication"—are not necessarily easy to access in a research context and need to be "operationalized." Existing ethnographic work on "socialist" or "progressive" experiments, such as David Kertzer's (1980) study of "Red Bologna," Roger Lancaster's (1992) ethnography of Managua neighborhoods during the revolution, C. M. Hann's (1993) political anthropology of eastern European socialism, and Michael Brown's (1997) study of AIDS activism in Vancouver, relies precisely on this premise. What ethnography promises in the context of "extended case methodology" is the reconstruction of theory with "local" or "grounded" categories. The most useful ethnographies in this context are those that allow enough of "local categories" to come through and link them to theory.

In the course of the ethnography, I attended as many district-level meetings as possible, where I eventually developed a rapport with a number of activists. I also came to participate in a number of smaller meetings in neighborhood associations, churches, and community centers. I occasionally acted as note taker for the meetings and sometimes helped with organizational tasks. I complemented the ethnography with life-history accounts, unstructured interviews, and conducted a number of surveys. I was able to interview almost all regular participants and "known" community activists in the three districts, as well as a number of key informants, amounting to a total of over 150 interviews, some of which lasted for hours. I carried out a number of archival searches, gathering several hundred documents from advisory groups, NGOs, and government bodies, as well as systematic research of newspapers from 1986 to 2000. I also carried out a series of surveys of OP participants, neighborhood activists, and citywide active associations.

Why Not Only Ethnography?

Nonetheless, this book may strike ethnographic purists as "not ethnographic enough." At times, I rely on a great deal of aggregate evidence, I spend much of my time in *too many sites*, and I constantly interpolate ethnographic with nonethnographic kinds of evidence. However, as noted above, because my units of observation were not the case, it was necessary to pursue ethnography with an eye to variance and sampling, as well as to draw on archival and aggregate evidence. "Variance and sampling" in ethnography means paying attention to what and whom you are observing and interviewing in the context of a larger social space. Just as one would not do an ethnography of a firm by only interviewing its directors (unless one were doing an ethnography of directors), it would not make sense to do a case study of a city by carrying out ethnography in one or two neighborhoods (unless one were carrying out a case study of one or two neighborhoods). In addition, while a study of neighborhood life in one or two neighborhoods would no doubt be interesting and important, I was concerned with just how unique the neighborhood might be in this context; I was also especially concerned with relationships among neighborhoods at the sites where they collectively interfaced with the state and with one another.

In the ethnographic research I pursued a "most-variance strategy," choosing to do ethnography in three districts of the city chosen for contrasting starting points, with OP meetings in each district as the focal point of investigation. Districts seemed the natural level for research; it is at the district level that activists from different neighborhoods meet, and it is there that much of the debating and wheeling and dealing over demands takes place. And it was at the district-level that the political intrigue around supposed patronage-schemes took place. I chose to also observe citywide council meetings of the Conselho do Orçamento Participativo (COP), or Budget Council, as a site for comparison, to have a sense of how demands from the districts scaled up or not, and whether there were distinctions in the interactions at that higher level.

This strategy involved a trade-off, of course, in that it meant relatively less attention to individual neighborhoods. It also involved a choice on my part about what to treat as "civil society": I chose to focus on what is sometimes referred to in Latin American Studies as the "popular sector"—that is, the working classes and the urban poor. Part of the choice was dictated to me by the field—in time I found that middle-class participants and organizations were relatively less represented in the district-level meetings of the OP that I was using as my focal point. Middle-class Brazilians, as discussed elsewhere, largely do not form neighborhood associations. Instead, they participate in settings such as trade and professional associations, which are less important in the OP. Rather than divert the study to organizations and activists that have been less involved in the OP, I chose to focus on popular sectors and neighborhood associations, choosing as my axis of comparison different relational configurations in the districts. The "urban poor" have also figured so prominently in discussions of Latin American cities that offering a different representation of them seemed a politically important thing to do.

I also carried out extensive archival research, came up with estimates of numbers of existing neighborhood associations, and fielded a number of surveys. This complementary research permitted broader claims about participants in the OP, civil society at large, and changes in associationalism over time. A number of the questions in the surveys were generated directly from the ethnography. Certain ways of posing questions and the kinds of potential answers to expect all came from the ethnography. The reverse was also true: it was enormously enriching to the interview process to have a sense both of the city's history (from the archival research) and of what some of the broad patterns were. I often used these data as "provocations" to start off interviews.

Sources of Bias

There were a number of potential sources of "bias," particularly in interviews about sensitive topics. I learned in the course of fieldwork what experienced ethnographers know: that there is no going around the process of developing rapport and trust—there is no trickery or perfect wording of questions that will compensate for mistrust. Many of the questions I was interested in were sensitive, and in a politically charged environment, where friends and foes of the administration might use information about delays in projects (or a crooked neighborhood association president) in partisan ways, it was not surprising that getting to some topics was sometimes challenging. Part of the problem also arose from a "triumphalist" bias—it was not uncommon for neighborhood association activists to exaggerate past woes and the role of the administration as "savior" of the community movement. Some tended to want to show a foreign scholar the best side of the city.

Even being aware of all these issues, the "presentation of self" in interviews created what I later would feel were distortions, or exaggerations, not to mention occasional attempts at deception. The only way to deal with this, and to feel confident about my interpretation, was systematically to cover enough of the social space. This meant tracking down neighborhood activists who didn't participate in the OP and those who still actively opposed the process. Finally, although thorough, systematic research involves effort, patience, and methodological sophistication, it does not absolve the researcher from the task of interpretation. No amount of survey data can make up for lack of a learned sense of the field that becomes partially instinctive.

The Research Strategy

In the course of the study, therefore, I collected life-history accounts, carried out interviews, did archival research, and conducted a number of surveys to supplement my ethnographic evidence. The bulk of my research was ethnographic observation in the three districts and in the COP. Meetings in the districts took place roughly once a week, and the COP's meetings took place twice a week, and it was not uncommon for discussions to go on elsewhere afterwards, at a bar or someone's house. For a while, I also attended meetings of the PT cell in two of the districts, but I eventually decided that this was having a chilling effect on non-PT members, who became more guarded with me as a result.

As a secondary priority, in light of the number of meetings I was already attending, I attended neighborhood association meetings, especially if the OP was being discussed, focusing on associations to which some of the key activists I was becoming friends with belonged. In almost two years of fieldwork, I attended meetings essentially every night of the week and came to appreciate the statement that the problem with socialism is that it takes up too many evenings! I tape-recorded some meetings but relied on notes in most cases.

I was able to interview almost all regular participants and "known" community activists in the three districts, amounting to a total of over 150 interviews, varying in length from half an hour to, in one case, eight hours, spread out over a few days.[6] The format of the interview was an unstructured conversation, usually provoked by a statement or, more often, by asking interviewees to tell me their stories. I also interviewed a few key activists of citywide renown and administrators. However, while a number of people in the administration showed me personal generosity and patience beyond any job description, I found as a rule, with a few notable exceptions, that they were generally not good interview subjects, because they felt obliged to put the administration in the best possible light. A research assistant carried out some additional structured interviews with people whom I had missed while in Porto Alegre. All of my interviews were then transcribed, and I carried out my analysis using both text and sound recording.

The second largest component involved archival work. A number of archival materials, numbering several hundred documents, from a variety of advisory groups and NGOs in Porto Alegre were available, as were documents from the administration and from neighborhood associations. I also utilized a number of important secondary works to complement these in order to reconstruct the history of social movements and neighborhood associations in Porto Alegre prior to 1989. These included several unpublished studies, cited throughout, and a few published reconstructions of neighborhood histories based on oral histories. In addition, I systematically reviewed Porto Alegre's largest newspaper, *Zero Hora*, from 1986 to 2000. From 1988 onwards, there were electronic records, but for the previous years, this required going through individual physical copies. These documents were coded and classified for thematic and geographical references. As documented by scholars who systematically review newspaper coverage of protest events (Koopmans 2002), there are many potential pit-falls in using newspaper sources in this way, most of which relate to underre-porting of protest activity and the political slant of the papers. Patterns attrib-uted to the way social movements or protest activity play out may simply be an artifice of newspaper biases. However, *Zero Hora* is a newspaper notoriously critical of the PT administration, which would suggest a bias toward overre-porting of municipal protest activity. Since my finding, as expected from inter-views, is a decline in protest activity, we can be fairly certain that it is unlikely to have been "produced" by the newspaper biases. I cross-checked two years of data against the records produced by another newspaper, the *Correio do Povo*, and the results were similar.

A series of surveys of participants, neighborhood activists, and active asso-ciations, carried out in conjunction with a local NGO and with my colleagues Benjamin Goldfrank and Marcelo K. Silva, were the third component of my re-search. These surveys were carried out between 1998 and 2001 and include a large survey of general participatory budget participants (carried out in 1998 and replicated in 2000 by CIDADE);[7] a survey of delegates (1998); a survey of councilors with Goldfrank (1999); a survey of associations in the three districts (1999); and a large municipal survey of active neighborhood associations with Silva (2002). In line with the methodological belief implicit in relational argu-ments that the "quantitative-qualitative divide" is artificial,[8] the aggregate evi-dence from the surveys is interspersed throughout the text rather than being relegated to a "quantitative chapter," as one might be tempted to do. For the sake of readability, only some of the results, and not the actual formal statistical tests, are reported here (see, however, Baiocchi 2001a and 2001b for further de-tails).

Each of the surveys employed a different sampling logic, in accordance with particular research needs and available resources. The 1998 survey of partici-pants was applied to a representative sample of OP participants drawn from first plenary meetings in March and April of 1998. Respondents were randomly selected from participants at each regional and thematic meeting and were asked to answer to a questionnaire. If the person had difficulty in answering the questionnaire in written format, an interviewer would apply the questionnaire. The sample of participants (1,039) was roughly 8 percent of the total number of participants for that year. The survey was designed and applied by myself, members of an NGO, CIDADE, in Porto Alegre, and municipal government employees. In the analysis, the data were weighted so as to avoid bias from the oversampling of participants who might come to both thematic and district meetings. Data from this survey were published by CIDADE in 1999 under the title *Orçamento Participativo—Quem e a População Que Participa e Que Pensa do Processo*, but without the weighting, giving somewhat different results. These data were also made publicly available at the CIDADE website.

The 1999 survey of delegates refers to a survey of delegates in three of the city's districts (Norte, Nordeste, Partenon) in May and June of 1999. This survey was applied to all the delegates present at a single meeting, randomly chosen, and the response rate (total $n = 104$), corresponded to over 75 percent of delegates in the three districts. The same survey was applied to councilors at the Budget Council (*n* = 39). The 1999 survey of neighborhood associations (n = 90) was carried out in the same districts between February and May. This survey was based on lists of associations available from UAMPA, the municipal administration, and popular councils. Each identified association was approached directly, and a representative of its directorate was interviewed. The response rate corresponded to over 75 percent of associations for the three districts. The logic of a survey in three districts, as opposed to a sample of all associations in the city, was to capture the variance within the districts, as well as to detect networks among associations.

The 2002 survey of associations (*n* = 167), carried out in conjunction with Marcelo K. Silva, was based on a sample of neighborhood associations and a number of sources, including municipal government, UAMPA, and listings in the phone book. Every association in the three districts was contacted, as was every fourth association in the remaining three districts of the city. Not every association's contact information was correct, and not every association eventually participated, but we reached a total of 75 percent of associations.

Earlier survey data are from surveys conducted in 1993 by the Municipal Administration and Luciano Fedozzi (Prefeitura Municipal de Porto Alegre and Luciano Fedozzi. 1993. "Participantes do Orçamento Participativo, Pesquisa.") and in 1995 by CIDADE and Rebecca Abers.

Estimating Civil Society Data

Estimating the number of functioning voluntary associations in Porto Alegre at different points in time is a challenging task, and the data given here are the best possible estimates, given the resource constraints. Studies of civil society in Brazil have utilized one of two sources to estimate associational activity, neither of which proved particularly useful by itself in the case of Porto Alegre. Scholars like Wanderley Guilherme dos Santos (1993) and Renato Boschi (1987) used municipal registries of associations in the offices of the city *cartórios* (notaries public). In the case of Porto Alegre, that strategy did not yield useful results. A sample of associations registered in the municipal *cartório* showed that many registered associations were "phantoms," often registered under the name of the same person. There are several explanations for this: in Porto Alegre, as may have been true in other cities, government agencies during the dictatorship went about "creating" sympathetic neighborhood associations, often writing the statutes; in addition, participation in some of the federally funded charity programs, such as the *ticket de leite* (milk ticket) program required official registration with the *cartório* (and nothing else) as a prerequisite. Such data did not, therefore, yield reliable estimates either of actually functioning associations in the present or of associational activity in the past. While the number of associations registered in the *cartório* had increased over the 1989–99 time period, it was theoretically possible that this was accompanied by an actual decline of associations.

The second source often used for associational activity in Brazil are two household surveys by the Instituto Brasileiro de Geografia e Estatística in 1988 and 1996. According to these, there was an increase in associational participation in the metropolitan region of Porto Alegre, and participation was higher there than in most other metropolitan regions in Brazil in 1996, when it essentially remained steady for the country as a whole, but the data are only disaggregated to the level of the metropolitan region. This makes the data unusable to test the argument advanced here, because the metropolitan region of Porto Alegre includes several additional municipalities in Porto Alegre's periphery, which does not allow an analysis of changes within the municipality itself.

The data for Porto Alegre's associational changes, then, are triangulated from available historical sources, cross-checking with retrospective data from currently functioning associations. Historically, I relied on City Hall lists and listings with the União das Associações de Moradores de Porto Alegre. UAMPA maintains a list of neighborhood associations registered with it, and requires payment of dues, which provides a filter for phantom associations. In 1987, the Collares administration carried out a survey of associations. This may have been biased toward more sympathetic associations (although it does include a number of PT associations), but it provides an additional measure of associationalism for the first year in my series, 1988. For the years following, if an entity described as a "neighborhood association" appeared for two years in a row as such in an OP listing, I considered it an active association for my count. Although these listings are potentially restrictive (for example, UAMPA may not list some conservative neighborhood associations, despite its nonpartisan stance), a restrictive method is preferable to an inflationary one. In addition, since there is no reason to believe that the standard of restrictiveness changed over time, we can assume that the growth in associations found here is real, and not an artifice.

In addition, as a measure of cross-checking, I used surveys of associations carried out in 1999 and 2002. Both surveys of neighborhood associations showed that almost 50 percent of associations currently functioning had been either founded or reactivated since 1989, which roughly supports the finding here that associationalism doubled in numbers in the time period in question. This mirrors the finding by Avritzer that of all associations encountered, and not only neighborhood associations, 37.5 percent had been founded in the 1990s.

Glossary

churrasco	barbecue
colarinho-branco	literally, "white-collar," i.e., a "suit"
companheiro	literally, "partner"; equivalent to "fellow citizen," or "brother"
conselho popular	popular council; these autonomous settings in civil society are similar to citizens' leagues in the United States or *consejos populares* in various Latin American countries
Dona	a term of respect for women, used with the first name; "Seu" is used for men
gaúcho	a native of Rio Grande do Sul
novela	soap opera
petistas	PT members
prefeito	mayor
prefeitura	city hall
vereador(a)	a member of the municipal legislature, equivalent to a city councilor in the United States
vila	a generic term encompassing working-class and poor neighborhoods; many vilas are self-constructed settlements in unzoned land; I use the terms "slum" and "favela" in the text to refer to substandard settlements

Notes

Preface

1. See "Lula's Message for Two Worlds," *Economist*, January 30, 2003.

2. See, e.g., the resolutions collected in Fisher and Ponniah 2003 or Cattani 2001, which read as "contemporary *Cahiers de doleánces*" (registers of grievances), according to Hardt and Negri 2003: xvii. For a discussion of the Global Social Justice movement, see Brecher, Costello, and Smith 2000 and Ancelovici 2002. See also the website of the World Social Forum, http://Forumsocialmundial.org.br.

3. Wallerstein 2002.

4. See Cohen and Rogers 1995.

5. Koopmans and Rucht 2002.

1. "Attention, Companheiros!"

1. Although most of the interviews I conducted and some of the meetings I attended were tape-recorded, interview and field note materials should not be taken as direct transcriptions. The names and identifying details of particular individuals have been changed, but names of districts, streets, and organizations have not.

2. On the "crisis" of democracy, see Markoff 1999; see also Jessop 1993; on innovations across the state-society divide, see Evans 1996.

3. Ferreira 2000.

4. See, e.g., Lagos 2001.

5. Habermas 1989. For the "SES Model" of civic engagement, see Marschall 2001; Verba and Nie 1972. For applications to Brazil, see Ferreira 1999, 2000; McDonough, Shin, and Moises 1998.

6. See Auyero 1999b for a discussion of this "metonymic prison." For a different, and convincing, rational-choice analysis of democratic action among the urban poor as a bounded-rationality problem, see Dietz 1998.

7. Fung 2003. See also Jean Cohen 1999b for a discussion of these "two faces."

8. Mansbridge 1980: 275.

9. The phrase is from Auyero 2001.

10. On the concept of "prefiguring," see Polletta 1999.

11. Doimo 1995; Dagnino 1994.

12. Fraser 1992.

13. The Empowered Participatory Governance, or EPG, approach of Fung and Wright 2003, which I take as an important starting point for the investigation here, does not centrally address the issue.

14. FESC 1999.

15. Already in 1988, for example, Porto Alegre's literacy rate was 93 percent in contrast with metropolitan Brazil's average of 87 percent, according to 1988 IBGE data.

16. Data according to UNDP 2004.

17. Perz 2000.

18. Neto and Araújo 1999.

19. Oliveira and Barcellos 1990.

20. Bak 1985.

21. Alvarez 1993; Nickson 1995; Montero 2001.

22. Brazil 1989. On the whole, Brazil's decentralization has had the result of "mixed but largely disappointing results in terms of service delivery, popular participation, strengthened local elites, and reform initiatives," according to Weyland 1999: 1006.

23. According to data from the Ministério da Fazenda.

24. IBASE 1992; Souza 2002. See also Pont 2000, who describes the situation as an unfunded mandate for municipalities.

25. Horn 1994.

26. Fischer, Colomer, and Teixeira, 1993.

27. See Instituto Pólis 2001; Jacobi 2000; Lebauspin 2000; Spink and Clemente 1997; Caccia Bava, Spink, and Paulics, 2001.

28. Ames 2002.

29. O'Donnell 1988, Pinheiro 1991, Weffort 1984.

30. Mainwaring 1986a, 1999; Weyland 1996; Ames 2002; Power 2000.

31. Ferreira finds that there was no significant growth in associational density in metropolitan regions between 1988 and 1996, while the percentage of persons participating in any group declined slightly between the years in question. Ferreira finds that the percentage of those participating in a neighborhood association in Brazil's six largest metropolitan regions increased from 2.3 percent to 2.5 percent, while the percentage of persons participating in any group in civil society declined from 14.3 percent to 12.1 percent. See Ferreira 2000. Some of the results of the 1996 survey are available in IBGE 2000.

32. Nylen 2002a.

33. Lagos 2001.

34. See, among others, Cardoso 1988; Diniz 1983; Durham 1984; Moises et al. 1982; Telles 1987.

35. Viola and Mainwaring 1987.

36. Pickvance 1999; Alvarez 1993.

37. Doimo 1995; Cardoso 1994; Telles 1994.

38. Moura and Pinho 1993.

39. Paoli 1992. Paoli has called this a "democratic invention" of social movements.

40. Dagnino 1994. See also Dagnino 1998, 2002.

41. Dagnino 1994: 108.

42. Shildo 1998.

43. Oliveira 1986: 16; Keck 1992.

44. Lowy 1987.

45. Beozzo and Lisboa 1983; Lowy 1987.

46. It elected 36 mayors in 1988; 54 mayors in 1992, 111 in 1996, and 187 in 2000. By 2001, 18 percent of Brazilians were under one of the 187 PT municipal administrations.

47. Menenguello 1989; A. Singer 2001.

48. It has been noted that the PT leadership tended to come less from the original basis of the union movement and more from the ranks of activists from the progressive church, the student movement, and other social movements, as well as garnering significant middle-class support. See Gaglietti 1999; Neves 1993; A. Singer 2001.

49. Magalhães et al. 1999.

50. Utzig 1996: 210.

51. Vacarezza et al. 1989.

52. See Grazia and Ribeiro 2001. By one estimate, over half of the 400 current (2001–4) municipalities with OP are not under the PT.

53. Conniff 1981; Cortes 1974.

54. Noll and Trindade 1995; Santos 2001.

55. Noll 1996; Araújo Passos and Noll 1996.

56. Goldfrank 2001.

57. Ribeiro 2000.

58. The numbers of registered participants in the first-round assembly were, for 1990, 628; for 1991, 3,086; for 1992, 6,168; for 1993, 6,975; for 1994, 8,011; for 1995, 8,495; for 1996, 7,653; for 1997, 11,075; for 1998, 11,790; for 1999, 14,776; and for 2000, 14,408. The number of *actual* participants is difficult to estimate, because these numbers ignore preparatory informal meetings, for which there is no count.

59. FESC 1999. "Minimum wage" is a convenient unit for measuring income in Brazil, given currency fluctuations. As of February 2001, it fluctuated around U.S.$70 per month, and "poverty" is often informally regarded as a household income of two minimum wages per month or less.

60. From 1993 to 1998, between 35 and 40 percent of participants were first-time participants, and between 18–20 percent had no affiliation in civil society. See Abers 2000; see also "Levantamento de Participantes do Orçamento Participativo; Quem são e que pensam do processo," 1999; "Participantes Do Orçamento Participativo, Pesquisa," 1993.

61. The relatively lower participation of women at the council level is explored statistically in Baiocchi 2001a.

62. Abers 2000; Marquetti 2001; Pozzobon 1998; Utzig 1999. See also the administration's own investment plans, available online at www.portoalegre.rs. gov.br

63. According to official data of the Ministério da Fazenda. According to the data, Porto Alegre's annual budget fluctuated between U.S.$210 and U.S.$785 million in the 1990s, with an average of U.S.$436 million.

64. In terms of amount of money spent, 35 percent of OP projects have been district-specific, and the remainder are "institutional projects," such as the renovation of an administration building, or projects that cover more than one district, like a thoroughfare. Investments per district per capita are up to five times higher in poorer districts.

65. According to Marquetti 2001: 141, by 2000 87 percent of planned projects were completed, 6 percent were in progress, and 6 percent were in the planning stage.

66. As documented by Regina Pozzobon and Adalmir Marquetti. Pozzobon finds, for instance, that 98 percent of households were connected to the sewer system by 1998, compared to 75 percent ten years earlier. Betweeen 1991 and 2000, homes with running water increased to 99 percent from 95 percent, and those with network sewage increased to 84 percent from 56 percent. Pozzobon 1998: 3–10; IBGE 1991, 2000.

67. Increasing to 46,505 from 14,838 according to Marquetti 2001: 152. Gross enrollment rates increased to 92.2 percent in 2000 from 82.6 percent in 1991, according to the IBGE.

68. The government built an average of 1,000 new homes a year for families in need, compared to an average of under 400 for the 1964–88 period.

69. According to DATASUS data, in 2000, Porto Alegre's per capita health expenditures were three and a half times the Brazilian average (http://www. datasus.gov.br/ [accessed December 3, 2003]). Part, but not all, of this is due to the fact that larger, southern cities, are privileged in Brazilian federal structures of distribution of funds. Based on IPEA data (http://www.ipea.gov.br/ [accessed December 3, 2003), a better comparison is possible against the two other state capitals in the south of Brazil, Curitiba and Florianópolis, which had similar per capita municipal budgets for the 1990s per capita annual budgets of R$377, 329, and 334 respectively. Porto Alegre's expenditures over the 1990s in per capita terms were 94 percent of those on education in Curitiba; its housing and urbanism expenditures were 118 percent, while its health and sanitation expenses were 292 percent. In comparison to Florianópolis, the numbers were 75 percent, 91 percent, and 533 percent, respectively.

70. See Marquetti 2001. For the 1989–2000 period, education was 19.1 percent of overall budget, housing 19.4 percent and health 18.8 percent; in 1984–88, the figures were, respectively, 13.2 percent, 18.8 percent and 14.0 percent.

71. Abers 2000; Fedozzi 1997, 2000; Baierle 1992.

72. Such as those in São Paulo under Mayor Erundina in 1989–92, the many other failed PT administrations in the 1989–92 and 1993–96 periods, and the more limited participatory experiments in Mexico City, Montevideo, and Córdoba, Argentina, among many others. On similar experiments in Brazil, see

Avritzer 2002; Souza 2002; Sanchez 2002; Baiocchi 2003; Lesbaupin 1996; Nylen 1997b, 2002a, 2002b. In addition to Porto Alegre, experiments in a number of other larger cities have been described. For São Paulo, see Couto 1995; Magalhães 1999; Macaulay 1996; Singer 1996, Santos Ferreira et al. 1994. For Santo André and Diadema, see Klink 1999; Ribeiro 1999; Simões 1992. For Belo Horizonte, see Avritzer 2000b; Azevedo 1997; Somarriba and Dulci 1997. For Fortaleza, see Pinto 1992. For Belém, see Guidry and Petit 2003. For smaller towns, see Silva 2003; Nylen 1995, 2002a, 2002b. For other examples from Latin America, see Schönwälder 1998; Harnecker 1991; Goldfrank 2002, 2003.

73. Novel institutional forms: Abers 2000; Santos 1998; Utizig 1998. Governmental performance: Marquetti 2000; Pozzobon 1998; Utzig 1996.

74. For such an empirical definition of the public sphere, see Baiocchi 2003. Examples exist in which government-sponsored assemblies and meetings have had such a limited democratic component, such as described for "Great Society Programs" in the United States. See Piven and Cloward 1979. In the context of socialist regimes, see Bengelsdorf 1994; Zhou 1993. The history of Latin America in particular is also replete with "participatory assemblies" sponsored by populist leaders or military dictators to simply legitimate governmental plans. See Bak 1985; Conniff 1981; Dietz 1998; Eckstein 1977; Hamilton 1984.

75. Genro 1999. See also Fischer and Moll 2000 with theoretical reflections on the theme.

76. Avritzer 2002: 79; Santos 1998.

77. For some of the current discussion, see Borja et al. 1997; Fisher and Kling 1993; Reilly 1995; Evans 1996; Fung et al. 2003.

78. Skocpol and Fiorina 1999.

79. Kriesi and Wisler 1999: p. xiii

80. See the special issue of *Sociological Forum* dedicated to this debate.

81. As echoed by scholars who have recently asked "How Social Movements Matter" and "the Impact of Social Movements." See Kriesi and Wisler 1999 and Giugni et al. 1999.

82. Somers 1993: 595.

83. In thinking about the state, for example, Bourdieu and Wacquant (1992: 111) insist that political and bureaucratic change remain a mystery if we assume that the state is a "well-defined, clearly bounded and unitary reality that stands in relation of externality with outside force." Similarly, a relational approach would challenge the "externality" of civil society.

84. Allowing us to explore what Cohen and Rogers (1992) call the "artifactuality" of civic engagement—how voluntary associations reflect a broader social context.

85. Migdal 2001.

86. See Laclau and Mouffe 1985 and Laclau 2000.

87. Institutional openings create incentives for certain kinds of collective action from below that aim to expand these openings, which then may have the effect of encouraging elite collective action to close off these openings. See Markoff 1997.

88. Dahl 1961's description of New Haven in the 1950s, in which associa-

tions of interest representation dialogue with representative institutions would be an example, as would many examples of liberal democracies, in which much of the input occurs through representative institutions.

89. The concept of a tutelage regime I develop is similar to clientelism, developed by political scientists, but while clientelism refers specifically to a patron-client dyad, tutelage regimes refer to the overall pattern of state openness to societal demands. See Migdal 2001.

90. See Davis 1994: 64, for a description of the Consejo Consultivo de La Ciudad de México in the late 1920s.

91. Other regimes documented in the literature vary from starkly authoritarian regimes that place high constraints on societal activity and are open to few societal demands, such as the tsarist regime described by Laclau 2000, to affirmative democratic regimes that place relatively few constraints on such activity and are highly open to societal demands, such as Scandinavian welfare states described in Esping-Anderson 1985.

92. Evans 2002: 22.

93. Mische forthcoming. See also Bourdieu 1977, 1990, 1998.

94. Mansbridge 1980: 160, 273.

95. Eliasoph 1990; Goffman 1959.

96. Auyero 1999a; Gay 1995; Gohn 1982; Zaluar 1985.

97. Burawoy 1991, 2000.

98. Dahl 1961.

99. On "most variance strategy," see Becker 1998.

2. A City Transformed

1. Schmidtt 1993: 72.

2. Rech 1988.

3. See "V Encontro Municipal do PT—Porto Alegre. Resolucoes," 1989, 1.

4. See "Resolucoes Do Encontro Municipal Do PT—Porto Alegre," 1993, 5–6.

5. Baierle 1992; Fedozzi 1997.

6. Goldfrank 2003; id. forthcoming. Goldfrank also argues that in comparative perspective, Porto Alegre's opposition parties were disorganized and did not work to undermine the OP as has been the case with similar participatory experiments by leftist administrations elsewhere in Latin America.

7. Conniff 1981.

8. Pont 1985.

9. "O Movimento Comunitario Em Porto Alegre" (internal document), 1986.

10. This pact between neighborhood associations and municipal government did, however, also foster some discord, with a few neighborhood associations founding an "anti-paternalist league" in the early 1960s in order to demand greater autonomy from municipal government. See ibid.

11. Nonetheless, in 1966, there was another municipal conference, in which a model statute for neighborhood associations was distributed and a "diploma of community leadership" for politically endorsed community leaders was introduced.

12. Guareschi 1980.

13. Doimo 1995. According to Baierle 1992, FRACAB supported an alternative May Day event in 1978 and a citywide strike of construction workers.

14. Menegat 1995; Guareschi 1980.

15. Guareschi 1980.

16. Ferreti 1984.

17. "Projeto Para a Zona Norte" 1981–82.

18. Alvarez 1993; Assies 1992; Cardoso 1998.

19. Dresch 1985: 1.

20. See "Seminario De Formacao Comunitaria Para Fortalecer a Associacao De Moradores," 1986; "O Momento Politico E O Movimento Comunitario," 1986; "Contribuicao Para Discussao Em Grupo No II Congresso Da Uampa," 1986; "II Congresso Da Uampa: Relatorio," 1986; "A Construcao Da Uampa Neste Momento Politico," 1986; "Conselhos Municipais: Como Devem Funcionar, O Que Devem Deliberar," 1986.

21. "O Movimento Comunitario em Porto Alegre" (internal document), 1986.

22. Baierle 1992.

23. "Movimento Popular," 1987.

24. Bava and Soares 1998; Gohn 1989.

25. "Conselhos Municipais: Democratizacao Administrativa," 1986, 2.

26. "Carta Ao Prefeito," 1985.

27. "Conselhos Municipais: Como Devem Funcionar, O Que Devem Deliberar," 1986, 7.

28. Moura 1989.

29. Community demands included dividing the city into twelve districts (as opposed to the four proposed by the administration) and instituting recall rules for councilors.

30. Rech 1988; Fedozzi 2000.

31. "Vitoria Da Vila Uniao," 1987.

32. Baierle 1992: 91.

33. "Obras do Mutirao da Zona Norte," 1987.

34. "Voce Sabia Que . . . ," 1987.

35. "Carta Ao Prefeito," 1988.

36. "III Congresso da Uampa: Os Numeros Falam," 1988.

37. "O Movimento Comunitario em Porto Alegre" (internal document), 1986, 6.

38. "Avaliação do Movimento na Zona Norte," 1987.

39. Filho 1994.

40. Utzig 1994.

41. For a review of recollections of the 1989–92 and subsequent administrations, see Baiocchi 2003: ch. 1.

42. Fedozzi 2000.

43. "Sobre O Processo De Discussao Do Orçamento," 1989.

44. Fedozzi 2000: 75.

45. Vice-mayor Genro later recalled that the public administration has "to respond to the demands that come to us, thinking of the whole of society, and

not only one segment. . . . This [conflict with CUT] did not mean a rupture, because there would have had to be an alliance, and there never was such an alliance. The administration does not establish alliances with unions. That is a completely distorted vision." Genro 1990: 57.

46. Sharão, cited in Harnecker 1993; "Processo De Avaliacao Da Gestao Da Frente Popular," 1992.

47. Baierle 1992; Abers 2000.

48. In one recollection "the popular movement is fragile, dependent, and defensive before the state. It has a culture of resistance, and is strongly passive and marked by a tradition where corporatism and clientelism reigned. Also, the union movement, with rare exceptions, even with the weight of two centrals, cannot overcome the defensive corporatism and affect an affirmative proposal of public policies." See Lima 1993: 10.

49. Goldfrank 2003.

50. In a policy brief, "Sobre o Processo de Discussao do Orçamento," FASE typically expressed the hope that the OP would strengthen and politicize civil society, arguing that under the current arrangement, "[t]he realization of only one initial meeting, where there is to be information about the budget, and a final municipal meeting, could restrict the process to presenting the information and the listing of community demands" (2).

51. Goldfrank 2003: 23.

52. Fedozzi 2000: 235.

53. Lima 1996: 122.

54. Goldfrank 2003; Fedozzi 2000; Abers 2000.

55. Fedozzi 2000: 95.

56. "Os Primeiros 15 Meses de Administracao Popular," 1990, 10.

57. "Conselho Municipal do Plano de Governo e Orçamento," 1990.

58. In fact, their literal title is "district-level councilor of the budget," but in order to keep them separate from the districts' elected representatives, the *concelheiros do orçamento*, or budget councilors (as well as from the *vereadores*, the members of the municipal legislature), I shall refer to them as facilitators.

59. "Processo De Avaliacao Da Gestao Da Frente Popular," 1992, 1.

60. Three factors explain this increase. First, municipal transfers from the federal government increased in 1990. Large, richer cities were favored in Brazilian decentralization because of the sorts of taxes they could raise and keep locally. Second, the administration's proposed tax raise came into effect for the year. In particular land-use taxes (IPTU) increased by 140 percent. Third, the administration stepped up efforts to increase tax compliance. As a result, by 1991, the amount available for investment was over 16 percent of the total budget, a figure four times higher than for 1989. The proportion of its budget raised locally increased from 48 percent to 59 percent in the same period, largely accomplished by increases in local land-use taxes. See Filho 1994; Horn 1994.

61. Dutra 1990: 49.

62. Schmidt 1993: 83.

63. Lima 1993: 6.

64. Fedozzi 1997.

65. Although districts include several neighborhoods and generally defy simple characterizations, such as "middle-class" or "poor" districts, per-district rates of poverty are highly correlated with per-capita rates of participation over the years. Districts with the highest levels of poverty, such as Nordeste (61 percent), Lomba (59 percent), and Restinga (54 percent), had, on average, per-capita participation rates for 1990–98 of 1.6 percent, 1.1 percent, and 0.86 percent. Districts with the lowest rates of poverty, such as Centro (15 percent), Noroeste (23 percent), and Sul (31 percent) had average participation rates of 0.08 percent, 0.14 percent, and 0.53 percent.

66. Baiocchi 2001a.

67. "Carta Denuncia," 1991.

68. Ribeiro 2000.

69. Harnecker 1993.

70. Pozzobon 1998.

71. Fedozzi 2000.

72. "Processo De Avaliacao Da Gestao Da Frente Popular," 1992.

73. Pont 1994: 1.

74. "Conselho Municipal Dos Direitos Da Cidadania," 1993, 2.

75. "II Congresso Municipal," 1995.

76. Passos and Brasil 2000.

77. While recognizing the difficulties in establishing precision, and agreeing in the direction of changes, Avritzer 2000b argues for a lower magnitude of the effect, roughly half of what I estimate. Our reliance on different methodologies and estimators accounts for the differences. As I discuss in the Appendix, I did not utilize retrospective interviewing because of morbidity bias, and I consider reactivations. My two surveys of associations in Porto Alegre in 1999 and 2001 (n = 100 and 240) offer evidence supporting these findings: in 2001, roughly half of all currently active associations had either been founded (26 percent) or re-activated (23 percent) since the introduction of the OP.

78. Examples such as this raise the issue of whether apparent associational growth is related to a fragmentation of civil society rather than an increase in civic activism per se. On the basis of the data presented here alone, it is difficult to conclusively decide, but the patterns are suggestive; the greatest growth in associational density has occurred in areas with the fewest number of organizations, and areas with the greatest level of organization have experienced the least growth, which is the opposite of what one would expect of splintering alone. In addition, associational density appears not to have increased much past one association per thousand in any district, which is also suggestive of a limit of associationalism. Interview evidence shows that while more than one association exists in several neighborhoods, parallel associations were often composed of new entrants into associational life.

79. Nordeste experienced an increase from 0.08 to 0.6 associations per thousand; Lomba rose from 0.12 to 0.8, while Restinga climbed from 0.1 to 0.7.

80. The question remains about whether this is a stepping-stone to political careers. As of 1998, three members of the municipal legislature had been OP

councilors at some point. It is too early to speculate on the long-term patterns of these trajectories.

81. Despite the difficulties in estimating protest events from newspaper reporting (see Koopmans 2002), in this particular case, because the newspaper in question, *Zero Hora*, is very critical of the administration and of the PT, the bias would lie in the overreporting protests during the PT years, therefore actually biasing *downward* the effect I note. See Appendix for further discussion.

82. Fedozzi 2000: 66.

83. Ibid., quoting Siqueira.

84. We cannot discount the possibility that more recent activists now "know not to" disclose clientelism.

85. Avritzer 2002: 37.

86. Goldfrank 2002: 301.

87. Setzler 2000.

88. Indeed, the types of favors neighborhood activists secured during my fieldwork were restricted to small items, such as funds for a party for children, paint for the neighborhood association building, and haircuts for the whole neighborhood.

89. Schmidtt 1993: 141.

90. "Conselho Popular," 1992.

91. "Tronco Postao," 1992.

92. Gildo Lima, interview 1999.

93. An average of 1.4 ties per general participant in 1998.

94. Baierle 1992.

95. "O Desafio do Comite Contra a Fome e Miseria," 1991.

96. Lichterman 2002.

3. New Actors and New Competencies

1. FESC 1999.

2. I am converting the median income to 1999 U.S. dollars from the awkward notation of multiples of the official minimum wage that is often used.

3. They were, respectively, in Batista Flores, in Residencial Machado, in Chácara da Fumaça, and in Safira Velha.

4. Marina, interview, August 1999.

5. Orgao Oficial da Associacao Riacho Doce (OCUPACAO), "Luta Pela Terra," 1991.

6. Gilson, interview 1998.

7. Maria, interview 1997.

8. FESC 1999.

9. Guareschi 1985.

10. Arnaldo, one of the founders of the Morro da Cruz association, said in an interview in 1999: "Mayor Villela gave us great support. And among the mayors of the dictatorship, he gave us a lot of help. . . . Then, after him, we started having problems with the administration. We would have a meeting, create a commission, and then go down to the DEMHAB office and we would have to wait for half a day sometimes."

11. Fei João, interview 1998.
12. "Propostas Para a Assembleia Popular E Democratica Do Partenon," 1984.
13. See Magalhães 1999.
14. Arnaldo, interview 1999.
15. Marcos, interview 1998.
16. Junio, interview 1997.
17. "Historia Do Movimento Popular (Atas Do Seminario De Reestruturacao Do Conselho Popular Do Partenon)," 1997.
18. "Carta ao Prefeito," 1991.
19. Ibid.; "Autonomia/Legitimidade/Democracia," 1992.
20. "Carta ao Conselho Popular Do Partenon," 1991.
21. Junio, interview 1999.
22. "Autonomia/Legitimidade/Democracia," 1992.
23. FESC 1999.
24. Porto Alegre is divided into voting subdistricts that do not necessarily overlap with the OP's divisions. Zonal 158 is almost entirely within the bounds of the Norte district.
25. Elza, interview 1999.
26. Wilson, interview 1998.
27. "Carta Da Grande Santa Rosa," 1985; "Nao Pague a Taxa Escolar," 1985.
28. "O Movimento Comunitario em Porto Alegre" (internal document), 1986.
29. "Carta Ao Prefeito," 1985; "Seminario Participacao Do Povo No Governo," 1986.
30. "Subsidios Para O Debate Sobre Os Conselhos Municipais," 1986.
31. "Relatorio Do Seminario: Conselhos Municipais," 1986.
32. "Preparacao do Encontro," 1988.
33. "Encontro de Formacao do Conselho Popular da Regiao," 1988.
34. "O Movimento Comunitario Em Porto Alegre" (internal document), 1986.
35. "Regimento Interno," 1988.
36. "I Encontro do Conselho Popular," 1988.
37. Wilson, interview 1999.
38. "Relatorio Dos Trabalhos Em Grupos Da Reuniao Do Conselho Popular," 1989.
39. "Projeto De Habitacao Popular Para a Zona Norte," 1989.
40. "Zona Norte Define Prioridades," 1989.
41. "Documento Do Conselho Popular Da Zona Norte Sobre Orçamento Municipal," 1989.
42. José, interview 1997.
43. Conselho Popular da Zona Norte, "Circular Interna 12/90," 1990.
44. Id., "Circular Interna 14/90," 1990.
45. Ibid.; id., "Circular Interna 05/90," 1990.
46. José, interview 1997.
47. Maria, interview 2000.

4. Deliberative Repertoires

EPIGRAPH: Marx 1978: 160.

1. The vast majority of OP participants declare membership in neighborhood associations, but almost half of those are not listed as belonging to any of the "formally registered neighborhood associations," choosing instead to form ad hoc "street commissions." Increasingly, in recent years, participants have chosen to declare themselves as belonging to groups other than neighborhood associations, such as school associations, parents' associations, and religious groups.

2. Joshua Cohen 1996; Mansbridge 1995; Guttman 1996. Authors generally juxtapose deliberative democracy against other types of democracy based on representation, majority rule, and competing interests. Mansbridge 1980 refers to "adversary democracy," and Cohen 1996 uses the broad umbrella term "aggregative conception of democracy" to refer to nondeliberative conceptions of democracy. See also Bohman 1997; Elster 1998a, 1998b; Guttman 1996; Macedo 1998.

3. Benhabib 1996.

4. Joshua Cohen 1996: 102. What "counts as a reason" is deeply dependent upon the "background context" of the deliberation, but it implies background conceptions of citizens as equal, free, and reasonable. See ibid., 106.

5. Mansbridge 1990: 24.

6. The evidence here also strongly suggests that the availability of time, and women's "second and third shifts" of household responsibilities, is a significant factor. One element that women, and sometimes men, brought up as an explanation for this was that of control over time, and specifically, the ability to be mobile, to which men have greater access. See Baiocchi 2001a.

7. In the regression models reported in Baiocchi 2001a, gender reduced the likelihood of election by 30 percent, and low education (up to 8th grade), reduced it by 27 percent. But each additional year of experience in the OP increased the chance of election by 25 percent, and each additional tie in civil society increased the odds by 51 percent. Being retired increases the odds by over 146 percent, and being self-employed by over 94 percent. The statistical models show that while people with few ties in civil society, women, and the less educated have a lower chance of election than their counterparts, increasing experience and increasing number of ties offset education and gender disadvantages. Statistical models also show that education effects have to do with a person's likelihood of being elected to a position in civil society and do not directly result from what "counts" in Participatory Budget meetings.

8. In 1999, the city council counted four women out of thirty-three councilors, only one of whom would have fitted the definition of "poor" and "nonwhite" used here.

9. The first 100 people at the meeting create 10 delegate positions; the next 150 persons, 7.5 delegate positions (one for 20); the next 150 create 5 (one for 30); from then on there is a delegate position for each 40 people present. The number of delegates for each association is based on a simple percentage of the total.

10. Unfortunately, there is no way to determine with precision how these decisions are made at the neighborhood level. The 1998 survey did reveal, however, that most delegates were chosen in open assemblies. Of those who answered the question, "How are delegates chosen?" 80 percent answered "in open assemblies," while 20 percent answered "by indication." This supports my fieldwork observations; in meetings I attended in neighborhood associations in all three districts, delegates were usually chosen at meetings after the number of delegates for each association was announced in the OP.

11. This second plenary meeting was abolished when the process was streamlined in 2001.

12. Mauro, interview. District-level meetings and the thematic fora continue to meet after this plenary meeting, although usually for informational purposes, or to monitor the construction of projects.

13. Once the Budget Council establishes municipal priorities for the year's budget, it divides specific investments among the city's districts according to three criteria: (a) lack of a specific public service (if up to 25 percent of its population: 1 point; 26 percent to 50 percent: 2 points, etc.); (b) total population of district in thousands (up to 30,999: 1 point; 31 to 60,999: 2 points; 61 to 119,999: 3 points; above 120,000: 4 points); and (c) how the district has prioritized the specific service area (fourth or below: 1 point; third: 2 points, etc.)

14. " Orçamento Participativo/94" (1993).

5. Emergent Public Spheres

1. See, e.g., Boyte and Evans 1986.

2. See Piven and Cloward 1979; Michels 1949; Habermas 1974; Cohen and Arato 1992. For a discussion of these criticisms, see Eliasoph 1998: 169, and Fraser 1992a.

3. Habermas 1989, 1969.

4. Habermas 1996: 360.

5. See Emirbayer and Scheller 1999.

6. Eliasoph 1998: 16.

7. See Joshua Cohen 1996.

8. Habermas, 1996: 360. This is a view between "thick" and "thin" publicity of political theorists. See Bohman 1999; Joshua Cohen 1996, 1998.

9. See Fraser 1992a, which notes that politicizing talk around "needs" has been an important way of expanding citizenship rights in the United States.

10. See Elster 1996; Polletta 1999; Putnam, Leonardi and Nanetti 1993; Somers 1994.

11. Habermas 1996.

12. Putnam 1995: 66.

13. Habermas 1996: 366.

14. See Bellah et al. 1985; Alexander and Smith 1993; Crook and Manor 1998; Dahl 1989; Tocqueville 1945, vol. 2.

15. Cardoso 1988.

16. Policing is not a municipal-level responsibility in Brazil but a state-level one. At the time of the study, the Workers' Party was in power at the state level, which put it in charge of police issues.

17. About 30 percent of associations in districts with popular councils had sent a representative to their local popular council. About 20 percent of associations had sent a representative to a meeting of the Union of Neighborhood Associations.

18. See Eliasoph 1998 for a discussion.

19. Arendt 1951, 1963; Dewey 1927; Habermas 1996. For a discussion of this, see Bohman 1999; Benhabib 1996; Emirbayer and Sheller 1999.

20. It is beyond the reach of this book to address this apparently surprising finding in light of theories of the "iron law of oligarchy" (e.g., see Lipset 1997). One plausible explanation is that this "self-discipline" emerges from the specific social movement traditions from which these activists come, here heavily influenced by participatory pedagogy. See Cardoso 1988. An alternative, of course, is that the time horizon for such "oligarchies" to emerge is longer than the years of the participatory experiment, and that they might appear in the future.

21. Bourdieu 1991; Lipset 1997; Michels [1915] 1999.

22. Auyero 1999a, 1999b; Gay 1995; Stokes 1995.

6. Militants and Citizens

1. Ray 1999: 8; Bourdieu and Wacquant 1992: 12.

2. The distinction is present in both the reflections of social movement activists ("Avaliação Do Movimento Na Zona Norte" [1987], and in academic writing on Porto Alegre (Abers 2000) and on Brazil's civil society at large (Alvarez 1993).

3. Jean Cohen 1999b.

4. For a discussion on estimating the number of associations, see Appendix.

5. This figure is higher than Avritzer's 2002 finding that 35 percent of associations had been founded since the establishment of the OP. See Avritzer 2002.

6. Vera, interview 1999.

7. Fontes 1990

8. Here openness to democracy is defined in normative terms as a reasonable openness to all to participate in a decision-making process. See Joshua Cohen 1994.

9. Associação Parque dos Maias, "Eleições" (1998). Porto Alegre. Photocopy.

10. Popular councils in Brazil date from the prodemocracy movement, and in Porto Alegre, they date from the late 1980s, just prior to the PT victory. Popular councils are autonomous of political parties and of the government and have no institutional power. See Azevedo 1988. They are analogous to North American "citizens' leagues," in that they are civic organizations with a social movement orientation. See Boyte 1992.

11. Although it is difficult to get precise answers, due to the nature of these relationships, it is worth noting that among neighborhood associations activated or reactivated since the OP's launching, only 2 percent of respondents to the association have received "a favor from a politician or secretary," as opposed to 18 percent among those whose associations predate participatory reforms.

12. In my interviews with older neighborhood activists, many described their privileged access to certain powerful political figures. One of them, Bernardo, said: "I had the card of the director of DEMHAB [in the 1980s]. He respected me and my work in the community, and I had his direct number. If we needed something, we would call him."

13. Adalto, City Hall facilitator, interview.

14. Abers 2000; Baierle 1998a; Fedozzi 1997.

7. The Civic Is the Political

1. UNDP 2004.

2. See, e.g., Patterson 2002; Putnam 2003.

3. Markoff 1999.

4. Habermas and Pensky 2001.

5. Logan and Molotch 1987: 136.

6. Fraser 1993.

7. Fraser 1992; Negt and Kluge 1993. The dilemmas of the PT in power are extensively analyzed by myself and others in Baiocchi 2003.

8. Tocqueville 1945, vol. 2.

9. Habermas 1989.

10. Warren 2001: 77; Joshua Cohen 1998: 186.

11. See discussions in Barber 1998; Crook and Manor 1998; Dahl 1989.

12. Emirbayer and Sheller 1999: 147; Evans and Boyte 1992; Polletta 1999.

13. Benhabib 1996; Fraser 1992.

14. It would have been possible to discuss a variety of such subaltern counterpublics, for instance, and the way they connect to these public spheres. This point is more fully explored elsewhere.

15. See Marschall 2001; Verba and Nie 1972; Ferreira 1999, 2000; McDonough et al. 1998.

16. Fung and Wright 2000.

17. Fraser 1992.

18. Putnam et al. 1993.

19. Putnam 2000.

20. Tarrow 1996.

21. Skocpol and Fiorina 1999: 18.

22. Fox 1996, 1999.

23. Booth and Richard 1998.

24. Piven and Cloward 1979; Domhoff 2002: 184.

25. Joshua Cohen et al. 1995; Hirst 1994; Fung and Wright 2000; Evans and Boyte 1992.

26. Fung and Wright 2003; Hirst 1994; Joshua Cohen and Rogers 1995.

27. See Fung and Wright 2003, esp. the introduction.

28. Migdal 2001.

29. Fung and Wright 2003.

30. Elster 1998.

31. Avritzer forthcoming.

32. Porto Alegre was the capital of the opposition to the attempted military

coup in August 1961, when Governor Leonel Brizola barricaded himself in the governor's palace and pledged that Porto Alegre would defend democracy until the end. Cortes 1974: 355.

33. See the reviews in Avritzer forthcoming and Baiocchi 2003.

34. Silva 2001.

35. There is a long tradition of this line of thinking buttressed by real experiences in Europe and elsewhere. In addition to Michels 1949, see Piven and Cloward 1979; Lipset 1997; Cohen and Arato 1992.

36. Roberts 1998.

37. See, e.g., Lowy 1987.

38. Keck 1992.

39. "Red Bologna" was split in the 1970s between the "world of the party" and the "world of the church." The Communist Party of Italy maintained control over organizations in civil society that were ultimately understood to be appendages of the party and bound by its political directives and hierarchy, and where "the authority and prestige of the party are reinforced" and "Party positions are extolled and the various party officers high status is validated." Kertzer 1980: 48. See also Jäggi et al. 1977.

40. Based on statistical analyses, not reported here, of 2001 data. See the website: www.participatorybudgeting.org.

41. Genro had left the post of mayor midterm to run for governor.

42. Nylen 2003.

43. Goldfrank and Schneider 2003.

44. Harnecker 1993: 23.

45. Assies 1992: 173.

46. http://www.internationalbudget.org (accessed August 3, 2004).

47. http://www.oidpart.com (accessed July 22, 2004).

48. http://www.budget-participatif.org/ (accessed August 3, 2004).

49. http://www.autoridadeslocais.com.br/ (accessed August 3, 2004).

50. DRD Charter 2002, http://www.budget-participatif.org/actualite.php3?com=6 (accessed July 23, 2004).

Epilogue: November 2004—The End of an Era?

1. http://www.diegocasagrande.com.br/pages/artigos/view.php?uid=956.

2. http://www.fogaca23.com.br/fogaca.php.

3. "Fogaça vai manter e aperfeiçoar o Orçamento Participativo." In http://www.fogaca23.com.br/noticias_ler.php?id=11. Last accessed September 1, 2004.

4. "OP une PT e PPS no Debate." In http://www.sintaf-rs.org.br/alfa/clip_clipping_detalhe.asp?cod_clipping=10471.

Methodological Appendix: Ethnography by Numbers

1. The few weeks during which I attempted this certainly led me to doubt the validity of international surveys about political values.

2. The problem is partially that, as John French has put it in personal conversation, the PT is a party of intellectuals in constant reflection and debate about the types of questions I pose in this book.

3. More than once, with my colleague Marcelo K. Silva, I received embarrassingly special treatment because I was from the United States. With my colleague and flatmate Ben Goldfrank, however, the situation was once reversed. We both once had interviews with the same person in the same municipal department to ask for some data; I came back with nothing but a request that I submit an official application from my university, doubt being cast on whether I really did attend a university in the United States. Ben came back with what seemed like a huge stack of books and documents. Being good progressives, however, we always "redistributed the wealth," sharing contacts, tips, and data. We even collaborated on one of the surveys here. Whatever competitive individualism we might have been socialized into in graduate school, we were much more inspired by the participatory ethic we were exposed to daily.

4. Fortunately, my dissertation committee provided plenty of inspiration. My two co-chairs themselves, one the original "multivariate Marxist" and the other an anthropologist in exile in sociology, were very helpful and methodologically demanding. The remaining members of the committee, an ethnographer, a comparative-historical sociologist, and a social historian, also helped to push questions of rigor and reflexivity involved in such an attempt.

5. The logic of Lichterman's arguments about participant observation is relevant to the results of the 1998 survey of OP participants. It is hardly surprising that if representatives of the municipal administration ask every tenth entrant to an assembly why it is that he or she has come, the answer may be "Citizenship."

6. I used a combination of "snowball" and survey techniques to identify people to interview. I interviewed at least one person from each neighborhood association and tried to interview all regular participants of the budget meetings. At the end of the interview, I asked for contacts with other people with "experience" in community activism. Eventually, the contacts were all for people already identified.

7. The data for the 2000 survey were generously made available to me by CIDADE.

8. This book attempts to carry out the "multivariate ethnomethodology" that Bourdieu and Wacquant 1992 call for.

References

Documents

1981–82

"Projeto para a Zona Norte." 1981–82. FASE—Federação de Orgãos para Assistencia Social e Educacional, Porto Alegre. Mimeo.

"Vila Nova Brasília." 1981–82. Vila Nova Brasília, Porto Alegre. Photocopy.

1984

"Boletim Informativo." 1984. União de Vilas Cruzeiro, Porto Alegre. Mimeo.

"Letter to Mayor Dib." 1984. Associação de Moradores Vila Brasília, Porto Alegre. Photocopy.

"Propostas Para a Assembleia Popular e Democrática do Partenon." 1984. Comissão Organizadora da Assembleia Popular e Democrática do Partenon, Porto Alegre. Mimeo.

1985

"Carta ao Prefeito." 1985. Associações de Moradores da Zona Sul, Porto Alegre. Photocopy.

"Carta da Grande Santa Rosa." 1985. COMPROMEL—Comissão Pró-Melhoria da Santa Rosa, Porto Alegre. Mimeo.

"Não Pague a Taxa Escolar." 1985. Círculo de Pais e Mestres da E.E. Santa Rosa, Porto Alegre. Mimeo.

1986

"A Construção da UAMPA Neste Momento Político." 1986. União das Associações de Moradores de Porto Alegre, Porto Alegre. Photocopy.

"Conselhos Municipais: Como Devem Funcionar, O Que Devem Deliberar." 1986. União das Associações de Moradores de Porto Alegre, Porto Alegre. Photocopy.

"Conselhos Municipais: Democratização Administrativa." 1986. Partido Democratico Trabalhista (P.D.T.), Porto Alegre. Photocopy.

"Contribuicao Para Discussão Em Grupo no II Congresso da UAMPA." 1986. União das Associações de Moradores de Porto Alegre, Porto Alegre. Photocopy.

"O Movimento Comunitário em Porto Alegre. Photocopy." 1986. Internal document. FASE—Federação de Orgãos para Assistencia Social e Educacional, Porto Alegre. Photocopy.

"O Momento Político e o Movimento Comunitário." 1986. União das Associações de Moradores de Porto Alegre, Porto Alegre. Photocopy.

"Regimento Interno." 1986. Conselho de Participação da Zona Comunitária 2C, Porto Alegre. Photocopy.

"Relatório do Seminário: Conselhos Municipais." 1986. Articulação de Associações de Moradores da Zona Norte, Porto Alegre. Photocopy.

"II Congresso da UAMPA: Relatório." 1986. União das Associações de Moradores de Porto Alegre, Porto Alegre. Photocopy.

"Seminário de Formação Comunitária Para Fortalecer a Associação de Moradores." 1986. União das Associações de Moradores de Porto Alegre, Porto Alegre. Photocopy.

"Seminário Participação do Povo no Governo." 1986. Prefeitura Municipal de Porto Alegre, Secretaria do Governo Municipal, Porto Alegre. Photocopy.

"Subsídios Para O Debate Sobre Os Conselhos Municipais." 1986. Comissão Mobilizadora da Zona Norte, Porto Alegre. Photocopy.

1987

"Avaliação do Movimento na Zona Norte." 1987. FASE, Porto Alegre. Photocopy.

"Movimento Popular." 1987. Centro de Assessoria Multi-Disciplinar, Porto Alegre. Photocopy.

"Obras do Mutirão da Zona Norte." 1987. União das Associações de Moradores de Porto Alegre, Porto Alegre. Photocopy.

"Vitória da Vila União." 1987. Associação de Moradores da Vila União, Porto Alegre. Photocopy.

"Você Sabia Que . . ." 1987. Associações de Moradores Zona Norte, Porto Alegre. Photocopy.

1988

"Ao Desrespeito, Respondemos Com Nossa União e Luta." 1988. Vila União, Porto Alegre. Photocopy.

"Carta ao Prefeito." 1988. Conselho Popular da Zona Norte, Porto Alegre. Photocopy.

"Encontro de Formação do Conselho Popular da Região." 1988. Articulação de Associações de Moradores da Zona Norte, Porto Alegre. Photocopy.

"I Encontro do Conselho Popular." 1988. Conselho Popular da Zona Norte, Porto Alegre. Photocopy.

"Preparação do Encontro." 1988. Articulação de Associações de Moradores da Zona Norte, Porto Alegre. Photocopy.

"Relatório do Encontro da Articulação das AMs da Zona Norte." 1988. Comissão de Coordenação Provisoria de Articulação das AM's da ZN, Porto Alegre. Photocopy.

"Regimento Interno." 1988. Conselho Popular da Zona Norte, Porto Alegre. Photocopy.

"III Congresso da UAMPA: Os Números Falam." 1988. União das Associações de Moradores de Porto Alegre, Porto Alegre. Photocopy.

1989

"V Encontro Municipal do PT—Porto Alegre. Resoluções." 1989. Partido dos Trabalhadores, Porto Alegre. Photocopy.

"Documento do Conselho Popular da Zona Norte sobre o Orçamento Municipal." 1989. Conselho Popular da Zona Norte, Porto Alegre. Photocopy.

"Nota." 1989. Associações de Moradores da Grande Santa Rosa, Porto Alegre. Photocopy.

"Projeto de Habitação Popular Para a Zona Norte." 1989. Conselho Popular da Zona Norte, Porto Alegre. Photocopy.

"Relatório dos Trabalhos em Grupos da Reunião do Conselho Popular." 1989. Conselho Popular da Zona Norte, Porto Alegre. Photocopy.

"Sobre o Processo de Discussão do Orçamento." 1989. Representantes de Micro Regioes de Porto Alegre, FASE.

"Zona Norte Define Prioridades." 1989. Conselho Popular da Zona Norte, Porto Alegre. Photocopy.

1990

"Circular Interna 05/90." 1990. Conselho Popular da Zona Norte, Porto Alegre. Photocopy.

"Circular Interna 12/90." 1990. Conselho Popular da Zona Norte, Porto Alegre. Photocopy.

"Circular Interna 14/90." 1990. Conselho Popular da Zona Norte, Porto Alegre. Photocopy.

"Conselho Municipal do Plano de Governo e Orçamento." 1990. Prefeitura Municipal de Porto Alegre, Porto Alegre. Photocopy.

Os Primeiros 15 Meses da Administração Popular. 1990. Prefeitura Municipal de Porto Alegre, Coordenação de Comunicação Social, Porto Alegre. Photocopy.

1991

"Carta ao Conselho Popular do Partenon." 1991. Centro Comunitário Africano, Porto Alegre. Photocopy.

"Carta Denuncia." 1991. Conselho Municipal do Orçamento Participativo, Porto Alegre. Photocopy.

"O Desafio do Comitê Contra a Fome e Miséria." 1991. Comitê contra a Fome e Miséria, Porto Alegre. Photocopy.

"Foro Contra a Recessão e Desemprego." 1991. Prefeitura Municipal de Porto Alegre, Porto Alegre. Photocopy.

"Luta Pela Terra." 1991. Orgão Oficial da Associação Riacho Doce (OCUPAÇÃO), Porto Alegre. Photocopy.

"Uma Proposta Para Avancar na Participação Popular." 1991. Prefeitura Municipal de Porto Alegre, Comissão de Participação Popular na Reforma Administrativa, Porto Alegre. Photocopy.

1992

"Autonomia/Legitimidade/Democracia." 1992. Conselho Popular do Partenon, Porto Alegre. Photocopy.
"Conselho Popular." 1992. COMUNIDADE—Conselho Popular da Gloria, Porto Alegre. Photocopy.
"Processo de Avaliação da Gestão da Frente Popular." 1992. Prefeitura Municipal de Porto Alegre—Gabinete do Prefeito: Coordenação de Relacoes com a Comunidade, Porto Alegre. Photocopy.
"Tronco Postão." 1992. COMUNIDADE—Conselho Popular da Gloria, Porto Alegre. Photocopy.

1993

"Conselho Municipal dos Direitos da Cidadania." 1993. Prefeitura Municipal de Porto Alegre, Porto Alegre. Photocopy.
"Orçamento Participativo/94." 1993. Conselho Popular do Partenon, Porto Alegre. Photocopy.
"Participantes do Orçamento Participativo, Pesquisa." 1993. Prefeitura Municipal de Porto Alegre and Luciano Fedozzi.
"As Plenarias Tematicas: Uma Nova Dimensão do Orçamento Participativo." 1993. Prefeitura Municipal de Porto Alegre—Secretaria do Governo Municipal, Porto Alegre. Photocopy.
"Resoluções do Encontro Municipal do PT—Porto Alegre. Photocopy." 1993. Partido dos Trabalhadores, Porto Alegre. Photocopy.

1994

"Lei Complementar 325: Politica Municipal dos Direitos da Cidadania." 1994. Prefeitura Municipal de Porto Alegre, Porto Alegre. Photocopy.

1995

Ciclo do Orçamento Participativo. July 1995. CIDADE—de Olho no Orçamento.
"II Congresso Municipal." Prefeitura Municipal de Porto Alegre, Porto Alegre. Photocopy.
Poder Local Participação Popular e Construção da Cidadania. 1995. FNPP, São Paulo.

1996

"Conselho Municipal dos Direitos da Cidadania Contra as Discriminacoes e Violência-CMDC: Relatório de Atividades." 1996. Prefeitura Municipal de Porto Alegre, Porto Alegre. Photocopy.

1997

Anuário Estatístico. 1997. Prefeitura Municipal de Porto Alegre—GAPLAN, Porto Alegre.

"História do Movimento Popular (Atas do Seminário de Reestruturação do Conselho Popular do Partenon)." 1997. Conselho Popular do Partenon, Porto Alegre. Photocopy.

1998

"Coordenação Municipal de Direitos Humanos e Cidadania." 1998. Prefeitura Municipal de Porto Alegre, Porto Alegre. Photocopy.

Regimento Interno do Orçamento Participativo. 1998. Prefeitura Municipal de Porto Alegre, Porto Alegre.

Resoluções de Encontros e Congressos. 1998. Diretório Nacional do PT, Secretaria Nacional de Formação Política. Editoria Fundação Perseu Abramo, São Paulo.

1999

Orçamento Participativo—Quem é a População que Participa e o que Pensa do Processo. 1999. CIDADE—Centro de Assessoria e Estudos Urbanos, Porto Alegre. Photocopy.

2001

"Banco de Dados: Participantes do OP, 1989–2001." 2001. CRC, Prefeitura Municipal de Porto Alegre. Photocopy.

"Resoluções de Encontros e Congressos." 2001. Diretório Nacional do PT, Secretaria Nacional de Formação Polítical. Editoria Fundação Perseu Abramo, São Paulo.

"Rompendo Nossos Limites: Avançando o OP." 2001. CRC: Grupo de Trabalho de Reforma do Orçamento Participativo, Prefeitura Municipal de Porto Alegre. Photocopy.

2002

"Radically Democratize Democracy" Network Charter. 2002. http://www.budget-participatif.org.

Articles and Books

Abers, Rebecca. 2000. *Inventing Local Democracy: Grassroots Politics in Brazil.* Boulder, Colo.: Lynne Rienner.

Alexander, Jeffrey, and Phillip Smith. 1993. "The Discourse of Civil Society: A New Proposal for Cultural Studies." *Theory and Society* 2: 151–207.

Alvarado, Arturo, and Dianne Davis. Forthcoming. "Citizen Participation, Democratic Governance, and the PRD in Mexico City: The Challenge of Political Transition." In *The Left and the City*, ed. D. Chavez and Benjamin Goldfrank. New York: Zed Books.

Alvarez, Sonia. 1993. "Deepening Democracy: Popular Movement Networks, Constitutional Reform, and Radical Urban Regimes in Contemporary Brazil." In *Mobilizing the Community: Local Politics in the Era of the Global City*, edited by Robert Fisher and Joseph Kling. Newbury Park, Calif.: Sage Publications.

Alvarez-Enriquez, Lucia. 1998. "Citizen Participation and New Political Culture in Mexico City; Participacion Ciudadana y Nueva Cultura Politica en la Ciudad de Mexico." *Acta Sociologica* 22: 9–24.

Amenta, Edwin, and Yvonne Zylan. 1991. "It Happened Here: Political Opportunity, the New Institutionalism, and the Townsend Movement." *American Sociological Review* 56: 250–65.

Ames, Barry. 2002. *The Deadlock of Democracy in Brazil.* Ann Arbor: University of Michigan Press.

Ancelovici, Marcos. 2002. "Organizing Against Globalization: The Case of Attac in France." *Politics and Society* 30: 427–63.

Andrews, George Reid. 1991. *Blacks and Whites in São Paulo, Brazil, 1888–1988.* Madison: University of Wisconsin Press.

Araujo, José. 1997. "Attempts to Decentralize in Recent Brazilian Health Policy." *International Journal of Health Services* 27: 109–24.

Araújo Passos, Manoel Caetano de, and Maria Izabel Noll. 1996. *Eleições municipais em Porto Alegre, 1947–1992.* Porto Alegre: Universidade Federal do Rio Grande do Sul, Programa de Pós-Graduação em Ciência Política.

Arendt, Hannah. 1951. *The Origins of Totalitarianism.* New York: Harcourt, Brace.

———. 1963. *On Revolution.* New York: Viking Press.

Arretche, Marta. 1999. "Social Policies in Brazil: Decentralization in a Federative State." *Revista Brasileira de Ciencias Socias* 14: 111–41.

———. 2000. *Estado Federativo e Politicas Sociais.* Rio de Janeiro: Editora Revan.

Assies, Willem. 1992. *To Get Out of the Mud: Neighborhood Associativism in Recife, 1964–1988.* Amsterdam: Center on Latin American Research and Documentation.

Attahi, Koffi. 2001–2002. *Urban Governance around the World.* Washington, D.C.: Woodrow Wilson International Center for Scholars, Comparative Urban Studies Project.

Auyero, Javier. 1999a. "'From the Client's Point(s) of View': How Poor People Perceive and Evaluate Political Clientelism." *Theory and Society* 28: 297–334.

———. 1999b. "'This Is a Lot Like the Bronx, Isn't It?': Lived Experiences of Marginality in an Argentine Slum." *International Journal of Urban and Regional Research* 23: 45–69.

———. 2001. *Poor People's Politics: Peronist Survival Networks and the Legacy of Evita.* Durham, N.C.: Duke University Press.

———. 2002. *La Protesta: Retratos de la Beligerancia Popular en la Argentina Democrática.* Buenos Aires: Universidad de Buenos Aires.

Avritzer, Leonardo. 1996. *A Moralidade da Democracia.* Belo Horizonte: Perspectiva.

———. 1997. "Um Desenho Institucional Para o Novo Associativism." *Lua Nova—Revista de Cultura Politica* 39: 149–74.

———. 2000a. *Teoria Social e Modernidade no Brasil.* Belo Horizonte: Editora UFMG.

———. 2000b. *Sociedade Civil, Espaço Público e Poder Local: Uma Análise do Orçamento Participativo em Belo Horizonte e Porto Alegre.* Relatório de Pesquisa: Belo Horizonte.

————. 2002. *Democracy and the Public Space in Latin America*. Princeton, N.J.: Princeton University Press.

————. Forthcoming. "O Orçamento Participativo e a Teoria Democrática: Um Balanço Crítico." In *A Inovação Institucional no Brasil: Um Estudo Comparado Sobre o Orçamento Participativo*, ed. id. São Paulo: Cortez.

Azevedo, Ricardo de. 1988. "Conselhos Populares: Uma Varinha de Condao?" *Teoria e Debate* 4.

Azevedo, Sérgio. 1997. "A Politica de Reforma Tributaria." *Revista Brasileira de Ciencias Socias* 12: 75–99.

Azevedo, Sérgio de. 1997. "Políticas Públicas e Governança em Belo Horizonte." *Cadernos IPPUR XI* 1: 63–74.

Azevedo, Sérgio, and Antônio Augusto Prates. 1991. *Planejamento Participativo, Movimentos Sociais e Ação Coletiva*. São Paulo: Anpocs-Vértice.

Baierle, Sergio Gregório. 1992. "A Explosão da Experiencia: A Emergência de um Novo Principio Etico-Político em Porto Alegre." Campinas: UNICAMP.

————. 1998a. "Experiência do Orçamento Participativo: Um Oásis no Deserto Neoliberal?" In *de Olho no Orçamento 6*. Porto Alegre: CIDADE.

————. 1998b. "The Explosion of Experience: The Emergence of a New Ethical-Political Principle in Popular Movements in Porto Alegre, Brazil." In *Cultures of Politics/Politics of Cultures: Revisioning Latin American Social Movements*, ed. E. D. Sonia E. Alvarez and Arturo Escobar, 118–38. Boulder, Colo.: Westview Press.

————. 2001. "Porto Alegre em Thermidor." Porto Alegre: FASE–CIDADE.

Baiocchi, Gianpaolo. 2001a. "Activism, Participation, and Politics: The Porto Alegre Experiment and Deliberative Democratic Theory." *Politics and Society*. March.

————. 2001b. "From Militance to Citizenship: The Workers' Party, Civil Society, and the Politics of Participatory Governance in Porto Alegre, Brazil." Ph.D. thesis, Department of Sociology, University of Wisconsin, Madison.

————, ed. 2003. *Radicals in Power: The Workers' Party (PT) and Experiments in Urban Democracy in Brazil*. New York: Zed Books.

Bak, Joan. 1985. "Political Centralization and the Building of the Interventionist State in Brazil." *Luso-Brazilian Review* 22.

Banck, Geert A. 1986. "Poverty, Politics and the Shaping of Urban Space: A Brazilian Example." *International Journal of Urban and Regional Research* 10: 522–40.

Barber, Benjamin. 1998. "Three Challenges to Reinventing Democracy." In *Reinventing Democracy*, ed. P. Hirst and S. Khilnani. Cambridge: Blackwell.

Bastos, Celso. 1985. "As Futuras Bases da Descentralização." *Revista Brasileira de Estudias Políticos* 60–61: 177–94.

Bava, Silvio C., and J. A. Soares. 1998. *Os desafios da gestão municipal democrática*. São Paulo: Cortez.

Bava, Silvio C., Peter Spink, and Veronika Paulics. 2002. *Novos Contornos da Gestão Local: Conceitos em Construção*. São Paulo: Instituto Pólis.

Bazdresch, Miguel. 2002. "Consejo Democratico en Cuquio, Jalisco." In *Innova-*

cion en Gobiernos Locales: Un Panorama de Experiencias Municipales en Mexico, ed. E. Cabrero. CIDE.

Becker, Howard. 1998. *Tricks of the Trade: How to Think About Your Research While You're Doing It.* Chicago: University of Chicago Press.

Bellah, Robert, Richard Madsen, William Sullivan, Ann Swidler, and Steven Tipton. 1985. *Habits of the Heart: Individualism and Commitment in American Life.* Berkeley: University of California Press.

Bengelsdorf, Carollee. 1994. *The Problem of Democracy in Cuba: Between Vision and Reality.* New York: Oxford University Press.

Bennett, Robert J. 1994. "An Overview of Developments in Decentralization." In *Local Government and Market Decentralization,* ed. id. New York: United Nations University Press.

Beozzo, José Oscar, and Apolo Heringer Lisboa. 1983. "PT: Avaliação Eleitoral." *Vozes* 77: 18–36.

Berezin, Mabel. 1997. "Politics and Culture: A Less Fissured Terrain." *Annual Review of Sociology* 23: 361–83.

Bohman, James. 1997. "Deliberative Democracy and Effective Social Freedom: Capabilities, Resources, and Opportunities." In *Deliberative Democracy: Essays on Reason and Politics,* ed. J. Bohman and W. Rehg, 321–48. Cambridge, Mass.: MIT University Press.

———. 1999. "Citizenship and Norms of Publicity." *Political Theory* 27: 176–203.

Booth, John A., and Patricia B. Richard. 1998. "Civil Society and Political Context in Central America." *American Behavioral Scientist* 42: 33–45.

Borja, Jordi, Mireia Belil, Chris Benner, and Manuel Castells. 1997. *Local and Global: The Management of Cities in the Information Age.* London: Earthscan Publications.

Boschi, Renato Raul. 1987. *A arte da associação: Política de base e democracia no Brasil.* Translated by Maria Alice da Silva Ramos. São Paulo: Vértice; Rio de Janeiro: Instituto Universitário de Pesquisas do Rio de Janeiro.

———. 1999. "Decentralization, Clientalism and Social Capital in Urban Governing." *Dados* 42: 655–90.

Boschi, Renato Rau, ed. *Movimentos Coletivos no Brasil Urbano.* Rio de Janeiro: Zahar.

Bourdieu, Pierre. 1977. *Outline of a Theory of Practice.* New York: Cambridge University Press.

———. 1984. *Distinction: A Social Critique of the Judgement of Taste.* Cambridge, Mass.: Harvard University Press.

———. 1989. "Social Space and Symbolic Power." *Sociological Theory* 7: 14–25.

———. 1990. *The Logic of Practice.* Stanford, Calif.: Stanford University Press.

———. 1991. *Language and Symbolic Power.* Cambridge: Polity Press.

———. 1998. *Practical Reason: On the Theory of Action.* Stanford, Calif.: Stanford University Press.

Bourdieu, Pierre, and Loïc J. D. Wacquant. 1992. *An Invitation to Reflexive Sociology.* Chicago: University of Chicago Press.

Boyte, Harry C. 1992. "The Pragmatic Ends of Popular Politics." In *Habermas and the Public Sphere,* ed. Craig Calhoun. Cambridge, Mass.: MIT Press.

Boyte, Harry C., and Sara M. Evans. 1986. *Free Spaces: The Sources of Democratic Change in America.* New York: Harper & Row.

Brazil. 1989. *Constituição da República Federativa do Brasil 1988.* Brasília: Centro Gráfico do Senado Federal.

Brecher, Jeremy, Tim Costello, and Brendan Smith. 2000. *Globalization from Below: The Power of Solidarity.* Cambridge, Mass.: South End Press.

Brenner, Neil. 1998. "Global Cities, Glocal States: Global City Formation and State Territorial Restructuring in Contemporary Europe." *Review of International Political Economy* 5, no. 1 (Spring): 1–37.

———. 1999. "Globalisation as Reterritorialisation: The Re-Scaling of Urban Governance in the European Union." *Urban Studies* 36: 431–51.

Brown, Michael P. 1997. *RePlacing Citizenship: AIDS Activism and Radical Democracy.* New York: Guilford Press.

Bruhn, Kathleen. 1999. "PRD Local Governments in Michoacán: Implications for Mexico's Democratization."In *Subnational Politics and Democratization in Mexico,* ed. Wayne A. Cornelius, Todd A. Eisenstadt, and Jane Hindley, 19–48. La Jolla, Calif.: Center for U.S.-Mexican Studies.

Buarque, Cristovam. 1999. "A Missão do PT e Seus Governos." In *Governo e Cidadania: Balanço e Reflexões Sobre o Modo Petista de Governar,* ed. I. Magalhães, L. Barreto, and V. Trevas, 46–50. São Paulo: Editora Fundação Perseu Abramo.

Burawoy, Michael. 1991. *Ethnography Unbound: Power and Resistance in the Modern Metropolis.* Berkeley: University of California Press.

———. 2000. *Global Ethnography: Forces, Connections, and Imaginations in a Postmodern World.* Berkeley: University of California Press.

Cabrero-Mendoza, Enrique. 1996. "Innovative Capacities of Mexican Municipalities; Capacidades Innovadoras de Municipios Mexicanos." *Revista Mexicana de Sociologia* 58: 73–97.

Caldeira, Teresa Pires do Rio. 1984. *A Política dos Outros: O Cotidiano dos Moradores da Periferia e o Que Pensam do Poder e dos Poderosos.* São Paulo: Brasiliense.

Calderon, Adolfo. 2002. *Gestão Municipal.* São Paulo: Cortez Editora.

Calhoun, Craig. 1994. *Neither Gods nor Emperors: Students and the Struggle for Democracy in China.* Berkeley: University of California Press.

Canty, Donald. 1993. "Seattle Conference on Reshaping Cities." *Progressive Architecture* 74: 25.

Cardoso, Ruth Corrêa Leite. 1988. "Os Movimentos Populares no Contexto da Consolidação da Democracia." In *A Democracia no Brasil: Dilemas e perspectivas,* ed. Fábio Wanderley Reis and Guillermo O'Donnell. São Paulo: Vértice.

———. 1994. "A Trajetória dos Movimentos Sociais." In *Os Anos 90: Política e Sociedade no Brasil,* ed. Evelina Dagnino, 81–90. São Paulo: Editora Brasiliense.

Carvalho, Inaia. 1997. "Decentralization and Social Policies in Bahia." *Caderno CRH* 26–27: 75–105.

Carvalho, Maria. 2002. *Orçamento Participativo nos Municipos Paulistas.* São Paulo: Polis.

Cassen, Bernard. 2002. "On the Attac." *New Left Review* 19: 41–61.

Cattani, Antonio David. 2001. "Fórum Social Mundial: A Construção de um Mundo Melhor." Porto Alegre: Editora Vozes.

Cohen, Jean L. 1985. "Strategy or Identity: New Theoretical Paradigms and Contemporary Social Movements." *Social Research* 52: 663–716.

———. 1996. "Rights, Citizenship and the Modern Form of the Social: Dilemmas of Arendtian Republicanism." *Constellations* 3: 164–85.

———. 1999a. "Changing Paradigms of Citizenship and the Exclusiveness of the Demos." *International Sociology* 14: 245–68.

———. 1999b. "Does Voluntary Association Make Democracy Work." In *Diversity and Its Discontents*, ed. N. J. Smelser and J. C. Alexander, 263–92. Princeton, N.J.: Princeton University Press.

Cohen, Jean L., and Andrew Arato. 1992. *Civil Society and Political Theory*. Cambridge, Mass.: MIT Press.

Cohen, Joshua. 1996. "Procedure and Substance in Deliberative Democracy." In *Democracy and Difference: Contesting the Boundaries of the Political*, ed. Seyla Benhabib, 95–109. Princeton, N.J.: Princeton University Press.

———. 1997. "Directly-Deliberative Polyarchy." *European Law Journal* 3: 313–42.

———. 1998. "Democracy and Liberty." In *Deliberative Democracy*, ed. J. Elster, 185–232. Cambridge: Cambridge University Press.

Cohen, Joshua, and Joel Rogers. 1995. *Associations and Democracy*. London: Verso.

Conniff, Michael L. 1981. *Urban Politics in Brazil: The Rise of Populism, 1925–1945*. Pittsburgh: University of Pittsburgh Press.

Coppedge, M. 1998. "The Dynamic Diversity of Latin American Party Systems." *Party Politics* 4: 547–68.

Cortes, Carlos. 1974. *Gaucho Politics in Brazil*. Albuquerque: University of New Mexico Press.

Costa, Nilson. 1996. "Policy Innovation, Distributivism and Crisis: Health Care Policy in the 1980's and 1990's." *Dados* 39: 479–511.

Costa, Ricardo. 2002. "Decentralization, Financing and Regulation Reform of the Public Heath System in Brazil During the 1990's." *Revista de Sociologia e Politica* 18: 49–71.

Couto, Claudio Goncalves. 1994. "Mudanca e Crise: O PT no Governo de São Paulo." *Luan Nova*: 145–64.

———. 1995. *O Desafio de Ser Governo: O PT na Prefeitura de São Paulo (1989–1992)*. Rio de Janeiro: Paz e Terra.

Crook, Richard, and James Manor. 1998. *Democracy and Decentralisation in South Asia and West Africa: Participation, Accountability and Performance*. Cambridge: Cambridge University Press.

Cuaresma, Jocelyn-C. 1993. "Reforms in Local Planning." *Philippine Journal of Public Administration* 37: 1–21.

Dagnino, Evelina. 1994. "Os Movimentos Sociais e a Emergência de Uma Nova Noção de Cidadania." In *Os Anos 90: Política e Sociedade no Brasil*, ed. Evelina Dagnino, 103–18. São Paulo: Editora Brasiliense.

———. 1998. "Culture, Citizenship, and Democracy: Changing Discourses and

Practices of the Latin American Left." In *Cultures of Politics/Politics of Cultures: Re-Visioning Latin American Social Movements*, ed. Sonia E. Alvarez, Evelina Dagnino, and Arturo Escobar, 26–56. Boulder, Colo.: Westview Press.

———. 2002. *Sociedade Civil e Espaços Públicos no Brasil*. São Paulo: Paz e Terra.

Dahl, Robert Alan. 1961. *Who Governs? Democracy and Power in an American City*. New Haven, Conn.: Yale University Press.

———. 1989. *Democracy and Its Critics*. New Haven, Conn.: Yale University Press.

Daniel, Celso. 2001. "Participatory Urban Governance: The Experience of Santo Andre." *UN Chronicle* 38: 28.

Davis, Diane. 1994. *Urban Leviathan: Mexico City in the Twentieth Century*. Philadelphia: Temple University Press.

Decalo, Samuel. 1994. "The Future of Participatory Democracy in Africa." *Futures* 26: 987–92.

Deegan, Heather. 2002. "A Critical Examination of the Democratic Transition in South Africa: The Question of Public Participation." *Commonwealth and Comparative Politics* 40: 43–60.

Dewey, John. 1927. *The Public and Its Problems*. New York: Holt.

Dias, Marcia Ribeiro. 2002. *Sob o Signo da Vontade Popular: O Orçamento Participativo e o Dilema da Câmara Municipal de Porto Alegre*. Belo Horizonte: Editora da UFMG.

Dietz, Henry. 1998. *Urban Poverty, Political Participation and the Sate*. Pittsburgh: University of Pittsburgh Press.

Dillinger, William. 1999. *Fiscal Management in Federal Democracies*. Washington, D.C.: World Bank.

Doimo, Ana Maria. 1995. *A Vez e a Voz do Popular: Movimentos Sociais e Participação Política no Brasil Pós-70*. Rio de Janeiro: ANPOCS: Relume Dumará.

Domhoff, G. William. 2002. *Who Rules America; Power and Politics*. Boston: Mc-Graw-Hill.

Dowbor, Ladislau. 1998. "Response to Critics." *Latin American Perspectives* 25: 49–52.

Drake, St. Clair, and Horace R. Cayton. 1945. *Black Metropolis: A Study of Negro Life in a Northern City*. New York: Harcourt, Brace.

Dresch, Giovanni. 1985. Untitled Article. *Debates Populares* 1: 1.

Durham, Eunice. 1984. "Os Movimentos Sociais: A Construção da Cidadania." *Novos Estudos CEBRAP*: 24–30.

Dutra, Olivio. 1990. "Depoimento de Olivio Dutra." In *A Intervenção nos Transportes Coletivos*, ed. Jõao Alves da Lima, 39–51. São Paulo: CEDI.

Eastis, Carla M. 1998. "Organizational Diversity and the Production of Social Capital: One of These Groups Is Not Like the Other." *American Behavioral Scientist* 42: 66–77.

Eckstein, Susan. 1977. *The Poverty of Revolution: The State and the Urban Poor in Mexico*. Princeton, N.J.: Princeton University Press.

———. 1998. "The Meaning of Mexican Democratization." *Research in Political Sociology* 8: 15–33.

Eley, Geoff. 1992. "Nations, Publics, and Political Cultures: Placing Habermas in the Nineteenth Century." In *Habermas and the Public Sphere*, ed. Craig Calhoun, 289–339. Cambridge, Mass.: MIT University Press.

Eliasoph, Nina. 1990. "Political Culture and the Presentation of a Political Self: A Study of the Public Sphere in the Spirit of Erving Goffman." *Theory and Society* 19: 465–94.

———. 1998. *Avoiding Politics: How Americans Produce Apathy in Everyday Life.* Cambridge: Cambridge University Press.

Ellner, Steve. 1986. "The Mas Party in Venezuela." *Latin American Perspectives* 13: 81–107.

Elster, John. 1996. "Introduction." In *The Roundtable Talks and the Breakdown of Communism*, ed. id., 1–20. Chicago: University of Chicago Press.

———. 1998. "Deliberation and Constitution Making." In *Deliberative Democracy*, ed. id., 97–122. Cambridge: Cambridge University Press.

Emirbayer, Mustafa, and Mimi Sheller. 1999. "Publics in History." *Theory and Society*: 145–97.

Enriquez, Laura Álvarez. 1998. "Participación ciudadana y la nueva cultura política en la Ciudad de México." *Acta Sociologica* 22: 9–24.

Esping-Anderson, Gosta. 1985. *Politics Against Markets: The Social Democratic Road to Power*. Princeton, N.J.: Princeton University Press.

Espinolda, Roberto. 2002. "Political Parties and Democratization in the Southern Cone of Latin America." *Democratization* 9: 109–30.

Evans, Peter. 1996. "Government Action, Social Capital, and Development: Reviewing the Evidence on Synergy." *World Development* 24: 1119–32.

Evans, Peter, Dietrich Reuschemeyer, and Theda Skocpol. 1985. *Bringing the State Back In*. New York: Cambridge University Press.

Evans, Sarah, and Harry Boyte. 1992. *Free Spaces: The Sources of Democratic Change in America*. New York: Harper & Row.

Fedozzi, Luciano. 1997. *Orçamento Participativo: Reflexoes Sobre a Experiencia de Porto Alegre*. Porto Alegre: Tomo Editorial.

———. 2000. *O Poder da Aldeia: Genese e História do Orçamento Participativo de Porto Alegre*. Porto Alegre: Tomo Editorial.

Ferreira, Marcelo Costa. 1999. "A Participação Política e os Seus Determinantes Socioeconômicos nas Regiões Metropolitanas Brasileiras: 1988–1996." *Opnião Pública* 5: 76–86.

———. 2000. "Associativismo e Contato Político nas Regiões Metropolitanas do Brasil, 1988–1996: Revisitando o Problema da Participação." *Revista Brasileira de Ciências Sociais* 14, no. 41: 80–102.

Ferretti, Rosemary Brum. 1984. "Uma Casa nas Costas. Análise do Movimento Social Urbano em Porto Alegre 1975–1982." MA thesis, Department of Sociology, Universidade Federal do Rio Grande do Sul, Porto Alegre.

FESCE. 1999. Fundação de Educação Social e Comunitária, Prefeitura Municipal de Porto Alegre. *Regioes do Orçamento Participativo de Porto Alegre—Alguns Indicadores Sociais*. Porto Alegre: FESC.

Figueiredo Júnior, José Rubens de Lima, and Bolivar Lamounier. 1996. *As cida-*

des que dão certo: Experiências inovadoras na administração pública brasileira. Brasília: MH Comunicação.

Filho, Arno Augustin. 1994. "A Experiencia do Orçamento Participativo na Administração Popular da Prefeitura Municipal de Porto Alegre." In *Porto Alegre: O Desafio da Mudanca*, ed. C. H. Horn and A. A. Filho, 49–68. Porto Alegre: Editora Ortiz.

Filho, Jao. 1998. "Critical Sociology of Social Engineering? Commentary on Ladislau Dowbor's 'Decentralization and Governance.'" *Latin American Perspectives* 25: 45–48.

Fine, Ben. 2001. *Social Capital Versus Social Theory*. London: Routledge.

Fischer, Nilton Bueno, and Jaqueline Moll. 2000. *Por uma nova esfera pública: A experiência do orçamento participativo*. Petrópolis, Brazil: Vozes.

Fischer, Tânia, Antônio Colomer, and Ângela Teixeira. 1993. "Gestão Municipal, Descentralização e Participação do Cidadão—Um Estudo Comparado Espanha/Brasil (Síntese de Resultados)." In *Poder Local: Governo e Cidadania*, ed. Tânia Fischer, 115–23 . Rio de Janeiro: Fundação Getúlio Vargas.

Fisher, Robert, and Joseph Kling, eds. 1993. *Mobilizing the Community: Local Politics in the Era of the Global City*. Newbury Park, Calif.: Sage Publications.

Fisher, William, and Thomas Ponniah. 2003. "Another World Is Possible: Popular Alternatives to Globalization at the World Social Forum." In *Another World Is Possible: Popular Alternatives to Globalization at the World Social Forum*, ed. id., xvi–xix. New York: Zed Books.

Fontes, Breno. 1995a. "Gestion Local en el Nordeste de Brasil: En Busca de Nuevos Paradigmas." *Revista Brasileiro de Ciencias Socias*: 123–42.

———. 1995b. "Local Administration in the Northeast of Brazil." *Revista Mexicana de Sociologia* 57: 123–42.

———. 1997. "Gestion Urbana y Participacion Popular." *Nueva Sociedad* 149: 179–89.

Fontes, Breno Augusto Souto-Maior. 1990. "Movimentos Reivindicativos Urbanos e Poder Local." *Caderno de Estudos Sociais* 6: 225–31.

Fox, Jonathan. 1995. "Governance and Rural Development in Mexico: State Intervention and Public Accountability." *Journal of Development Studies* 32: 1–30.

———. 1996. "How Does Civil Society Thicken? The Political Construction of Social Capital in Rural Mexico." *World Development* 24: 1089–1103.

Fox, Jonathan, and Luis Hernandez. 1992. "Mexico's Difficult Democracy: Grassroots Movements, NGOs, and Local Government." *Alternatives* 17: 165–208.

Fraser, Nancy. 1992. "Rethinking the Public Sphere: A Contribution to the Critique of Actually Existing Democracy." In *Habermas and the Public Sphere*, ed. Craig Calhoun, 109–42. Cambridge, Mass.: MIT Press.

Fraser, Nancy, and Sandra Lee Bartky. 1992. *Revaluing French Feminism: Critical Essays on Difference, Agency, and Culture*. Bloomington: Indiana University Press.

Fukasaku, Kiichiro. 1998. *Democracy Decentralisation, and the Deficits in Latin America*. Paris: Inter-American Development Bank.

————. 1999. *Fiscal Decentralization in Emerging Economies*. Paris: Development Center of the Organisation for Economic Co-Operation and Development.

Fung, Archon. 2003. "Associations and Democracy: Between Theories, Hopes, and Realities." *Annual Review of Sociology* 29: 515–39.

Fung, Archon, and Erik Olin Wright. 2003. *Deepening Democracy: Institutional Innovations in Empowered Participatory Governance*. New York: Verso.

Gaglietti, Mauro. 1999. *PT: Ambivalências de uma Militância*. Porto Alegre: Dacasa Editora / Unicruz.

Gay, Robert. 1990. "Community Organization and Clientelist Politics in Contemporary Brazil: A Case Study from Suburban Rio de Janeiro." *International Journal of Urban and Regional Research* 14: 648–66.

————. 1990. "Popular Incorporation and Prospects for Democracy: Some Implications of the Brazilian Case." *Theory and Society* 19: 447–63.

————. 1992. "Hierarchy and Trust in Modern Mexico and Brazil." *American Journal of Sociology* 97: 1149–50.

————. 1995. "Democracy, Clientelism, and Civil Society." *Contemporary Sociology* 24: 769.

————. 1998. "Rethinking Clientelism: Demands, Discourses and Practices in Contemporary Brazil." *Revista Europea de Estudios Latinoamericanos y del Caribe/European Review of Latin American and Caribbean Studies* 65: 7–24.

————. 1999. "The Broker and the Thief: A Parable (Reflections on Popular Politics in Brazil)." *Luso Brazilian Review* 36: 49–70.

Genro, Tarso. 1990. "Licoes da Intervencao." In *A Intervencao Nos Transportes Coletivos*, ed. João Alves da Lima, pp. 51–63. São Paulo: CEDI.

————. 1999. "Um Debate Estratégico." In *Governo e Cidadania: Balanço e Reflexões Sobre o Modo Petista de Governar*, ed. I. Magalhães, L. Barreto, and V. Trevas, 11–17 . São Paulo: Editora Fundação Perseu Abramo.

Gilbert, Alan, and Peter Ward. 1984. "Community Action by the Urban Poor: Democratic Involvement, Community Self-Help or a Means of Social Control." *World Development* 12: 769–82.

Giugni McAdam, Marco, and Charles Tilly, eds. 1999. *How Social Movements Matter*. Minneapolis: University of Minnesota Press.

Goffman, Erving. 1959. *The Presentation of Self in Everyday Life*. Garden City, N.Y.: Doubleday.

Gohn, Maria da Gloria. 1982. *Reinvidicações Populares Urbanas*. São Paulo: Cortez.

————. 1989. "Conselhos Populares, Participação e Gestão de Bens Coletivos." In *XIII Encontro Anual da ANPOCS*. Caxambu, Minas Gerais.

Goldfrank, Benjamin. 2001. "Deepening Democracy Through Citizen Participation? A Comparative Analysis of Three Cities." In *Annual Meeting of the Latin American Studies Association*. Washington, D.C.

————. 2002. "The Fragile Flower of Local Democracy: A Case Study of Decentralization/Participation in Montevideo." *Politics and Society* 30: 58–83.

————. 2003. "Making Participation Work in Porto Alegre." In *Radicals in Power: The Workers' Party (PT) and Experiments in Urban Democracy in Brazil*, ed. Gianpaolo Baiocchi, 27–52 . New York: Zed Books.

———. Forthcoming. "The Difficulties of Deepening Democracy: La Causa R Meets Caracas the Horrible." In *The Left in the City*, ed. id. and D. Chavez. London: Latin American Bureau.

Graham, Carol. 1992. *Peru's Apra*. Boulder, Colo.: Lynne Reinner.

Graham, Lawrence S. 1997. *Social Policy Dilemmas under Decentralization and Federalism: The Case of Brazil*. Seoul: Korea Institute for International Economic Policy.

Gramsci, Antonio. 1971. *Selections from the prison notebooks of Antonio Gramsci*, ed. Quintin Hoare and Geoffrey Nowell-Smith. New York: International Publishers.

Gret, Marion, and Yves Sintomer. 2002. *Porto Alegre: L'Espoir d'une autre démocratie*. Paris: La Découverte.

Guareschi, Pedrinho. 1980. "Squatter's Movements in Brazil." Ph.D. thesis, Sociology, University of Wisconsin, Madison.

———. 1985. *A Cruz e o Poder: A Irmandade da Santa Cruz no Alto Solimões*. Petrópolis: Vozes.

Guidry, John A., and Pere Petit. 2003. "Faith in What Will Change: The PT Administration in Belém." In *Radicals in Power: The Workers' Party (PT) and Experiments in Urban Democracy in Brazil*, ed. Gianpaolo Baiocchi. New York: Zed Books.

Guttman, Amy, and Dennis Thompson. 1996. *Democracy and Disagreement*. Cambridge, Mass.: Belknap Press of Harvard University Press.

Habermas, Jürgen. 1969. *Die Linke Antwortet Jürgen Habermas. Mit Beiträgen von Wolfgang Abendroth*. Frankfurt am Main: Europäische Verlagsanstalt.

———. 1974. "The Public Sphere: An Encyclopedia Article." *New German Critique* 3: 49–55.

———. 1989. *The Structural Transformation of the Public Sphere*. Cambridge, Mass.: MIT Press.

———. 1996. *Between Facts and Norms: Contributions to a Discourse Theory of Law and Democracy*. Cambridge, Mass.: MIT Press.

Habermas, Jürgen, and Max Pensky. 2001. *The Postnational Constellation: Political Essays*. Cambridge, Mass.: MIT Press.

Hamilton, Nora. 1984. *The Limits of State Autonomy: Postrevolutionary Mexico*. Princeton, N.J.: Princeton University Press.

Hanchard, Michael. 1994. *Orpheus and Power: The Movimento Negro of Rio de Janeiro and São Paulo, Brazil, 1945–1988*. Princeton, N.J.: Princeton University Press.

Hann, C. M., ed. 1993. *Socialism: Ideals, Ideologies, and Local Practice*. New York: Routledge.

———. 1996. "Introduction: Political Society and Civil Anthropology." In *Civil Society: Challenging Western Models*, ed. id. and Elizabeth Dunn, 1–26. London and New York: Routledge.

Hardt, Michael. 1987. "The Withering of Civil Society." In *Masses, Classes, and the Public Sphere*, ed. Mike Hill and Warren Montag, 158–76. New York: Verso.

———. 1995. "The Withering of Civil Society." *Social Text* 45: 27–44.

————. 1998. "The Global Society of Control." *Discourse* 20: 139–52.

————. 2002. "Today's Bandung?" *New Left Review* 14: 112–18.

Hardt, Michael, and Antonio Negri. 2000. *Empire*. Cambridge, Mass.: Harvard University Press.

————. 2001. "Adventures of the Multitude: Response of the Authors." *Rethinking Marxism* 13: 236–43.

————. 2003. "Foreword." In *Another World Is Possible: Popular Alternatives to Globalization at the World Social Forum*, ed. William Fisher and Thomas Ponniah, xvi–xix . New York: Zed Books.

————. 2004. *Multitude: War and Democracy in the Age of Empire*. New York: Penguin Press.

Harnecker, Marta. 1991. *Frente Amplio: Los Desafios de un Izquierda Legal. Segunda Parte: Los Hitos Mas Importantes de Su História*. Montevideo: Ediciones La Republica.

————. 1993. *Alcadia de Porto Alegre: Aprendiendo a Gobernar*. Havana: MEPLA.

————. 1994. *El Sueño Era Posible*. Havana: Editorial Cultura Popular.

Higgins, Michael James, and Tanya L. Coen. 1992. *Oigame! Oigame!: Struggle and Social Change in a Nicaraguan Urban Community*. Boulder, Colo.: Westview Press.

Hinders, Duane Charles. 1996. "Low-Income Urban Housing Policy at the Intersection of State and Society Political Decentralization, Grassroots Participation and New Policy Actors in Brazil." MA thesis, Public Affairs, University of Texas at Austin.

Hirst, Paul Q. 1994. *Associative Democracy: New Forms of Economic and Social Governance*. Amherst: University of Massachusetts Press.

Horn, Carlos Henrique, and Augustin Filho Arno. 1994. *Porto Alegre: O Desafio da Mudança: A Políticas Financeira, Administrative e de Recursos Humanos no Governo Olívio Dutra, 1989–92*. Porto Alegre: Editora Ortiz.

Hunter, Floyd. 1953. *Community Power Structure: A Study of Decision Makers*. Chapel Hill: University of North Carolina Press.

IBGE. 1988. Instituto Brasileiro de Geografia e Estatlstlca. *Indicadores Sociais: Regioes Metropolitanas, Aglomeracoes Urbanas, Municipios Com mais de 100,000 Habitantes*. Rio de Janeiro: IBGE.

————. 1991. "Anuário Estatístico do Brasil." Rio de Janeiro: IBGE.

————. 2000. Pesquisa Nacional de Amostra de Domicílios 1996: Suplemento. www.ibge.gov.br (accessed July 3,2002).

————. 2001. "Anuário Estatístico do Brasil." Rio de Janeiro: IBGE.

Instituto Pólis. 2001. *125 Dicas do Instituto Pólis*. São Paulo: Instituto Pólis.

Jacobi, Pedro. 2000. *Politicas Socias e Ampliação da Cidadania*. Rio de Janeiro: FGV Editora.

Jacobi, Pedro Teixeira, and Marco Antônio Carvalho. 1996. "Orçamento Participativo: Co-Responsabilidade na Gestão das Cidades." *Cadernos CEDEC, São Paulo* 55.

Jäggi, Max, Roger Müller, and Sil Schmid. 1977. *Red Bologna*. London: Writers' and Readers' Cooperative. Originally published as *Das rote Bologna: Kommu-*

nisten demokratisieren eine Stadt im kapitalistischen Westen (Zurich: Verlags-genossenschaft, 1976).

Jessop, Bob. 1993. "Towards a Schumpeterian Workfare State? Preliminary Remarks on a Post-Fordist Political Economy." *Studies in Political Economy* 40: 7–39.

———. 2000. "The Crisis of the National Spatio-Temporal Fix and the Tendential Ecological Dominance of Globalizing Capitalism." *International Journal of Urban and Regional Research* 24: 323–60.

Johnston, Hank, and Bert Klandermans. 1995. *Social Movements and Culture.* Minneapolis: University of Minnesota Press.

Keck, Margaret. 1984. "Update on the Brazilian Labor Movement." *Latin American Perspectives* 11: 27–34.

———. 1992. *The Workers' Party and Democratization in Brazil.* New Haven, Conn.: Yale University Press.

Kenney, C. 1998. "Outsider and Anti-Party Politicians in Power." *Party Politcs* 4: 57–75.

Kerbuay, Maria. 2001. "Federalism, Decentralization and Democracy." *Estudos de Sociologia* 6: 51–61.

Kertzer, David I. 1980. *Comrades and Christians: Religion and Political Struggle in Communist Italy.* Cambridge: Cambridge University Press.

Kingstone, Peter R., and Timothy J. Power. 2000. *Democratic Brazil: Actors, Institutions, and Processes.* Pittsburgh: University of Pittsburgh Press.

Klein, Naomi. 2003. The Hijacking of the World Social Forum. http://www. nadir.org/nadir/initiativ/agp/free/wsf/naomiklein.htm (accessed May 1, 2003).

Klink, Jeroen. 1999. "The Future Is Coming. Economic Restructuring in the São Paulo Fringe: The Case of Diadema." *Habitat International* 23: 325–28.

Koopmans, Ruud, and Dieter Rucht. 2002. "Protest Event Analysis." In *Methods of Social Movement Research*, ed. Bert Klandermans and Suzanne Staggenborg, 231–59. Minneapolis: University of Minnesota Press.

Kriesi, Hanspeter, and Dominique Wisler. 1999. "The Impact of Social Movements on Political Institutions: A Comparison of the Introduction of Direct Legislation in Switzerland and the United States." In *How Social Movements Matter*, ed. Marco Giugni McAdam and Charles Tilly, 42–65. Minneapolis: University of Minnesota Press.

Kugelmas, Eduardo. 1999. "Recentralization/Decentralization Dynamics of the Federative Regime in 1990's Brazil." *Tempo Social* 11: 63–81.

Laclau, Ernesto. 2000. "Constructing Universality." In *Contingency, Hegemony, Universality: Contemporary Dialogues on the Left*, ed. Judith Butler, Ernesto Laclau, and Slavoj Žižek, 281–308. London: Verso.

Laclau, Ernesto, and Chantal Mouffe. 1985. *Hegemony and Socialist Strategy.* London: Verso.

Lagos, Marta. 2001. "Between Stability and Crisis in Latin America." *Journal of Democracy* 12, no. 1 (Jan.): 137–45.

Lancaster, Roger. 1992. *Life Is Hard: Machismo, Danger, and the Intimacy of Power in Nicaragua.* Berkeley: University of California Press.

Lanegran, Kimberly. 1996. "Civic Associations in Transitional Local Government Structures in South Africa." *Critical Sociology* 22: 113–34.

Lanzaro, Jorge. 1998. "Uruguay: The Alternatives of Pluralist Presidentialism." *Revista Mexicana de Sociologia* 60: 187–215.

Leite, Ilka Boaventura. 1996. *Negros no sul do Brasil: Invisibilidade e territorialidade.* Ilha de Santa Catarina, SC: Letras Contemporâneas.

Lesbaupin, Ivo, ed. 1996. *Prefeituras do povo e para o povo.* São Paulo: Edições Loyola.

———. 2000. *Poder local x exclusão social: A experiência das prefeituras democráticas no Brasil.* Petropolis: Vozes.

Lessa, Sergio. 2001. "'Immaterial Labor': Negri, Lazzarato and Hardt; "Trabalho Imaterial": Negri, Lazzarato e Hardt." *Estudos de Sociologia* 6: 119–43.

Lichterman, Paul. 1996. *The Search for Political Community.* Cambridge: Cambridge University Press.

———. 1998. "What Do Movements Mean? The Value of Participant Observation." *Qualitative Sociology* 21: 401–18.

———. 1999. "Talking Identity in the Public Sphere: Broad Visions and Small Spaces in Sexual Identity Politics." *Theory and Society* 28: 101–41.

———. 2000. "Integrating Diversity: Boundaries, Bonds, and the Greater Community in the New Golden Rule." In *Autonomy and Order: A Communitarian Anthology*, ed. E. W. Lehman, 125–41 . Lanham, Md.: Rowman & Littlefield.

———. 2002. "Seeing Structure Happen: Theory-Driven Participant Observation." In *Methods of Social Movement Research*, ed. Bert Klandermans and Suzanne Staggenborg, 118–45. Minneapolis: University of Minnesota Press.

Lima, Gildo. 1996. "A Experiencia da Prefeitura de Porto Alegre." In *Prefeituras do Povo e Para o Povo*, ed. I. Lesbaupin. São Paulo: Edições Loyola.

Lima, Gilson. 1993. "Entrevista: Administração Popular em Porto Alegre: Dilemas e Desafios." In *Uma Aventura Responsavel: Novos Desafios das Administracoes Populares*, ed. E. Luzzatto. Porto Alegre: Sagra-DC Editores.

Lipset, Seymour Martin. 1990. "The Death of the Third Way." *National Interest* 30: 25–38.

———. 1997. "The Iron Law of Oligarchy." In *Social Movements: Perspectives and Issues*, ed. Steven M. Buechler and F. Kurt Cylke Jr., 385–92. Mountain View, Calif.: Mayfield Publishing.

Logan, John R., and Harvey L. Molotch. 1987. *Urban Fortunes: The Political Economy of Place.* Berkeley: University of California Press.

Lopez, Luiz Roberto. 1993. "Brasil o Federalismo Mal Costurado." *Vozes* 87: 79–82.

Lopez-Monjardin, Adriana. 1999. "The Accords of San Andres and the Autonomous Governments in Chiapas; Los Acuerdos de San Andres y Los Gobiernos Autonomos en Chiapas." *Espiral: Estudios sobre Estado y Sociedad* 5: 127–45.

Lovell, Peggy. 1994. "Race, Gender, and Development in Brazil." *Latin American Research Review* 29: 7–35.

Lowy, Michael. 1987. "A New Type of Party: The Brazilian PT." *Latin American Perspectives* 14: 453–64.

Lynd, Robert S., and Helen M. Lynd. 1929. *Middletown: A Study in Contemporary American Culture.* New York: Harcourt, Brace.

Lyndon B. Johnson School of Public Affairs. 1997. *Policymaking in a Redemocratized Brazil.* Policy Research Project Report No. 119. Austin: University of Texas.

Lyons, Michal, Carin Smuts, and Anthea Stephens. 2001. "Participation, Empowerment and Sustainability: How Do the Links Work?" *Urban Studies* 38: 1233–51.

Macaulay, Fiona. 1996. "Governing for Everyone: The Workers' Party in São Paulo, 1989–1992." *Bulletin of Latin American Research* 15: 211–29.

Magalhães, Inês, Luiz Barreto, and Vincente Trevas. 1999. *Governo e Cidadania: Balanço e Reflexões sobre o Modo Petista de Governar.* São Paulo: Editora Fundação Perseu Abramo.

Mainwaring, Scott. 1986a. *The Catholic Church and Politics in Brazil, 1916–1985.* Stanford, Calif.: Stanford University Press.

———. 1986b. *The Consolidation of Democracy in Latin America: A Rapporteur's Report.* Notre Dame, Ind.: Helen Kellogg Institute for International Studies, University of Notre Dame.

———. 1999. *Rethinking Party Systems in the Third Wave of Democratization.* Stanford, Calif.: Stanford University Press.

Maira, Luis, and Guido Vicario. 1991. *Perspectivas de la izquierda latinoamericana: Seis diálogos.* Santiago, Chile: Fondo de Cultura Económica.

Mansbridge, Jane. 1980. *Beyond Adversary Democracy.* Chicago: University of Chicago Press.

———. 1990. "Democracy and Common Interests." *Social Alternatives* 8: 20–25.

———. 1995. Does Participation Make Better Citizens. http://www.cpn.ort/cpn/cpn.html (accessed November 2001).

Maree, Johann. 1998. "The Cosatu Participatory Democratic Tradition and South Africa's New Parliament: Are They Reconcilable?" *African Affairs* 97: 29–51.

Markoff, John. 1997. "Peasants Help Destroy an Old Regime and Defy a New One: Some Lessons from and for the Study of Social Movements." *American Journal of Sociology* 102: 1113–42.

———. 1998. "Globalization and the Future of Democracy." *Journal of World-Systems Research* 2: 281–98.

Marquetti, Adalmir. 2000. "Participatory Budgeting in Porto Alegre." *Indicator S A* 17: 71–78.

———. 2002. "Participação e Redistribuição: O Orçamento Participativo em Porto Alegre." In *A Inovação Democrática no Brasil: O Orçamento Participativo,* ed. L. Avritzer and Z. Navarro, 129–56. São Paulo: Cortez.

Marschall, Melissa J. 2001. "Does the Shoe Fit? Testing Models of Participation for African-American and Latino Involvement in Local Politics." *Urban Affairs Review* 37: 227–48.

Martines Fabre, José. 1996. "The 1988 Brazilian Constitution and the Real Plan Contradictions and Challenges." *Ceteris Paribus* 6: 43–68.

Marx, Karl, and Frederick Engels. 1978 [written 1845–46]. *The German Ideology.* Part I. In *The Marx-Engels Reader,* ed. R. C. Tucker. New York: Norton.

McDonough, Peter, Doh C. Shin, and José Alvaro Moises. 1998. "Democratization and Participation: Comparing Spain, Brazil, and Korea." *Journal of Politics* 60, no. 4 (November): 919–53.

Medeiros, Antonio Carlos. 1994. "The Politics of Decentralization in Brazil." *Review of Latin American and Carribean Studies* 57: 7–27.

Melo, Marcus. 1990. "A Formação de Politicas Publicas e a Transicao Democrática." *Dados* 33: 443–70.

Menegat, Elizete. 1995. "Fios Condutores da Participação Popular em Porto Alegre: Elementos Para um Debate." *Proposta* 9: 34–40.

Meneguello, Rachel. 1989. *PT: A Formação de um Partido, 1979–1982.* Rio de Janeiro: Editora Paz e Terra.

Michels, Robert. 1949. *First Lectures in Political Sociology.* Translated by Alfred de Grazia. Minneapolis: University of Minnesota Press.

———. [1915] 1999. *Political Parties: A Sociological Study of the Oligarchical Tendencies of Modern Democracy.* Translated by Eden and Cedar Paul. Reprint. New Brunswick, N.J.: Transaction Publishers.

Migdal, Joel. 2001. *State in Society: Studying How States and Societies Transform and Constitute One Another.* Cambridge: Cambridge University Press.

Mische, Ann. Forthcoming. "Cross-Talk in Movements: Reconceiving the Culture-Network Link." In *Social Movement Analysis: The Network Perspective,* ed. M. Diani and D. McAdam. London: Oxford University Press.

Mitlin, Diana, and John Thompson. 1995. "Participatory Approaches in Urban Areas: Strengthening Civil Society or Reinforcing the Status Quo?" *Environment and Urbanization* 7: 231–50.

Mizrahi, Yemile. 2004. "Twenty Years of Decentralization in Mexico: A Top-Down Process." In *Decentralization, Democratic Governance, and Civil Society in Comparative Perspective: Africa, Asia, and Latin America,* ed. Philip Oxhorn, Joseph S. Tulchin, and Andrew D. Selee, 39–74 . Washington, D.C.: Woodrow Wilson Center Press; Baltimore: Johns Hopkins University Press.

Moctezuma, Pedro. 2001. "Community-Based Organization and Participatory Planning in South-East Mexico City." *Environment and Urbanization* 13: 117–33.

Moises, José Alvaro, Luiz Gonzaga de Souza Lima, Tilman Evers, Herbert José de Souza, and Ximena Bazzarra. 1982. *Alternativas Populares da Democracia: Brasil Anos 80.* São Paulo: Vozes.

Montero, Alfred. 2001. "After Decentralization: Patterns of Intergovernment Conflict in Argentina, Brazil, Spain, and Mexico." *Publius* 31: 43–64.

Montoro Filho, André. 1994. "Federalismo e Reforma Fiscal." *Revista de Economia Politica* 14: 20–30.

Negt, Oskar, and Alexander Kluge. 1993. *Public Sphere and Experience: Toward an Analysis of the Bourgeois and Proletarian Public Sphere.* Translated by Peter Labanyi, Jamie Owen Daniel, and Assenka Oksiloff. Minneapolis: University of Minnesota Press.

Neto, Silva, and Lauro de Araújo. 1999. *Derivativos: Definições, Emprego e Risco.* São Paulo: Atlas.

Neves, Gleisi. 1993. *Descentralização Governmental Municipio e Democracia.* Rio de Janeiro: Instituto Brasileiro de Administração Municipal.

Nickson, Andrew. 1995. *Local Governments in Latin America.* Boulder, Colo.: Lynne Rienner.

———. 2002. *Decentralization: The Quiet Revolution.* Pittsburgh: University of Pittsburgh Press.

Noll, Maria Izabel. 1996. Eleições em Porto Alegre, Um Pouco de História. www.tche.ufrgs.br/nupergs/ (accessed August 12, 2000).

Noll, Maria Izabel, and Hélgio Trindade, eds. 1995. *Estatísticas eleitorais comparativas do Rio Grande do Sul, 1945–1994.* Porto Alegre: Editora da Universidade, Universidade Federal do Rio Grande do Sul; Estado do Rio Grande do Sul, Assembléia Legislativa.

Novaes, Carlos Alberto M. 1993. "PT: Dilemas da Burocratização." *Novos Estudos Cebrap* 35: 217–37.

Nylen, William R. 1995. "The Workers' Party in Rural Brazil." *NACLA Report on the Americas* 29: 27–32.

———. 1997a. "Reconstructing the Workers' Party (PT): Lessons from North-Eastern Brazil." In *The New Politics of Inequality in Latin America: Rethinking Participation and Representation,* ed. Douglas A. Chalmers et al., 421–46. New York: Oxford University Press.

———. 1997b. "Popular Participation in Brazil's Worker's Party: Democratizing Democracy in Municipal Politics." *Political Chronicle* 8: 1–9.

———. 2002. "Testing the Empowerment Thesis: The Participatory Budget in BH and Betim." *Comparative Politics* 34, no. 2: 127–45.

———. 2003. "An Enduring Legacy? Popular Participation in the Aftermath of the Participatory Budgets of João Monlevade and Betim." *Radicals in Power: The Workers' Party (PT) and Experiments in Urban Democracy in Brazil,* ed. Gianpaolo Baiochchi, 91–112. London: Zed.

O'Donnel, Guillermo. 1988. *Transicoes do Regime Autoritario: Primeiras Conclusoes.* São Paulo: Vertice.

O'Hare, Greg. 2001. "Urban Rennaissance: New Horizons for Rio's Favelas." *Geography* 86: 61.

Oliveira, Francisco de. 1986. "e Agora PT?" In *e Agora PT? Caráter e identidade,* ed. Emir Sader. São Paulo: Brazilense.

Oliveira, Jose Antonio Puppim de. 2002. "Implementing Environmental Policies in Developing Countries Through Decentralization." *World Development* 30: 1713.

Oliveira, Naya, and Tanya Barcellos. 1990. *O Rio Grande do Sul Urbano.* Porto Alegre: FEE.

Oliveira, Ney dos Santos. 1996. "Favelas and Ghettos: Race and Class in Rio de Janeiro and New York City." *Latin American Perspectives* 23: 71–89.

Olma, Sebastian. 2001. "Globalization, the Pudding and the Question of Power." *Theory, Culture and Society* 18: 111–22.

Paoli, Maria Célia. 1992. "Citizenship, Inequalities, Democracy and Rights: The Making of a Public Space in Brazil." *Social and Legal Studies*, 143–59.

Parnell, Susan, Edgar Pieterse, Mark Swilling, and Dominique Woolridge. *Democratising Local Government: The South African Experiment*. Cape Town: University of Cape Town Press.

Passos, André, and Assis Olegário Brasil. 2000.

Patillo-McCoy, Mary. 1998. "Church Culture as a Strategy of Action in the Black Community." *American Sociological Review* 63: 767–84.

Patterson, Thomas E. 2002. *The Vanishing Voter: Public Involvement in an Age of Uncertainty*. New York: Knopf.

Perz, Stephen G. 2000. "The Rural Exodus in the Context of the Economic Crisis, Globalization and Reform in Brazil." *International Migration Review* 34: 842–81.

Pickvance, Christopher G. 1999. "Democratisation and the Decline of Social Movements: The Effects of Regime Change on Collective Action in Eastern Europe, Southern Europe and Latin America." *Sociology* 33: 353–72.

Pinheiro, Jair. 1998. *Burocracia e Poder Local*. São Paulo: Marco Markovitch.

Pinheiro, Paulo Sergio. 1991. "Police and Political Crisis: The Case of the Military Police." In *Vigilantism and the State in Modern Latin America: Essays on Extralegal Violence*, ed. M. K. Huggins. New York: Praeger.

Pinto, Valeska P. 1992. *Prefeitura de Fortaleza: Administração Popular—1986/88*. São Paulo: Pólis.

Piven, Frances Fox, and Richard Cloward. 1979. *Poor People's Movements: Why They Succeed and How They Fail*. New York: Vintage Books.

Polletta, Francesca. 1999. "Free Spaces in Collective Action." *Theory and Society* 28: 1–38.

Pont, Raul. 1985. *Da Critica ao Populismo a Construção do PT*. Porto Alegre: Seriema.

———. 1994. "Incorporando Novos Atores Sociais." Prefeitura Municipal de Porto Alegre, Porto Alegre. Photocopy.

———. 2001. "Porto Alegre e a Luta Pela Democracia, Igualdade e Qualidade de Vida." In *Porto Alegre: Uma Cidade Que Conquista*, ed. R. A. Pont and A. Barcelos, 11–28. Porto Alegre: Artes e Oficios.

Power, Timothy. 2000. "Political Institutions in Democratic Brazil: Politics as a Permanent Constitutional Convention." In *Democratic Brazil: Actors, Institutions, and Processes*, ed. Peter R. Kingstone and Timothy J. Power, 17–35. Pittsburgh: University of Pittsburgh Press.

Pozzobon, Regina. 1998. *Porto Alegre: Os Desafios da Gestão Democrática*. São Paulo: Instituto Polis.

Przeworski, Adam. 1985. *Capitalism and Social Democracy*. New York: Cambridge University Press.

Putnam, Robert. 1995. "Bowling Alone: America's Declining Social Capital." *Journal of Democracy* 6: 65–78.

———. 2000. *Bowling Alone: The Collapse and Revival of American Community*. New York: Simon & Schuster.

Putnam, Robert D., Robert Leonardi, and Raffaella Nanetti. 1993. *Making*

Democracy Work: Civic Traditions in Modern Italy. Princeton, N.J.: Princeton University Press.

Ramirez-Saiz, Juan-Manuel. 1999. "Civil Political Practices and Local Power in the Metropolitan Area of Guadalajara, 1995–1997; Practicas politicas ciudadanas y poder local en el area metropolitana de Guadalajara, 1995–1997." *Estudios Sociologicos* 17: 441–72.

Ray, Raka. 1999. *Fields of Protest: Women's Movements in India*. Minneapolis: University of Minnesota Press.

Rech, Marcelo. 1988. "Movimento Comunitário: Força Nova na Politica." *Zero Hora*, December 18, pp. 2–3. Porto Alegre.

Reilley, Flavio. 1997. "Descentralização, Gastos Publicos e Preferencias." *Dados* 40: 413–40.

Reilly, Charles. 1995. *New Paths to Democratic Development in Latin America: The Rise of NGO-Municipal Collaboration*. Boulder, Colo.: Lynne Reiner.

Ribeiro, Luiz Cesar de Queiroz, and Luciana Correa do Lago. 1995. "Restructuring in Large Brazilian Cities: The Centre/Periphery Model." *International Journal of Urban and Regional Research* 19: 369–82.

Ribeiro, Matilde. 1999. "Gênero e Raça no Processo do Orçamento Participativo de Santo André, 1997–1998." MA thesis, Psicologia Social, PU-SP, São Paulo.

Roberts, Kenneth. 1998. *Deepening Democracy? The Modern Left and Social Movements in Chile and Peru*. Stanford, Calif.: Stanford University Press.

Sanchez, Felix. 2002. *Orçamento Participativo*. São Paulo: Cortez.

Santos, Boaventura de Souza. 1998. "Participatory Budgeting in Porto Alegre: Toward a Redistributive Democracy." *Politics and Society* 4: 461–510.

Santos, Wanderley Guilherme dos. 1993. *As Razoes da Desordem*. Rio de Janeiro: Rocca.

Schmidtt, David. 1993. "A 'Desitiotização da Cidadania': A Formação do Cidadao Para a Coisa Publica, Atraves de Sua Participação no Processo do Orçamento Participativo de Porto Alegre, entre 1989 e 1992." MA thesis, Education, Universidade Federal do Rio Grande do Sul, Porto Alegre.

Schmitt, Carl. 1996. *The Concept of the Political*. Chicago: University of Chicago Press.

Schönwälder, Gerd. 1997. "New Democratic Spaces at the Grassroots? Popular Participation in Latin American Local Governments." *Development and Change* 28: 753–70.

Setzler, Mark. 2000. "Democratizing Urban Brazil: Institutional Legacies and Determinants of Accountability in Local Elections and Legislatures." In *Annual Meeting of the Latin American Studies Association*. Miami, Fla. March 16–18.

Shidlo, Gil. 1998. "Local Urban Elections in Democratic Brazil." In *Urban Elections in Democratic Latin America*, ed. Henry A. Dietz and Gil Shidlo. Wilmington, Del.: Scholarly Resources.

Silva, Marcelo Kunrath. 2003. "Participation by Design? The Workers' Party in the Metropolitan Region of Porto Alegre." In *Radicals in Power*, ed. Gianpaolo Baiocchi. New York: Zed Books.

Simoes, Julio Assis. 1992. *O Dilema da Participação Popular*. São Paulo: Editora Marco Zero.

Singer, André. 2001. *O PT*. São Paulo: Publifolha.

Singer, Paul. 1996. *Um Governo de Esquerda Para Todos: Luiza Erundina na Prefeitura de São Paulo*. São Paulo: Brasiliense.

Skocpol, Theda, and Morris P. Fiorina. 1999. "Making Sense of the Civic Engagement Debate." In *Civic Engagement in American Democracy*, ed. id., 27–80. Washington, D.C.: Brookings Institution Press; New York: Russell Sage Foundation.

Somers, Margaret R. 1993. "Citizenship and the Place of the Public Sphere: Law, Community, and Political Culture in the Transition to Democracy." *American Sociological Review* 58: 587–620.

———. 1994a. "The Narrative Constitution of Identity: A Relational and Network Approach." *Theory and Society* 23: 605–49.

———. 1994b. "Rights, Relationality, and Membership: Rethinking the Making and Meaning of Citizenship." *Law and Social Inquiry* 19: 63–112.

———. 1995. "Narrating and Naturalizing Civil Society and Citizenship Theory: The Place of Political Culture and the Public Sphere." *Sociological Theory* 13: 229–73.

Souza, Celina. 1996. "Redemocratization and Decentralization in Brazil the Strength of the Member States." *Development and Change* 27: 529.

———. 2002. "Brazil: The Prospects of a Center-Constraining Federation in Fragmented Polity." *Publius* 32: 23.

Souza, Celina de. 1997. *Constitutional Engineering in Brazil*. London: Macmillan.

Spink, Peter, and Roberta Clemente. 1997. *20 Experiências de Gestão Pública e Cidadania*. Rio de Janeiro: Fundação Getulio Vargas Editora.

Staggenborg, Suzanne. 1989. "Stability and Innovation in the Women's Movement: A Comparison of Two Movement Organizations." *Social Problems* 36: 75–92.

Stepan, Alfred. 2000. "Brazil's Decentralized Federalism." *Daedalus* 129: 145.

Stokes, Susan Carol. 1995. *Cultures in Conflict: Social Movements and the State in Peru*. Berkeley: University of California Press.

Suttles, Gerald. 1976. "Urban Ethnography: Situational and Normative Accounts." *Annual Review of Sociology* 3: 1–18.

Tarrow, Sidney. 1996. Making Social Science Work across Space and Time: A Critical Reflection on Robert Putnam's *Making Democracy Work.*"*American Political Science Review* 90, no. 2: 389–97

Telles, Edward. 1992. "Residential Segregation and Skin Color in Brazil." *American Journal of Sociology* 57, no. 2: 186–97.

Telles, Vera da Silva. 1994. "Sociedade Civil e a Construção de Espaços Públicos." In *Os Anos 90: Política e Sociedade no Brasil*, ed. Evelina Dagnino, 91–102. São Paulo: Editora Brasiliense.

Tilly, Charles. 1978. *From Mobilization to Revolution*. Reading, Mass.: Addison-Wesley.

Tilly, Charles, and Edward Shorter. 1974. *Strikes in France, 1830–1968*. Cambridge: Cambridge University Press.

Tocqueville, Alexis de. [1835–39] 1945. *Democracy in America*. New York: Knopf.

UNDP (United Nations Development Program). 2004. *Democracy in Latin America*. New York: UNDP.

Utizig, José Eduardo. 1994. "Notas Sobre of Governo do PT em Porto Alegre." *Novos Estudos Cebrap* 45: 209–22.

———. 1998. "La Izquierda en el Gobierno: Notas Sobre el PT en Porto Alegre." *Nueva Sociedad* 157: 107–24.

Utzig, José. 1996. "Notas Sobre o Governo do PT em Porto Alegre." *Novos Estudos Cebrap* 45: 209–22.

———. 1999. "Orçamento Participativo e Performance Governamental." Report. Prefeitura Municipal de Porto Alegre, Porto Alegre. Photocopy.

Verba, Sidney, and Norman H. Nie. 1972. *Participation in America: Political Democracy and Social Equality.* New York: Harper & Row.

Viola, Eduardo, and Scott Mainwaring. 1987. "Novos Movimentos Sociais: Cultura Politica e Democracia." In *Uma Revolucao no Cotidiano? Os Novos Movimentos Sociais na America Latina*, ed. I. Scherer-Warren and P. Krische. São Paulo: Brasiliense.

Wallerstein, Immanuel. 2002. "New Revolts Against the System." *New Left Review* 18: 29–37.

Walters, Shirley. 1987. "A Critical Discussion of Democratic Participation Within Community Organisations." *Community Development Journal* 22: 23–30.

Walton, John. 1992. "Making the Theoretical Case." In *What Is a Case? Exploring the Foundations of Social Inquiry*, ed. C. C. Ragin and H. S. Becker, 121–37. New York: Cambridge University Press.

Weffort, Francisco. 1984. *Por Que Democracia?* São Paulo: Brasiliense.

Weyland, Kurt. 1999. "Constitutional Engineering in Brazil." *American Political Science Review* 93: 1006.

Wood, Richard. 2002. *Faith in Action: Religion, Race, and Democratic Organizing in America.* Chicago: University of Chicago Press.

Zaluar, Alba. 1985. *A Máquina e a Revolta: As Organizações Populares e o Significado da Pobreza.* São Paulo: Brasiliense.

Zaret, David. 1992. "Religion, Science, and Printing in the Public Spheres in Seventeenth Century England." In *Habermas and the Public Sphere*, ed. Craig Calhoun, 212–35. Cambridge, Mass.: MIT University Press.

Zhou, Xuegang. 1993. "Unorganized Interests and Collective Action in Communist China." *American Sociological Review* 58: 54–73.

Index

In this index an "f" after a number indicates a separate reference on the next page, and an "ff" indicates separate references on the next two pages. A continuous discussion over two or more pages is indicated by a span of page numbers, e.g., "57–59."